PRAISE FOR
CRISIS TALES

"Written in clear, quick, conversational prose, *Crisis Tales* provides a wealth of sensible advice for handling crises of all sizes and shapes."

—*The Washington Times*

"Our company turned to Lanny Davis when we faced a legal problem in Washington. He found a way to combine his considerable legal, media, and political skills to find a solution satisfactory to all parties. This book demonstrates the effectiveness of his multi-disciplinary approach to crisis management."

—John P. Mackey, co-founder and co-CEO, Whole Foods Market

"*Crisis Tales* offers simple crisis management rules, told through riveting true-to-life stories, that can help everyone facing a business, governmental, or personal crisis. In my experience, Lanny applies his unique combination of legal and media experience to get the facts out early, develop the right strategy to communicate them effectively, and find the 'sweet spot' solution among competing viewpoints to solve the problem."

—Gary Lauer, chairman and CEO, eHealth, Inc.

CRISIS TALES

*Five Rules for Coping with Crises in
Business, Politics, and Life*

LANNY J. DAVIS

THRESHOLD EDITIONS

New York   London   Toronto   Sydney   New Delhi

Threshold Editions
A Division of Simon & Schuster, Inc.
1230 Avenue of the Americas
New York, NY 10020

First Threshold Editions paperback edition January 2014

THRESHOLD EDITIONS and colophon are trademarks of Simon & Schuster, Inc.

For information about special discounts for bulk purchases, please contact Simon & Schuster Special Sales at 1-866-506-1949 or business@simonandschuster.com.

The Simon & Schuster Speakers Bureau can bring authors to your live event. For more information or to book an event, contact the Simon & Schuster Speakers Bureau at 1-866-248-3049 or visit our website at www.simonspeakers.com.

Designed by Claudia Martinez

Manufactured in the United States of America

10   9   8   7   6   5   4   3   2   1

Library of Congress Cataloging-in-Publication Data

Davis, Lanny J.
   Crisis tales : five rules for coping with crises in business, politics, and life / Lanny J. Davis.
      p.   cm.
   1. Public relations—Case studies.   2. Crisis management—Case studies.   3. Scandals—Case studies.   4. Davis, Lanny J.   I. Title.
   HD59.D337 2013
   658.4'056—dc23   2012026475

ISBN 978-1-4516-7928-1
ISBN 978-1-4516-7929-8 (pbk)
ISBN 978-1-4516-7930-4 (ebook)

AUTHOR'S NOTE

In this book, I have described true-to-life stories of high-profile legal crises I have handled over the past twelve years, as best as I can remember them. Any quotations in the book are not from notes, which it has been my practice for many years not to retain, but are to the best of my recollection.

I took care to avoid revealing any legal advice I offered clients or any confidential or sensitive nonpublic communications from clients revealed to me. I have tried to be fair and tell the tales accurately and factually, with as few editorial comments as possible.

To truth and fairness, which should still matter in the media—
especially on the Internet and in social media

CONTENTS

RULE 5: NEVER REPRESENT YOURSELF IN A CRISIS

AFTERWORD

ACKNOWLEDGMENTS

INDEX

Tell It All, Tell It Early, Tell It Yourself

Welcome to my world. It's January 2002, and the phone rings late at night, and Martha Stewart is on the line. "Sorry to call you so late. Is this Lanny Davis? I need your help getting the truth out. My lawyers are telling me I can't. Will you help?"

Or it's December 2005 and the chairman and CEO of Royal Caribbean Cruise Lines calls: "We had a tragic incident on board one of our ships—a young man recently married on his honeymoon went overboard last July, we still don't know what happened, and the cable TV shows and media are criticizing us. We decided to say nothing out of sensitivity to the family. What should we do?"

Or Representative Charlie Rangel wants to know how to respond to a *New York Times* article saying he never paid taxes he owed on a condo over a twenty-year period.

Or Senator Trent Lott wants advice on having made an embarrassing public utterance—and should he return a call from civil rights icon Rev. Jesse Jackson Sr.

Or I myself wake up to find I'm on page one of the *New York Times*—falsely accused of something that people will now believe is true.

What do you do? How do you respond? How do you fight back?

My work in crisis management has taught me a series of rules and one overall guiding principle. The guiding principle: *Tell it all, tell it early, tell it yourself.*

The rules and how I learned them are what I tell in my *Crisis Tales*.

CRISIS TALES

The Five Rules of Crisis Management

The phone call I received in November 1996 from then White House counsel Jack Quinn not only changed my profession; it also changed my life.

Quinn, a distinguished Washington, D.C., attorney and an old friend from Democratic politics for thirty years, called me shortly after the November 5, 1996, presidential election. After some small talk, he offered me the job of White House special counsel defending President and Mrs. Clinton in the media from expected Republican attacks and congressional investigations.

I had known the Clintons for more than twenty-five years. I first met Hillary Rodham when I was in my "senior" (third) year at Yale Law School; she had just arrived as a freshman in the fall of 1969. We became good friends—she was the smartest, funniest, and most public-service-committed person I knew at Yale Law School. Bill Clinton arrived in September 1970 as a first-year—I had graduated in June 1970. I met him when we worked together briefly on the Joe Lieberman (now a former four-term U.S. senator) insurgent primary campaign for the Connecticut State Senate, and for an anti–Vietnam War Senate candidate for the Connecticut Democratic Party nomination.

Now it was twenty-six years later. I had spent the previous twelve months appearing on TV, as a volunteer, to defend my still good friend Hillary Clinton, now First Lady, from attacks concerning a twenty-plus-year-old land deal called Whitewater in which the Clintons had invested and lost money.

I thought then that the entire blown-up Whitewater "scandal" was bogus—an egregious example of scandalmongering by the media machine. As it turned out, I was right. After thousands of headlines and editorials by the nation's leading investigative reporters, dozens of Republican-partisan congressional hearings on the Clintons' Whitewater investment, spending tens of millions of dollars of taxpayer funds, and another $70 million–plus spent by Independent Counsel Kenneth Starr on Whitewater, not one charge of wrongdoing regarding Whitewater was ever filed against the Clintons.

So the nonscandal of Whitewater that preoccupied the media and the public for years taught me the most important lesson about crisis management: Fight back with facts, no matter how many leading media organizations pile on, and with persistence and patience, the conventional wisdom accepting the notion "where there's smoke there's fire" can be challenged, if not permanently defeated.

Besides Whitewater, in 1996, another alleged "scandal" was building in the nation's political media. The Clinton fund-raising apparatus for the 1996 reelection campaign was accused of campaign finance violations. Dozens of stories had appeared in the fall of 1996, but the Clinton reelection campaign was not responding, understandably keeping focused on the reelection messages people cared about.

Once President Clinton was reelected over Republican senator Bob Dole by a healthy margin, the pressure cooker of unanswered questions and unwritten stories on the Clinton campaign fund-raising practices seemed ready to blow.

The White House lawyer who had served as a spokesperson primarily for Whitewater had announced his resignation. When White House counsel Jack Quinn called shortly after the election, he asked me to become White House "special counsel"—specifically to speak for the White House on scandal-related and legal issues, primarily, we expected, regarding the alleged campaign finance abuses during the 1996 Clinton reelection campaign.

Why me? I asked, resisting, not wanting to give up my law practice and my leisure time with my wife and family. "You are the only one the Clintons can think of who meets three requirements—a lawyer, who understands and can deal with the media, and who also understands politics."

I accepted, knowing this would be a difficult job. But I had my doubts. Many Clinton White House senior staffers, I knew, had accumulated hundreds of thousands of dollars of legal fees defending themselves during congressional investigations over the bogus Whitewater issue. So I was reluctant to take the job.

But I was concerned also about the line of demarcation between my role as White House spokesman on scandal issues and that of the widely respected White House press secretary, Mike McCurry.

So before I accepted the job, I went to McCurry to ask his advice. He urged me to take the job. Clearly he wanted to clear out all the "scandal" questions from the podium he commanded every day when he briefed the White House press corps.

So I asked McCurry, "We both speak for the White House, Mike. But where does your job end and my job begin?"

McCurry put his legs up on his desk. He smiled that mischievous and evil smile I came to know . . . and fear.

"Have you ever seen the bumper sticker 'Shit Happens'?"

I said, "Yes."

"Well," he said, "when 'shit happens,' you speak!"

Ouch, I thought. Some job. I immediately thought of the old cartoon character in *Li'l Abner*, the character who, on a sunny day, walked around with a dark storm cloud over his head. That would be my job at the White House, I thought.

As it turned out, that was an understatement.

I began my job and quickly became known within the White House as "Mr. Bad News" or, as the *New Republic* referred to me in a cover story published some months later, "the minister of scandal."

I must admit there were times that I had the feeling that people were afraid of me when I appeared anywhere in the White House complex. I remember sometimes walking down the hallways of the West Wing on my way to the White House counsel's office or sometimes the Oval Office to discuss the latest breaking "bad news" scandal story on campaign finance issues and to get answers to hundreds of reporter questions. I began to notice that when people saw me coming, they would quickly close their doors.

I thought: What am I—a walking infection?

From the start, McCurry and I devised a preemptive strategy that was counterintuitive: We needed to help reporters write bad stories as completely and quickly as possible. We knew that there were plenty of "bad" documents, as in embarrassing and raising legal questions, that had been turned over to various Republican-controlled congressional investigative committees. We knew that two committees—the Senate committee led by Republican senator Fred Thompson and the House committee led by Republican congressman Dan Burton—had scheduled hearings in the early summer that would almost certainly be nationally televised.

So what to do? Wait and let the documents we had turned over to the Republicans be leaked, a few at a time, dribbling out stories and building up the importance of the TV hearings? Or call reporters, "leak" the stories (without attribution), and invite them to write the bad stories in the winter and early spring so by the time the hearings were held, these stories would be "old news"?

To anyone familiar with media and politics, the answer was clear:

preemption, making "bad news" "old news" by the time the Republicans held their hearings. And that is what we did.

From that strategy came my mantra within the White House for getting the truth out, which remains to this day, in my judgment, the starting point for all good crisis managers regarding the truth: "Tell it all, tell it early, tell it yourself."

The first step in implementing this strategy—or in being ready to respond in the event preemption didn't make any sense—was to gather facts to be ready for the story.

The White House fact machine I relied on was a group of lawyers under the leadership of another lawyer named Lanny—Lanny Breuer, a brilliant white-collar Washington lawyer and former New York prosecutor who also carried the title of "special counsel to the president." (As of the end of 2012, Mr. Breuer still served as assistant attorney general for the Criminal Division of the Justice Department in the Obama administration.)

I needed to be part of this legal fact-gathering process. I was talking to the media and I knew what they wanted. I knew what was hot and what was not. From listening to reporters, I knew what would have "legs" (as in, be picked up by other news organizations) and knew what the Republicans in the investigation committees were planning to emphasize to a national TV audience. I also wanted to confirm the facts myself.

After gathering what we hoped were all the facts, good and bad, of interest to reporters and the public, the second step was to try to boil them down to a simple set of messages that people could understand. As Mike McCurry phrased it, we had to "put a waterfall of facts into a garden hose" to produce simple messages that reporters and readers could easily understand.

Next we had to get the story out proactively before the Republicans did. We usually did so by "placing" the story, or, to use the colloquial word most often used, "leaking" the story to a reporter with a respectable news organization. That way, it could be written, out, over with, and thus be "old news" before the expected summer 1997 nationally televised Republican hearings.

We would call a reporter and often would give the reporter the documents and facts on a "deep background" basis—meaning the reporter could write the facts without disclosing the original source of the documents. We called this a "deep background private placement." If we were successful, we referred to the resulting story as a "predicate" story—one that summarized all the facts, good and bad, so it could be used as a foundation for other reporters and then there was virtually nothing new to report.

Sometimes our "leaks" had to be done without the knowledge of senior White House lawyers so they would have "deniability" when confronted by the Republicans (who, hypocritically, would be angry because they would be denied doing the leaking with a more negative spin). I felt uncomfortable about this, and it was rare, but this was my instruction from senior political and media White House officials.

Unfortunately, this practice of operating without the knowledge and approval of senior lawyers may have been okay as an exception, because the White House was a political institution. But it might have created in my mind a basis for doing so again if it appeared to be necessary.

I preferred to engage in debate with my fellow lawyers on how to get facts out proactively without significant legal risks. McCurry would warn me when I was on my way to a meeting of White House lawyers: "Davis, don't leave the room full of all these lawyers without your blood being left on the floor!" "That's easy for you to say, McCurry," I would ritualistically respond. "That's my blood you are talking about." What McCurry meant was that as a press person, he couldn't be in the room with the lawyers, and I had to be his agent to make the political and media arguments for our proactive strategy.

What blocked McCurry from being in the room was that he wasn't an attorney. He couldn't challenge lawyers when they objected to disclosures to the media for legal reasons, such as executive privilege. That would be a showstopper, McCurry would point out. End of discussion. Whereas I, as an attorney, could ask my fellow lawyers: "Executive privilege? What are you talking about? That's BS. There is no executive privilege for a political memo between staff." Whether my position was accepted or not, at least my fellow lawyers would have to engage and debate. Also, any nonattorney in the room can risk the waiver of attorney-client privilege—the rule that communications between a client and an attorney rendering legal advice are immune from subpoenas or compelled testimony. With a nonattorney PR person in the room, most lawyers worry there could be a complete "subject matter" waiver—meaning anyone in the room, including attorneys and clients, could be forced to testify as to the legal advice and produce all documents underlying the advice to the adversary.

So McCurry had the wisdom to see—way before I did—that an attorney who understood media and politics had a great crisis management advantage. He or she could be in the room with the attorneys, argue with them, test legal judgments through a media-political filter, and at least have a fighting chance to convince the instinctively opaque attorneys to go transparent.

Without realizing it at the time, my work at the White House—where the three disciplines of legal, media, and politics inevitably crossed my desk every day, often every hour—was the basis for a new model for crisis management, one that as far as I knew had never been combined or tried before, using all three disciplines at once to produce an effective crisis management strategy.

I announced I was leaving to return to my law firm in December 1997, after the campaign finance hearings fizzled out and most people in Washington believed that the Clintons had survived a bunch of largely bogus, partisan-driven scandal charges. After I left the White House, I spent most of 1998 as a volunteer defender of President Clinton from impeachment proceedings. After he was acquitted in early 1999, I was able to develop this new three-pronged legal/media/political approach to traditional crisis management.

The key new element was taking advantage of the "attorney-client privilege" to be able to get access to all the facts, good and bad.

The "privilege," as it is called by attorneys, derives from centuries of tradition based on a confidentiality principle that has long been accepted—not just in the law, but in religion and medicine as well.

For example, when a priest hears confession, he is bound to maintain the secrecy of the confessor, and the confessor is able to rely on that and, thus, is willing to be completely honest. The same principle applies to the patient, who must be completely forthright with a physician or psychiatrist if he or she is going to get effective medical help. An attorney must also be able to assure a client in trouble that the client must be 100 percent truthful to get the best legal advice, and if he or she is, the facts disclosed cannot be compelled to be disclosed (with rare exceptions), even if the attorney is served with a subpoena.

Over the years, I learned that the traditional advice of a lawyer to avoid public comment during a legal crisis had become outdated, especially with the impact of the Internet at the turn of the twenty-first century.

It was no longer viable for a lawyer to tell a client, "We'll win it in the courtroom—we won't litigate this in the media." There were too many ways for the judge and the jury to be influenced by public opinion, consciously or unconsciously; too many ways for prosecutors and regulators to be persuaded by adverse media coverage to launch an investigation or to bring a case, as broadcast news once a day became 24/7 cable, and then within just a few years, the Internet led to websites and then some blogs and then the blogosphere and then Google, Twitter, YouTube, WiFi, and social networks.

Over more than a decade since leaving the White House, the foundation rule—"Tell it all, tell it early, tell it yourself"—in practice broke down to five simple rules of crisis management. These five emerged from the actual crisis tales I experienced, handling scandals in politics, business, and life. They are:

RULE 1: GET ALL THE FACTS OUT

The first and mandatory question is: What are the facts? And the best way for a crisis manager to get access to all the facts directly and reliably is to be a practicing attorney protected by the attorney-client privilege. (It's not enough to do public relations and have a law degree—the courts require actual law practice and legal advice to obtain the protection of the "privilege.")

This does not mean that public relations and political advisors aren't needed. To the contrary. But ideally there are attorneys who can be a bridge between the two worlds—an agent for the PR team to convince the attorneys they need to get the facts out; and an agent for the attorneys with the PR team to be sure that what is said to the media is factual and complete and won't carry legal risk.

Good examples of fact-gathering that could not have been done without the attorney-client privilege were the Martha Stewart and HealthSouth controversies. My first set of interviews with both Ms. Stewart and the CEO of HealthSouth, Richard Scrushy, had to be done myself, under the protection of the privilege. I knew there was a potential that a full accounting of the facts might lead to legal exposure in the case of each—so before I knew all the facts, I had to have the protection of the attorney-client privilege and then be able to decide what could, or could not, be disclosed to the media to handle the crisis—or whether to have any media strategy at all.

RULE 2: PUT THE FACTS INTO SIMPLE MESSAGES

Second, once the legal crisis manager has all the facts—meaning documents, emails, and other verification that the facts are true—the next step must be to craft a simple message.

The best way to approach this task is to write the message or messages as brief headlines for the story you would like to see written.

Ultimately reporters are no different from members of Congress or even regulators: You have to simplify your facts into a concise, easy-to-understand message.

For example, how do you summarize the message when a cruise ship loses a passenger in the middle of the night and the young man's family hires a lawyer and accuses the ship of botching the investigation? The facts are complex and the cruise ship does not want to seem insensitive to the grieving family, including the grieving widow, who lost her husband and their honeymoon cruise. So when the Royal Caribbean crisis tale is told, we will see that the message wasn't easy to summarize in a simple headline. Then we found it—and once we did, we knew we had it. "We're a cruise ship—not *CSI*."

Once the core messages are developed, the attorneys must confirm verifiable facts to support those messages, with documents and sources that a reporter will find believable.

The end result for effective crisis management at this point is what we came to call "The Book"—core messages on the first page, then bullet points supporting each core message on the next pages, and tabs of documents supporting each bullet-point fact. Ideally, attorneys should approve the facts and media strategy. On one occasion I have violated that policy of working closely with attorneys—and in that case, as will be told in my tale about Martha Stewart, I regretted doing so.

RULE 3: GET AHEAD OF THE STORY

There are many techniques for getting the facts out, using "The Book" as your "fact box"—meaning, getting the messages and facts contained in "The Book" published, and limited to those contained there, since they have been approved by the attorneys and client and it is dangerous to go outside them.

When you have the luxury of proactively "placing" a story with a reporter, you are ready to place your predicate story.

The advantage is not only preemption—giving all other reporters one place to go to read all the facts and understand the most favorable narrative thread—but the ability to take your time and work with a reporter to make the story complete and effective, since the reporter can take his or her time preparing the story without an immediate deadline. It also allows you to get your viewpoint—your "spin," so to speak—into the story in a way that is credible, since that viewpoint should be a plausible argument drawn from the facts of the story.

A classic predicate story was written by the *New York Times* about the accusation that Macy's Herald Square (the famous Macy's store in New York City that is the sponsor of the annual Thanksgiving Parade) had been guilty of racial profiling of its minority customers when it came to shoplifting apprehensions. The Macy's crisis tale describes the second-guessable decision to allow the *Times* reporter and a photographer access to the holding room for shoplifting suspects, together with cells and handcuffs. But the predicate story that was ultimately written by the *New York Times* proved the value of giving a reporter total access to all facts, individuals in the company, and the full context of the alleged shoplifting incident that was the basis of a racial discrimination lawsuit—getting an entire story written, all at once, with all good and bad facts summarized fairly and accurately.

Of course, if it is too late and the story has already broken, "The Book" will still be useful for responding to a deluge of questions in a "war room" or "rapid response" room of lawyers and PR consultants. And it will not be too late to try to stanch the bleeding and dribbling out of information after a bad news story has broken by finding a reporter from an influential newspaper or Internet site to write the complete story and—the crisis management objective—get the story behind you.

RULE 4: FIGHT FOR THE TRUTH USING LAW, MEDIA, AND POLITICS

Sometimes, a single tool will not be effective to solve a crisis, especially a high-profile civil case or regulatory prosecution in Washington. Usually companies hire separate teams of lawyers to do the litigating, public relations advisors to talk to the press, and public policy or lobbying experts to deal with the politics of the crisis—addressing the concerns of various constituencies affected by the crisis, whether shareholders, voters, or even governments.

This multidisciplinary strategy is sometimes very risky, since lawyers and media strategists and politicians or diplomats in the international arena accustomed to secrecy may all be at cross-purposes. Two tales—one domestic (a U.S. CEO accused of accounting fraud and with suspicious facts from the start) and the other international (Hondurans caught in the middle of a coup—or was it a coup?)—demonstrate that the multidisciplinary approach done by one individual, while risky, is sometimes the best way to solve a crisis, or at least minimize the damage.

RULE 5: NEVER REPRESENT YOURSELF IN A CRISIS

It is all too easy and common for an individual in the middle of a crisis, such as a CEO used to commanding the heights and leading a major corporation, to rely on his or her own instincts and experience to solve a media crisis. This is a mistake—especially when it is the crisis manager who finds himself or herself as the subject of the media storm.

I learned this lesson the hard way, as one chapter of this book demonstrates. There was a story written about me in the *New York Times* in which I did not have a chance to present to the *Times* reporters all the facts up front, because I was working behind the scenes to assist the U.S. State Department in facilitating the exit of an Ivory Coast strongman who had lost an election. I also was ill prepared to counter other characterizations of my previous clients that were not accurate. But in the final analysis, I had only myself—not the *Times*—to blame for violating all the crisis management rules that I advise others to follow.

WHEN WILL THEY EVER LEARN?

More than a quarter century ago, the Nixon crisis managers in the Watergate scandal made all the fundamental mistakes that make a bad crisis worse: deny, deny, deny; then the "limited modified hang-out" of partial disclosure, then the cover-up; and finally, after the inevitable dribble, dribble, dribble of facts leading to critical mass and the final explosion, the resignation of a president of the United States.

The crisis management mistakes made in Watergate have been repeated in the corporate arena—from the mismanagement of the media and message after the *Exxon Valdez* oil tanker grounded on a sandbar, beginning a massive oil leak that soiled Alaskan shorelines and wildlife, to the difficulties experienced by BP during and after the Deepwater Horizon oil spill. What is most remarkable is that after so many years of repeating the same mistakes in mismanaging high-profile crises, they continue to be made—denial, delay in getting the facts out, letting the legal concerns trump the brand and media perceptions, and then watching helplessly as the truth inevitably dribbles out in Chinese-water-torture fashion—as if no one has any memory, or has learned anything from the past. There are plenty of examples of this amnesia and blindness to the fundamental rules of crisis management in recent years, through 2012. For example:

- Former senator John Edwards believed for too long (as he would admit) that his affair with a campaign worker and the birth of their child could be kept a secret. Given how smart a man and politician he is, it's hard to imagine why he thought that sooner or later (and it could have been in the middle of his campaign as the Democratic Party's nominee for president) the truth would not come out.

• Similarly, during the 2011 Republican contest for the presidential nomination, former Republican presidential candidate Herman Cain seemed to believe that he could ride out the specific allegations made public by individuals that he had engaged in sexual harassment and personal indiscretions and that the media would lose interest if he just nailed down the hatches and ducked for cover. Of course, as inevitably as the sun rising in the east, several more shoes dropped—and it was Mr. Cain's presidential campaign, not the story, that died relatively quickly.

• Another example in 2011 and through 2012 was the Obama White House's handling of the issue of the Solyndra government-guaranteed loan, which ended up in an embarrassing bankruptcy after being touted by the Obama White House as a great success story (and one pushed by the White House for media events, including one involving the president personally). But we saw the common pattern when bad stories arise, whether in the White House or corporate suites—first the White House resisted turning over emails and other documents to the Republican oversight committee. Was anyone surprised that sooner or later these emails actually leaked and most had to be turned over, after all was said and done? Shocking! Then the White House press office referred most questions to the Energy Department. Was anyone surprised that doing so left the impression that the White House seemed to be hiding something or evading the topic?

I am sure, in hindsight, that the White House press office realized that they would have been better off doing what we at the Clinton White House called a "document dump"—collect all the emails and documents, put them on a conference room table, invite in all the reporters, and stand there and answer all nasty questions and refuse to leave until everyone was done, and then the story can be over with quickly. (Regarding the document dump technique, I was once complimented when a reporter covering the Bush White House called me and said, "Today in the press room, someone actually stood up and said [about the Vice President Dick Cheney Energy Task Force documents, which were being withheld from disclosure]: 'Why don't you do a Lanny Davis?'" I was amazed—my name had become a crisis management term of art.)

· Typically for most political "crises," there was really no story at all on Solyndra once all the emails were dribbled out a little at a time: that is, there was absolutely no evidence of political corruption—maybe a bad business judgment, but not a sliver of evidence that there was any quid pro quo between an Obama donor and a decision made to loan money to Solyndra. This only confirms that sometimes not-bad stories are turned into worse stories by delays in going transparent.

· In late 2011 and early 2012 there was the mishandling of the decision by the leaders of the Susan G. Komen for the Cure foundation to cut off funding for Planned Parenthood. The Komen leaders initially were evasive about acknowledging that the decision had anything to do with politics. The first explanation was that the funding was cut off pending the results of an "investigation" announced by Florida Republican congressman Cliff Stearns. (This was the same Representative Stearns who was subsequently defeated in an August 2012 Republican primary when he sought reelection. His so-called investigation ultimately went nowhere.) Then the public subsequently learned from the media that a senior official of Komen, Karen Handel, was part of the decision-making process that led to the funding cutoff. And that the same Ms. Handel, an anti-abortion, "prolife" advocate, had stated during her unsuccessful campaign for Georgia governor: "Since I am prolife, I do not support the mission of Planned Parenthood."

Would it not have been better crisis management— "tell it all, tell it early . . . etc."—for Komen to disclose immediately that Ms. Handel, with a known anti-abortion, anti–Planned Parenthood history, was at least involved in the decision to cut off Planned Parenthood funding by the Komen Foundation?

Weeks later, Komen founder and leader Nancy Brinker (sister of Susan Komen, who passed away tragically of breast cancer and who inspired the start-up of the organization) announced restoration of Planned Parenthood funding. But Komen never acknowledged that Ms. Handel may have influenced the decision.

• The 2012 Romney campaign failed for many reasons, but two of the major mishandled crises that might have affected the outcome were the failure to publish prior tax returns way before the 2012 campaign heated up—even before the 2011 Republican nomination contests; and second, Governor Romney's failure to step up to the line—"get in front of the story"—when he was caught on a cell phone camera at a private fund-raiser commenting, in effect, that 47 percent of the electorate were for President Obama and wouldn't change their minds because they were dependent upon government to sustain them. Romney's strategy was to describe his comments as "inelegantly expressed"—and that only caused the story to blow up on him more, since it seemed to confirm that he really meant what he said, but he just it expressed it badly.

On the other hand, I would have advised him—assuming he would have believed these words—to say, simply: "You know, that was a stupid mistake and I didn't mean it —of course those 47 percent are composed of a variety of voters who have many reasons for not being for me not relating to government, and I want to apologize to them for my mistake."

I am convinced that the 47 percent issue would have gone away almost instantly had he said this or something similar. After all, there were plenty of examples of President Obama making gaffes behind closed doors (such as his famous "they get bitter, and they cling to guns," et cetera, during the Democratic nomination race in 2008; or Senator Biden implying that Republicans favor keeping people in "chains" while talking to a minority audience). Gaffes can be excused—Americans are a forgiving lot. But it requires an authentic admission, "I screwed up"—and let's move on.

So, in short, my advice to Mr. Romney—as well as to Vice President Biden and any other politician who makes an embarrassing gaffe—is what I should have told myself when I found myself the subject of a negative story before I was ready, as I describe in detail at the end of this book to "Tell it all, tell it early, tell it yourself."

When will they ever learn?

Maybe all of us caught in a crisis—beginning when we were young and our mothers caught our hands in the cookie jar—will continue to repeat the same mistakes that violate the time-tested, fundamental rules of crisis management. Perhaps this book, and the five basic rules of crisis management that emerge from these crisis tales, will become a template for what to do—and not to do—the next time the "$#&@" hits the fan—whether in business, politics, or life.

GET ALL THE FACTS OUT

I.

MARTHA STEWART

Fighting Prosecutors . . . and Her Lawyers

"Sorry to call you so late. Is this Lanny Davis? I need your help getting the truth out into the media. My '%#@!' lawyers are telling me I can't. I am told by one of my company's major investors that you disagree. Will you help?"

Those were the first words I heard Martha Stewart speak late one night over the phone in the late fall of 2002.

The phone rang close to midnight, waking me and my wife up. "Someone's on the phone who says she is Martha Stewart, and she asked me what time it was—as if she didn't know," my wife said, after waking me up. "I'm sure it's not *the* Martha Stewart. Tell her not to call so late."

But I wasn't surprised. I knew it was *the* Martha Stewart. As was often the case when people are in bad headlines, I had received several calls from friends of Ms. Stewart and a major shareholder on her company's board of directors asking me whether I was available to help her in her legal and media crisis.

The stock in the company that bore her name had plunged in the winter of 2001 after she was accused of insider trading, and she was in the headlines nonstop for weeks, without adequate factual response from her. The media strongly suggested that Ms. Stewart had sold her stock in a cancer-research company, ImClone, founded and run by her friend Sam Waksal. The stories suggested that she had sold about fifty thousand dollars' worth of stock on December 27, within a day or two of the announcement by the U.S. Food and Drug Administration that ImClone's anticancer drug had been denied approval. Once that announcement was made, the stock dropped precipitously.

I followed the story and I knew the optics were terrible—the innuendo was that somehow Ms. Stewart had gotten inside information from her friend Sam Waksal about the pending FDA negative decision and had sold her stock before the bad news broke in the media, and thus, ahead of the inevitable drop in share value caused by the bad news. Other stories suggested that she had heard that the Waksal family was dumping its shares, and that she inferred the FDA would be turning ImClone's anticancer drug down.

Either way, the New York media jumped all over the story, in a typical feeding frenzy where rumor and innuendo are far in front of facts. Most people were led to believe that Martha Stewart had acted on "inside information" illegally.

But Martha Stewart's comments in the media to explain her reasons for selling when she did were either missing entirely or incomplete. The usual over-the-top tabloid headlines from the *New York Post* were the worst: MARTHA'S PRISON EVERYDAY COLLECTION, MARTHA'S STEWING, and MARTHA IN HELL'S KITCHEN. The rival *New York Daily News* couldn't resist sinking to the *Post*'s depths: DIVA MARTHA'S NOW IN THE SOUP. The fact that headlines suggested guilt even before Ms. Stewart had been indicted for, much less convicted of, insider trading is a sad habit of not only tabloid newspapers, but mainstream media too.

So my wife handed me the phone and when I said, "Hello," I heard a familiar voice. Ms. Stewart said she needed my help getting her story out into the media, telling me she wanted to tell the truth, adding that she didn't think she did anything wrong but her lawyers wouldn't let her talk to the media to get her story out.

As she had said publicly, she wanted to tell her story but the lawyers opposed her doing so, given that she was under investigation. She did tell the media, however, that she had told her broker to sell ImClone stock when it hit sixty dollars in price—which was also part of a year-end investment strategy which, she told the media, had been previously discussed with her financial advisor. She had said publicly that when she got a message from her broker that the stock was declining in value. She gave her instructions to sell the stock when it went below $60. (He ultimately did.) She didn't explicitly deny that she might have also known that the founder and CEO of the company was selling his stock.

I had seen Ms. Stewart appear to be embarrassed when she did her regular appearance on the CBS *Early Show*, demonstrating her various recipes and "every person" household and party suggestions that had made her so famous and successful. But after the massive media frenzy about her possibly selling her stock on the basis of insider information, the hostess for the CBS show asked her to comment about the headlines while she was making a salad, literally cutting lettuce as she kept saying in answer to repeated questions that she couldn't comment. It was awful—for her and for everyone watching.

I repeated my usual standard advice about establishing an attorney-client privilege by expressing a desire to retain me as an attorney, thus protecting me from compulsory testimony about anything she told me. After she had expressed her desire to retain me, we discussed the media's negative portrayal of her as having engaged in illegal insider trading—having sold her ImClone stock with the benefit of nonpublic, material information from a company "insider," which, if so, might have been illegal. So far, I had seen no response in the media on whether Ms. Stewart actually had received what is defined as an "insider" versus getting a "tip" from a broker, who was not legally an "insider," just like millions of Americans every year, and thus, the tip might not have constituted, under the law, "inside information."

Then, Ms. Stewart—assured she was talking to me with the protection of attorney-client privilege (since she said she was considering retaining me)—told me her version of what had happened for the next two hours or so, until after 2:00 a.m.

VIOLATING ONE PART OF RULE #1—TRYING TO GET FACTS WITHOUT THE ATTORNEY'S COOPERATION

I knew that I needed to gain the full cooperation of her New York criminal attorney, the late Robert Morvillo (who passed away in February 2012), if I was to follow my model and always be in the room with my fellow lawyers, sharing attorney-client privilege, so I could get access to all the facts. And this rule was much more important in a criminal case, where one mistake to a reporter in a conversation that is not privileged could risk my client going to jail.

Mr. Morvillo was one of the top criminal defense attorneys in New York City, highly respected as a former prosecutor and highly skilled in dealing with juries. I had no reason to believe he wouldn't welcome my assistance, first to evaluate the facts as he understood them, and then to determine what was safe and which undisputed facts could be put out to the media to help balance the media coverage, and possibly influence the prosecutors' decision whether to indict Martha. My expectations were based on my White House experience and my other experiences to date—attorneys just don't trust the media to get it right (often for good reason), and in a criminal case, it's too risky to allow clients to be quoted in the media, as their words may come back to be used against them by the prosecution if the case gets to trial.

I asked Ms. Stewart to call Mr. Morvillo to ask him to confide in me under shared attorney-client privilege, tell him she had already retained me as an "attorney advisor," and direct him (she was, after all, the client paying his bills) to take my call so I could explain my desire to work with him *before* making any judgments about whether to go to the media.

The next morning she called me and told me to call Mr. Morvillo—that he was expecting my call.

I immediately called him. I introduced myself and told him that Ms. Stewart had asked me to meet with him as an attorney, and thus subject to attorney-client privilege, and discuss the facts and whether there was any basis for going to the media to get her story out and correct some of the misreporting that had occurred to date.

There was silence on the phone.

I repeated that no decision would be made to talk to the media without his approval and all I wanted to do was understand the facts and concerns so we could make a mutual decision on whether a media strategy made sense.

More silence.

I was on a cell phone in a cab in New York City and I thought I was having bad cell service. "Hello, Mr. Morvillo?"

Then he spoke, succinctly and to the point.

"I am not going to meet with you, Mr. Davis," he said. "I don't believe going to the media is wise. Good-bye. Have a good day."

I started to answer, to remind him that no decision to go to the media would be made without his approval and supervision of all facts and messages. I just needed to know all the facts to help make the best judgment about whether—and if so, how—to go to the media but Mr. Morvillo had already hung up the phone.

I called Ms. Stewart back and told her.

She was stunned, angry. "But I am the client and I want him to meet with you and I want to get my story out—I want to defend myself, my reputation," she said, with obvious frustration in her voice.

After all, it was her reputation and her name on the famous "Martha Stewart" company brand that was threatened.

I told her I believed Mr. Morvillo was not interested in meeting with me and that was that.

She restated that she wished me to represent her, and that I proceed to try to get her narrative out into the mainstream media so she could give her side of the story. I resisted.

I was opposed to doing anything without the full cooperation of her attorneys, especially the criminal attorney.

But she insisted that I could represent her personally—that she didn't need to ask anyone's permission and would pay me, if necessary, from her personal (as opposed to her company's) funds.

She reminded me that the night she had called me I told her she needed to get her side of the story out, that she was being hammered by media coverage that implied that she was guilty of insider trading, and that I would help her. "Don't give up on me and go back on what you promised," she said, with real pain in her voice.

I told her I would think about it.

I was concerned. Everything told me that it was very difficult and risky for me to work for her without the knowledge and cooperation of her attorneys. But I returned to my law firm and discussed the situation with my partners and colleagues there. I was advised by a few that the company bore her name, and she owned the controlling shares of stock, and she had a personal interest in clearing her name and her company's, too. But still I was worried. It broke my basic rule, learned at the White House, that I couldn't do a legal crisis management project without working closely with all attorneys involved.

Finally, after another conversation with Ms. Stewart, I decided I would help her without the approval or knowledge (per her instructions) of her attorneys.

We established the game plan according to the usual crisis management rules. First we would try to get the facts by interviewing Ms. Stewart and checking out whatever documents she had that supported her version of what happened, coming up with a simple message, such as: a tip from a broker with no knowledge of a pending adverse FDA decision concerning ImClone, i.e., inside information, might not be a crime. Then, depending on what we learned, we would make a decision whether to go to a reporter who could do the fact-checking and corroboration without Ms. Stewart having to speak on the record and prejudice her legal defense. I already had someone in mind who fit the bill almost perfectly. But my plan was that, once the article was published, I would seek again to try to confer with Mr. Morvillo and the company's in-house general counsel and external civil attorneys. I was determined not to go forward at that point if I couldn't get all the attorneys on board with my media strategy. If they agreed, we would then follow up that print story with a few high-impact TV interviews—such as with Barbara Walters on ABC's *20/20*, or Larry King on CNN—but only if I could obtain the full cooperation at that point of the attorneys.

So I decided to go ahead with the first step—without the knowledge or approval of Mr. Morvillo or her other attorneys. It was a major mistake on my part—one I vowed I would never make again. And never have since.

GETTING THE PREDICATE STORY WRITTEN: "LUNCHING AT MARTHA'S"

I and my three colleagues at my law firm spent the next several weeks interviewing Ms. Stewart and reading relevant documents and emails.

Our legal research revealed that even if she had received a "tip" from her stockbroker, as was published in the newspapers, that the Waksal family was selling stock and had acted on the tip, acting on that type of information would not necessarily fit the definition of illegal "insider trading."

An "insider" is supposed to be a senior official of a company with access to "material" nonpublic information. The definition of "material" is rather loose, but usually the law defines it to mean information that if known by a prudent shareholder might affect his or her decision to buy or sell the stock. Clearly information about a favorable or unfavorable decision by the FDA about allowing ImClone's anticancer drug to be sold would be material information. But would information that the CEO of a company and his family members had decided to sell their company stock at year's end, which just happened to be shortly before an expected crucial decision by the FDA to approve the anticancer drug on which the company's future heavily depended, constitute "inside" information? Unclear, we thought. And since the tip came from her broker, not a company official, it seemed, in any event, that the broker would probably not be considered an "insider" as that word was defined under at least many legal cases.

There had been published reports that Ms. Stewart had heard about the selling of ImClone shares by the Waksals. If she had been told this, it was at least conceivable that Ms. Stewart might have reasonably wondered whether the Waksals were selling stock for other reasons besides advance knowledge of a negative FDA decision—such as year-end tax reasons, or regularly scheduled year-end cashing out on a stock-sales program to liquidate some share holdings. (In fact, it was reported that the CEO, Sam Waksal, retained considerable shares despite his pre-Christmas sales.)

After consulting experts, our legal team came to believe that it appeared that the prosecutors would have a tough time bringing a case of violation of the anti–insider information law and rules because it seemed the information provided to her was neither "inside" nor provided by an insider. Even if she had been given a "tip" by her broker that the Waksals were selling their shares, as appeared to be the case, many experts advised that it would be difficult to call that information direct "inside" information, or to argue that the broker could be considered a corporate "insider" conveying "inside information" in this circumstance.

Moreover, given the small amount of money that Martha Stewart "saved" by selling her minor position in that company—estimated at the time to be about fifty thousand dollars—before the bad news was announced that the drug had not been approved, it was also hard to see why a federal prosecutor would bother to bring a case against her on such an indirect "inference" of bad news, with so little motive.

So we decided we had enough facts to seek a well-respected legal affairs reporter, preferably a journalist who was also an experienced attorney before becoming a journalist, to probe the issue himself of whether Ms. Stewart had been guilty under the legal definition of "insider trading." It was our hope that such a journalist would talk to and hear from legal experts what we had heard—that the "insider trading" case would be, at best, weak, and, thus, that the prosecutors might be persuaded not to bring it.

Did we believe that prosecutors would reach a judgment based solely on media coverage, not on the facts as they understood them, about whether to indict Ms. Stewart? No. But did we also believe that decision might be influenced—consciously or unconsciously, if the decision to indict was a borderline, close-call decision—by an overwhelming public perception that Martha Stewart was *not* guilty of insider trading?

Yes.

In my view, there was nothing untoward or improper about prosecutors' considering public perceptions in a close-call decision. After all, many prosecutorial decisions, subject to discretion on whether to go forward with seeking an indictment, consider the deterrent effect of bringing the case on other future perpetrators.

So we decided to proceed. The reporter we thought would be best was a former prosecutor and outstanding legal affairs reporter for *The New Yorker* magazine, Jeffrey Toobin, who also was a legal analyst for CNN. That was a dual advantage, since we thought it was likely that he would be invited to discuss his article on Ms. Stewart on CNN.

We set up the "deep background" (not-for-attribution) interview with Toobin to take place at Ms. Stewart's house in southern Connecticut on a Sunday morning, January 26.

THE "DEEP BACKGROUND" INTERVIEW
AND THE SILVER CHOPSTICKS

On early Sunday morning, January 26, I and two colleagues flew to the Westchester, New York, airport and a car picked us up and took us to Ms. Stewart's beautiful, country-style home just over the border in Connecticut.

Ms. Stewart greeted us cheerfully and served us a delicious continental-style breakfast. We had about an hour to prepare before Toobin's expected arrival.

It was a memorable experience listening to Martha tell her story to Jeffrey Toobin over her dining room table, with coffee and Danish and fruit, followed by a multicourse (twelve? who could count?) Thai lunch in her kitchen, served by her Thai cook.

I remember we all laughed when Ms. Stewart commented on her especially thin sterling silverware chopsticks as Mr. Toobin picked up one to use. She explained that thin chopsticks in ancient China were used by royalty and upper-class Chinese to impress their visitors.

At some point during the lunch, I excused myself and fulfilled my promise to my wife, calling her on my cell to describe all the details. I couldn't tell her anything about the substance of what Ms. Stewart was saying, but I told her that the lunch was delicious and that Ms. Stewart was a gracious and lively hostess. My wife made me promise to look closely at the napkins and be able to describe exactly how they were folded!

The understanding (what we call "ground rules") for the interview with Mr. Toobin was that he could report on Ms. Stewart's "feelings" about the situation she faced. But he could not directly use any "fact" that she asserted. In order to use the facts he heard asserted, he had to confirm their truth with a third party. This is a classic example of a "deep background" rule. As Toobin wrote in his article, which appeared in the February 3 issue of *The New Yorker*:

> I first asked to speak to Stewart shortly after the ImClone investigation began, and it wasn't until recently that some of her advisers, frustrated by the bad publicity, saw that there might be advantages for their client in such an interview. Under the terms of my agreement with these advisers, who were present for our conversation, Stewart would discuss her feelings about the investigation, and the public reaction, but wouldn't speak on the record about the facts.

For example, she said she had received a message from her broker that the ImClone share price was "declining." Under the ground rules, for Toobin to report that fact, he had to get someone else to confirm its truth—for example, one of the prosecutors (who presumably already had access to that message slip through a subpoena), or Ms. Stewart's assistant who had taken down the message, or the broker himself. This is the sort of thing reporters do, and Mr. Toobin was not only a great lawyer but a great reporter—which is of course why we selected him to do the story.

That ground rule was legally important. I did not want Ms. Stewart's credibility to be at issue in what Toobin wrote, since if she was brought to trial the article might be used against her if the facts turned out to be different from what was written in the article. I wanted Toobin's article to be based on what others told him, with Ms. Stewart's role being only to guide him on what to look for and ask for to confirm the facts independently.

Despite the friendly atmosphere over lunch, Toobin asked tough questions. After all, he was a former prosecutor and an outstanding lawyer. At times his questions resembled a cross-examination more than a conversation. But Ms. Stewart didn't seem to mind. She followed our instruction (for the most part) to stick to expressing her feelings about what she was going through, and let Mr. Toobin investigate and confirm the facts.

THE NEW YORKER PUBLISHES—AND THE CRISIS MANAGEMENT SHUTDOWN

The article that Toobin wrote for *The New Yorker*, published online the following Sunday morning, February 2, and in the magazine the next day, was aptly titled "Lunching at Martha's."

We found Toobin's article fair. It spelled out her version of events, especially that she had no knowledge of the FDA decision, and raised the doubts that we had hoped for, based on good reporting based on expert opinions, that Ms. Stewart could or should be charged with criminal "insider trading" as strictly defined by the law. Not only was Toobin's solid reputation for thorough, factual reporting borne out, but the advantage of his being a first-rate lawyer and former prosecutor was clear in the way he addressed that crucial issue. He wrote:

> How could this woman, who appears to stay in touch with everything that affects her, not know that her good friend Sam Waksal was trying to dump his stock at the same time that she was selling hers? Even if she did, knowing that is not necessarily the same thing as breaking insider-trading laws—laws that operate by specific rules.

Toobin then quoted, as we hoped he would, an expert to address the apparent weakness of the "insider trading" case. He quoted William R. Baker III, who, he wrote, had recently stepped down as associate director of the division of enforcement at the Securities and Exchange Commission. "Insider treading is a form of fraud, and you have to have some fraudulent intent." Then Toobin wrote just what I had been told and noted in a legal memorandum about the facts necessary to prove criminal "insider trading":

> In other words, in order to prove that Stewart engaged in insider trading, the government would have to prove several things: that she received information from someone with a legal duty to keep it confidential, that she knew this person was making an improper disclosure, and that she traded on the basis of that information. It might be difficult for the government to prove any of this, much less all of it, about Stewart's sale of ImClone.

Bingo! I thought as I read this sentence.

Toobin also proved himself to be the great reporter I knew him to be by finding additional sources to verify that Ms. Stewart had also been engaging in year-end portfolio stock selling for financial-planning reasons—which would further undermine the assertion that she had sold her ImClone stock only because of receipt of "inside" information. Toobin quoted a major shareholder in her company—San Francisco–based investor Jeff Ubben, who gave her advice in November 2001, just a month before her sale of ImClone stock:

> "I approached her in November 2001 [a month before her ImClone stock sales], and said: 'You've never sold any of your own stock,'" Ubben told me. " 'You should take some money off the table as an insurance policy. You're still paying mortgages on your properties.' She was a reluctant seller. She asked me if I knew any money managers and said she was in the process of getting out of the stock market. The implication was that she was selling all of her individual stock holdings."

Toobin went on to refer to Stewart's business manager, who Stewart had told me had recommended these year-end sales as well. Toobin used his own "deep background" sourcing to verify the business manager's advice: "She has confirmed to investigators, a person close to her says, that Stewart sold 'a lot' of stock in late 2001."

Toobin also quoted another securities law expert on the importance of her plan to do late-year selling. He wrote that the prosecutors faced a "greater problem" as a result of those year-end plans, if she could corroborate that those plans at least influenced her decision to sell ImClone, in addition to the fact of the price's declining below sixty dollars. " 'If she can show that she has a preexisting plan to sell the stock, she doesn't have to abort that plan because of some intervening information that she receives,' " said Adam Pritchard, a former SEC lawyer who was then a professor at the University of Michigan law school.

Double bingo!

We looked forward to the following Sunday morning, February 2, when we knew the Toobin story would be posted on the Internet, the day before it would appear on newsstands in *The New Yorker*. When we read it in its entirety, we were overjoyed—it clearly cast doubt on whether there was an insider case to be brought, and we saw it as a good foundation to raise further doubts about whether anyone other than Martha Stewart, or someone equally famous, would be charged with insider trading given these facts and circumstances.

I couldn't wait to call Ms. Stewart to share our satisfaction with the story and belief that it would be a foundation for the next steps, putting her on TV to tell her story personally. But what I heard wasn't all positive. She was upset about the "silver chopsticks" paragraph. I raced to the article to reread it, and there it was:

When we took a lunch break, it was clear that the wounds of the past year ran deep. After I admired the silver chopsticks that had been set out, Stewart said: "You know, in China, they say, 'The thinner the chopsticks, the higher the social status.' Of course I got the thinnest I could find."

I had the "déjà vu all over again" sensation. I remembered working into the wee hours of the morning to try to get a very negative story about President Clinton as neutral and fair as I could, and waking up early in the morning to read, with relief, that it came out even somewhat positive. But in the last paragraph there was one quotation that was nasty. Sure enough, later in the day when I saw President Clinton and asked him what he thought of the story, his reaction was negative regarding that last paragraph quotation—not too different from every other crisis client I have had since (including me, when I found myself in the middle of my own crisis of my own making).

Welcome to my world.

The Monday magazine publication of the article in *The New Yorker* caused a media stir. It was reported in other publications and, as we expected, Toobin went on CNN to comment on the story. His comments raised questions about the strength of the "insider trading" case—just as we hoped.

A day or so later, I received a phone call from Barbara Walters, anchor of ABC's *20/20* newsmagazine program—just what I had hoped for and planned for. She described the Toobin article as "great"— "about time Martha got her story out"—and congratulated me. "But you can't stop now, Lanny—not everyone reads *The New Yorker*. You need to put her on national TV—she is the best TV communicator on the planet, next to your former client, Bill Clinton, that is." She pitched *20/20* as the program she should choose first.

I of course agreed that Ms. Stewart was a gifted TV communicator and should go on *20/20*—as well as on *Larry King Live* on CNN.

But not, I was 100 percent determined, before I talked to and received approval from the legal team, especially Robert Morvillo, who had refused to talk to me or see me when I made my first call to him a month before.

I then heard from a company source that Mr. Morvillo was so unhappy that she had authorized me to proceed with *The New Yorker* without his knowledge that he was seriously thinking of resigning. I must say I wasn't surprised—and couldn't blame him. I understood that he must have felt blindsided not only by his client, Ms. Stewart, but by me.

My excuse was that I was under strict instruction not to tell him or any of her other lawyers until after the Toobin article was published. But I still felt bad. I tried to call Mr. Morvillo several times that day and the next to apologize and explain, but couldn't get through.

I felt terrible. I knew it could hurt Ms. Stewart's standing with the public and perhaps with the prosecutors if Mr. Morvillo resigned. So I immediately told her that, without Mr. Morvillo's cooperation, I could not proceed with our media strategy and had to cease my work. I knew she agreed—it seemed reluctantly.

I believed then and now that we could have built on Toobin's stories with appearances on *Larry King Live* and *20/20* with Barbara Walters and elsewhere in the media, and this might have helped convince the public and perhaps the prosecutors that the insider trading case was weak. But now that could not be done. *The New Yorker* story alone, I knew, wouldn't have the effect we were looking for.

THE SEC QUESTIONS . . . OF ALL PEOPLE . . . ME

Unfortunately, my involvement in the Martha Stewart crisis tale was not yet over.

First Mr. Morvillo came to interview me in Washington about what Martha had told me and Toobin to be sure that he knew what I knew. I was relieved that he was cordial and gracious, and appreciated that.

Then I was informed, to my chagrin, that the SEC wanted to interview me under oath about what I had told Jeffrey Toobin and about a document I had sent to him that was a rough draft of my understanding from published reports about Martha's explanation for the sale of the stock based on a tip from her broker. I had sent the document January 25, the night before the Sunday lunch interview, to make the interview go more smoothly and so that he could have an understanding of the basic public facts. We marked the document "draft" since there were a few items that needed to be reconfirmed. I knew that sending this document to a reporter meant it would not be attorney-client privileged, i.e., thus available to be "discovered" if there were litigation or regulatory investigations. But I had no concerns—it was a factual chronology that we had checked out and we were careful to describe it as a "draft" to be checked out for 100 percent accuracy. But as careful as we were, we subsequently discovered one factual error in that rough-draft narrative—relating to the first question she asked the broker she talked to on the phone before her stock sale. But when she read the draft that morning, Ms. Stewart immediately corrected the error—in fact, she had not asked about the FDA decision when she talked to the broker—she asked about the price of the stock and whether it had gone down to the "sell" price of sixty dollars, which she believed she had previously discussed with her broker.

Fortunately, after the Toobin Sunday interview, the very next day—Monday—I fixed this error in the narrative document, deleting reference to her question about the FDA. And my computer fortunately had a record of the two documents—one with the previous error and one corrected after the Toobin interview at Ms. Stewart's home.

I write "fortunately" because that error was the key subject of the SEC interview. It isn't pleasant for an attorney to be subject to sworn testimony—usually the attorney is defending a client in that situation. But I knew that, as someone who chose to be both an attorney and a media specialist in crisis communications, I would have to be prepared to do so, since my conversations and communications with reporters were not protected by attorney-client privilege. The SEC had copies of the rough-draft narrative I had sent to Toobin with the single error as well as the corrected version. So my explanation was corroborated.

The other good news—great news for me—was that they honored my attorney's assertion of attorney-client privilege when they asked me about any legal advice I had given to Ms. Stewart about protecting her reputation (including discussions of media strategy that directly pertained to legal concerns about correcting distortions in the media), and thus, I was not required to answer such questions.

It was great news because this was one of my first tests of the research I had done that indicated that I would not lose the attorney-client privilege protection regarding legal advice and media strategy related to legal strategy—even though I was questioned about conversations and communications with the media. This, after all, was the new model of crisis management I had created. And I believed having the "privilege" was essential to my gaining access to all the facts, which I also believed—from my Clinton White House experience—was essential to effective crisis management.

The last fear was that I would be called before a grand jury to explain the discrepancy between the two drafts. But this did not happen. Thank goodness that, in the written narrative, we had remained faithful to our rule of sticking to facts, avoiding adjectives and characterizations—and that we had immediately corrected the factual error.

NO CHARGES OF "INSIDER TRADING" FILED

The final outcome of the trial, as most people know, is that Martha Stewart was never indicted for inside information trading. I felt vindicated in that respect.

But that was no solace—Ms. Stewart was still indicted, not for the alleged "crime" for which she had been unjustly accused in the media all these months, but for alleged "false statements" made to investigators. I remember being troubled about one reality in our criminal justice system—when prosecutors don't indict on the core crime that led to their investigation, they too often vindicate all their time and resources spent by indicting on "false statements" or perjury that they allege occurred during the course of the investigation. I always thought there was something borderline wrong about that prosecutorial judgment. It reminded me of what I regarded as one of the worst injustices perpetrated by the prosecution team working for independent counsel Ken Starr during the Whitewater investigations—prosecuting, and reprosecuting, former associate attorney general Webster Hubbell not for crimes involved in cover-up of Whitewater-related crimes, but for alleged false statements on what appeared to be trivial issues.

I understand why that is so, and I certainly believe—as an attorney and a citizen—that making false statements to prosecutors or lying under oath is not defensible. However, I doubted the validity of charging her with false information after the prosecutors finally came to realize there was no "inside information" case that could be brought.

As it turned out, Martha Stewart was convicted of making false statements to investigators. She was not called to testify in her own defense, on the advice of her attorneys. I always wondered whether one of the best communicators in the world would have been better off if she had been allowed to testify. Despite instructions to jurors not to hold her not testifying against her, I always wondered whether they unconsciously did—or at least, whether she could have done some good by turning to them and admitting some of her mistakes, but insisting that she had not sold based on "inside" information.

But hindsight is twenty-twenty. I am sure Mr. Morvillo and his defense team had good reasons for making their decision and, for sure, I am not a criminal lawyer, and I concede that most criminal lawyers agreed with Mr. Morvillo's decision.

In the final analysis, I was very sad that Ms. Stewart was indicted for making false statements to prosecutors. I liked Ms. Stewart. I admired her. I still do.

After she was convicted of that charge, I believed then that she would not have been indicted in the first place had her name been Jane Doe or Max Stewart, rather than Martha Stewart.

And I still do to this day.

2.

HEALTHSOUTH

Trying to Find the Truth

It was six o'clock in the morning one day in August 2002. The Signature Terminal for charter jets at Dulles Airport was virtually empty. I sleepily walked in, looking for the captain of the private jet I was supposed to take to Birmingham, Alabama, to be interviewed by a possible new "crisis management" client.

As I looked around the terminal, there were only two other people there. Across a relatively darkened room, I recognized one of them: the late Jody Powell, former press secretary to President Jimmy Carter. He saw me about the same time. I walked over to say hi to him. "What are you doing here so early in the morning?" I asked Jody, whom I had met several times after the Carter years when he started his own PR firm.

"Some possible new client in a PR crisis wants my advice," Jody said, not naming the client. I didn't ask.

"What are you doing here?" Jody asked me.

"Coincidentally, same reason," I said.

I looked across the room and recognized the third person sitting on a couch across the room.

"Say, isn't that Mike Deaver?" I asked Jody.

Mike Deaver, now also deceased, was a hero of mine. I considered Mr. Deaver one of the geniuses in our business. He was the earliest advisor to then actor Ronald Reagan and had helped influence his public image and persona through two terms as California governor and two terms as president.

"Yes, it is," said Jody. We both walked across the room—I to introduce myself, since I had never met Mr. Deaver, and Jody to say hello, since he knew Mike pretty well.

After the introduction and hellos, Jody asked Mike the same question I had asked Jody, "What are you doing here so early in the morning?"

Deaver smiled and said only, "I really can't say. A possible new client." He, too, wouldn't mention the name.

I was beginning to get a sensation that there was an echo chamber going on in this private charter plane waiting room.

I decided to break the ice. "It's kind of coincidental the three of us are all here for a mysterious client to pick us up on a charter plane, isn't it?" I asked.

Mike and Jody looked at each other, and back at me. It was clear they were suspecting the same thing I was now suspecting.

"So let's all hold hands, count to three, and say it at once—who invited us here to help him with a crisis?"

We held hands, and said: "Richard Scrushy." And laughed.

"Well, I'll be goddamned," said Jody.

Mike Deaver smiled, seeming to be less surprised. "We shouldn't be surprised."

We looked at each other grinning, but not quite knowing what to say next.

Scrushy had been headlined in the *New York Times* a few days before as being under investigation by the Securities and Exchange

Commission for possible insider trading. He had sold a large block of HealthSouth stock just before a public announcement that the federal Medicare agency had made a technical rule change involving what was reimbursable for "rehabilitation" services for the elderly, which might include physical therapy that sometimes seemed to be the functional equivalent of a fitness program. The rule change, if read literally, would cost HealthSouth considerable revenue, since the company depended heavily on Medicare reimbursements for its local outpatient surgical centers, clinics, and rehabilitation centers.

The stock market reacted badly to news of the Health Care Financing Administration (HCFA) rule change, and HealthSouth's New York Stock Exchange share value dropped drastically the very next day. The fact that Scrushy had sold his stock just a day or two before the announcement looked, at the very least, suspicious—as if he had inside knowledge—news of the rule change and its negative financial impact before the rest of the market.

The *Times* story did not explain why Scrushy had sold the stock just before the announcement of the bad news, nor was there any denial that he had had any advance knowledge. Indeed, there was no comment at all from Scrushy, despite the implication in the article that Scrushy had known the bad news was coming and dumped his stock—an illegal act, if true.

It was obvious that Scrushy needed some crisis management advice—how to deal with the nasty media, casting aspersions on his honesty and fostering the suspicion that he had engaged in illegal insider trading.

Obviously each of us had been invited, secretly, without being told about the others, to visit Scrushy at his HealthSouth offices in Birmingham for what felt like a competitive auction, since none of us had been told we had been hired.

It made me uncomfortable to participate in such an auction, without being told ahead of time, and I said so.

"I'm not real happy about this secrecy thing," said Jody.

"Same here," Mike said.

I wondered aloud whether I was willing to make the trip under these circumstances. But as soon as I made the comment, a young man dressed in whites who looked like a pilot approached the three of us and asked us whether we were "Deaver, Powell, and Davis." I joked that it sounded like a bad law firm. We nodded, and he told us to follow him to the plane on the runway. We looked at each other, shrugged, figured we were up so early anyway, were curious about Scrushy, and decided to take the plane ride to Birmingham and see what happened.

DEVISING A LEGAL-MEDIA TRANSPARENCY STRATEGY

The flight down was uneventful. We discussed what we had read in the paper about Scrushy, agreed that Scrushy had done a poor job of telling his side of the story, and snoozed until, ninety minutes later, the plane landed at the Birmingham airport. As we got off the plane, we were immediately guided by the pilot to a large waiting helicopter.

"How far is HealthSouth from the airport?" I asked, surprised to see that a helicopter would be delivering us to the offices.

"By car about ten minutes," the pilot said, surprising me even further that Scrushy and HealthSouth used an expensive helicopter to deliver us to the offices when a cab or car would have taken so little time.

The helicopter ride took only a few minutes, and it landed next to a large office building that was two to three stories high but extended over a large area in the middle of what seemed more like a college campus than an office building complex.

We exited the helicopter and were met by a young man who introduced himself as head of HealthSouth "security." We followed him one flight up in an elevator, and then across the hall to Richard Scrushy's CEO offices.

As we entered, we found couches, a large conference table, and a huge desk, with a fair-haired, attractive man sitting behind it. He immediately stood up, broke into a big smile, and held his arms open, welcoming us with a booming announcement:

"I feel like O. J. Simpson. The three best in the business. You're going to be my 'Dream Team,'" he exclaimed.

Deaver, Powell, and I were shocked at this casual affirmative reference to the man who had perhaps the most negative public image of any American alive. We looked at each other and, as we later discovered when we shared our thoughts on the flight back to Washington, we had exactly the same thought:

"This guy needs crisis management."

USING ATTORNEY-CLIENT PRIVILEGE TO QUESTION SCRUSHY

The three of us agreed we needed to convince Scrushy to "go transparent" if ever anyone was going to believe that he was telling the truth. As the only attorney among us, I was worried about Mike and Jody not having the protection of attorney-client privilege—meaning that if Scrushy had in fact committed the crime of insider trading, then he could not admit it to them. Without the privilege, they could be forced to testify against him, and he would in all likelihood go to jail.

I explained this to them and to Scrushy and asked them to step outside so I could interview him alone.

When they left, Scrushy stood up behind his desk, an intimidating man physically—six feet or so, muscular, piercing eyes, and an aura of power and charisma.

"You're not worried that I am a crook, are you, Mr. Davis?"

"I only need you to tell me the truth," I responded.

He said that he didn't know for sure that it would be interpreted the way it had been by the Medicare agency. He initially knew only that they were redefining what was eligible to be reimbursed. He began to realize the possible serious impact on his company only some time after he had sold his stock. And he was pretty sure the new Medicare rule limiting reimbursement in this type of situation would not stand up since it didn't make any sense.

As to why he sold his stock after he had heard something about the rule change, he said that was consistent with a previously existing financial plan, not a decision linked to the possible impact of a Medicare rule change.

If that checked out, it was a good answer. It's a frequently used excuse by people who have engaged in illegal insider trading just before a bad news event. It also could be an honest answer, with the timing coincidental.

Now we had to investigate the facts and determine which was the right interpretation.

"If you sold your stock because of a previously existing plan, then why didn't you tell the *New York Times* reporter this—so you could have refuted the impression from the story that you had inside information and sold your stock illegally?" I asked.

"Well, now, that's where y'all came in—that's why I need the 'Dream Team,' " he said with a broad smile.

I called Powell and Deaver back into the room, told them Mr. Scrushy had told me a few things that I needed to check out with an independent investigation, and if I could verify that Mr. Scrushy had told the truth, then I would tell them, and the three of us would recommend a "get it out" media strategy.

I was, in effect, testing Scrushy to find out whether he would say that he didn't need an independent investigation. Instead he nodded— and said he had nothing to fear from an independent investigation. A good sign.

Scrushy called in his general counsel, and I spent the next several hours with him looking over Scrushy's documents and stock sale transactions over the past several years, while Deaver and Powell sat with Scrushy regaling him with White House war stories.

By the end of the day, I was relatively satisfied—subject to my bringing down an SEC expert in my law firm to review what I had reviewed and question Scrushy more expertly than I had so I could have the comfort of a second opinion. I returned to Scrushy's huge office to tell him that if everything checked out, I thought we could work together—meaning the three of us and him—to come up with a strategy to get his facts out into the media at the same time that we called the SEC and offered to cooperate fully in any investigation.

"What SEC investigation?" he asked me.

"The one that is coming for sure," I responded. "If everything checks out, you'll need to start off persuading them that you have nothing to hide—and we'll need to find a credible way to persuade the public and your shareholders that you are telling the truth as well."

Scrushy had an unhappy look on his face.

"You're not talking about hiring more lawyers to conduct an investigation, are you?" he asked.

"That's exactly what I have in mind—an independent investigation by a reputable law firm, reporting to your board and not to you, is probably the best way to convince your shareholders and the public that you have nothing to hide."

I raised the bar more than a little with one more suggestion.

"In fact, if we confirm what I have just seen that backs up your story about a regular trading program, and interview your top executives, who confirm you did not know about the real economic effects of the Medicare agency rules change, then I might recommend to you that after the investigation is over, the board waive attorney-client privilege and turn at least a summary of the report over to the SEC—and announce that ahead of time to the media."

I waited to see his reaction.

Scrushy knew I was waiting to see his reaction.

Long pause.

"Sounds like a plan to me," he said, triumphantly, surprising me a little.

On the flight home, Jody and Mike agreed that he had reacted credibly under pressure—and we began to discuss the full scenario of going to the board of directors, hiring a law firm to conduct the investigation, and getting the full story out by selecting one or more reporters to sit with Scrushy, review the documents, and write the complete story, with his explanation of his trading program. This would be what we call the "predicate" story—the baseline story that clears the fog created by the failure to comment and explain in the first stories—and it would be the basis of the rest of our crisis management plan going forward.

As we departed from Signature Terminal at Dulles, with the sun going down, we realized this was going to be a challenge—Scrushy was smart and always seemed to be one step ahead in anticipating what I had to say—but it was also going to be fun.

"Fun," Powell said, in his typical wry smile, "if nothing surprising happens."

SHOCKING THE SEC

The "rest of the story" in this crisis tale, unfortunately for Scrushy as well as for us, had a lot of surprises.

One of the first realities that struck the three of us—it was Mike Deaver who said it first—was that until all the legal issues were cleared up, he and Jody Powell couldn't play much of a role, since they couldn't get exposure to the facts, and possible evidence of Scrushy's culpability, if he had any, whereas I could because of the protection of the attorney-client privilege.

I agreed to check with them regularly and did—first on the overall strategy and then on developing messages and responses to media inquiries when I was comfortable with the fact that Scrushy appeared to be ignorant of the true economic impact of the Medicare rule change.

They warned me, and they were right, that no matter how the legal issues were sorted out, the public perception was horrible. Scrushy was a larger-than-life character, with his palatial house in Birmingham, Alabama, his big cars, helicopters, and beautiful wife and family. But that also made him a target for envy and resentment.

The first overall strategy that Deaver, Powell, and I developed was an "independent" investigation to confirm that Scrushy was telling the truth about not having inside knowledge about the effects of the Medicare rule change. A special committee of "independent directors" on the HealthSouth board of directors needed to be formed ("independent" in this context meant having no business—as in external businesses—or family relationship with Scrushy or HealthSouth); and that special committee would then hire another law firm to conduct an investigation, independent of me and Scrushy, who would stay at arm's length.

In a way, this was our first test of Scrushy. If he had lied to us about his lack of inside knowledge of the federal government's rule change, he might resist allowing an independent investigation to proceed. But his quick agreement to proceeding with such an investigation as the best way to deal with the crisis reinforced our belief that he had been telling us the truth.

I recommended to the board's special committee several law firms to choose from—including the famous Dallas, Texas, firm of Fulbright & Jaworski. I knew a partner there—Hal Hirsch—whom I respected greatly (and still do, to this day), having worked with him on another matter. He was an expert on bankruptcy and company restructurings. He was smart and savvy and I knew he had conducted many independent investigations as part of his restructuring practice, since he often inherited problems from companies in bankruptcy where there were many possible fraud activities that needed to be looked at.

Most of all, I knew that Fulbright & Jaworski was a famous national firm—and would instantly bring credibility to the investigation.

I and my law firm at the time, Patton Boggs, would represent both Scrushy and the company, with the understanding that if Fulbright or my firm uncovered any wrongdoing by Scrushy, there would be a conflict of interest between Scrushy and the company (meaning that the board of directors would become adverse to Scrushy, and, as we agreed in the legal engagement letter, I would continue to represent Scrushy personally and the company would have to hire a new law firm).

Once Hirsch had been hired and agreed to the plan and the independent investigation, the two of us agreed that we had to keep a distance between us. I did not want to be at all involved in the investigation except to be kept informed about its status. We both knew that for the investigation to have any credibility, that was the way it had to be. In substance and in optics, the investigation had to be in fact completely independent.

With Scrushy's and the board's permission, I then made an unusual phone call, late on a Sunday night, to a senior staff member of the Atlanta office of the SEC (I had set up the call ahead of time, and he had given me the number at which to reach him on a Sunday night). I told him we might give him a copy of the Fulbright report once it was completed and waive attorney-client privilege—assuming of course that the independent investigation confirmed that Scrushy had done nothing wrong. I told him I had done my own investigation and was convinced that Scrushy did not trade on inside information.

The effect was as I wanted. "That is unusual," he said. "That tells me that you are confident that Scrushy hasn't done anything wrong."

I didn't comment—but that was precisely the inference I hoped he would draw.

"SHREDDING"?

The plan was executed as we had initially discussed—first a straight-forward story in the *New York Times* and the *Wall Street Journal*, with the facts about Scrushy's pre-planned trading program to sell Health-South shares and his statement that he had not known about the adverse economic impact of the complicated Medicare federal agency rule change.

Meanwhile, Hal Hirsch had a half-dozen lawyers going through documents and papers, interviewing senior company officials, reading emails from everyone's hard drives, all with the objective of determining whether they could find any evidence that Scrushy had advance knowledge of the economic impact of the HCFA rule change.

But things didn't work out as we had carefully planned them.

One dramatic part of the narrative was the call I received early one morning from Hal Hirsch, after a couple of months, toward what we both thought would be the end of the investigation. He told me that he had discovered something that might be a problem (or might not be) and needed to be sure I was alone.

I closed the door and returned to my desk to listen.

Hirsch then told me that late the previous evening, one of his investigating attorneys had walked by a closed room, heard a strange whirring/vibrating sound, opened the door, and saw one of Health-South's security officials feeding documents into a shredder.

Shredder? I asked. The word itself was hair-raising. Memories of Watergate immediately hit me, recalling the shredding at CREEP (Committee to Re-elect the President) headquarters by Gordon Liddy and others involved in the third-rate burglary at the Watergate.

Oh, my God, I thought, I hope it wasn't the worst case of a cover-up as opposed to the usual destruction of documents that involved patient privacy information.

Hirsch and I discussed the potential legal ramifications.

If in fact there was a destruction of relevant documents to cover up the insider-knowledge issue on the U.S. government rule change that could adversely affect HealthSouth, and thus potentially impede Hirsch's (and the SEC's) inquiry, it would mean possible criminal conduct. And, of course, I would have to resign unless Scrushy could document that the shredding was in the ordinary course of protecting patient privacy rights and had nothing to do with destroying evidence of his possible insider trading that was under investigation.

Hirsch and I agreed that we both should consult with a criminal attorney about what we should do as attorneys as we explored what really happened, and why, regarding the shredded documents.

I called a criminal lawyer in my firm and consulted with the managing partner of the firm and the firm's counsel, before deciding that Hirsch needed to ask the independent board to begin an investigation of the shredding, the results of which might have to be reported to the SEC.

So here is where crisis management becomes riskiest. Is the client, to whom I always feel a total, 100 percent loyalty, owed my loyalty if he is involved in committing a crime? If he has lied to me?

An attorney's canon of ethics requires him or her to be loyal to a client, but there is ambiguity and some debate as to an attorney's obligation when he or she starts to suspect his or her client has committed a crime. The classic example: If an attorney (or a priest or a physician) is told in confidence the location of a ticking atomic bomb, of course the ethical obligation to maintain the confidence must give way to the moral imperative.

But when a client lies to an attorney and the attorney finds out, then the attorney must resign—at least as far as I am concerned. Moreover, since my hybrid legal crisis management discipline sometimes means I am both a defense attorney and a public advocate, my rule is: I cannot advocate anything publicly that I do not believe to be a provable fact or reasonable inference.

But without doubt, this shredding incident proved the absolute necessity for me to be an attorney with privilege and a crisis manager at the same time—otherwise Hirsch could not have shared the knowledge of the shredding and I could not have been in the best position to decide on a legal and crisis management strategy. But first I had to find out what happened and why—and whether any laws had been violated.

Am I living through a real-life version of a John Grisham movie? I thought.

The most stressful moment came when I confronted Scrushy with the question about the shredding, with Hal Hirsch on the phone. Scrushy's response was so quick and so casual that it struck us that he was telling the truth. He explained that the company was required every night to shred individual medical records that were old and closed under federal health records secrecy laws. (This was still the era of mostly paper records and before full digitization of such data became prevalent.)

Since Hirsch and Fulbright & Jaworski were still the attorneys working for the board's independent committee investigating all these matters, Hirsch and I agreed that the shredding incident should be made part of a separate independent investigation report by Fulbright, and I stood down and let him and his team proceed to get to the bottom of the shredding.

I informed Richard Scrushy of this additional investigation. I didn't ask for him to react, although he did say a few words indicating his unhappiness with more legal fees.

Hirsch kept me informed in the next several weeks about the shredding investigation. Interviews with the security official found at the shredding machine and others, as well as a review of prior practices and of privacy laws regarding medical records, confirmed that there was a need under federal medical privacy regulations to protect and possibly to destroy medical records of individual patients.

But there seemed no way to confirm what records were actually being shredded at such a coincidental and untimely moment, when there was an order from outside attorneys, standard when a company is in litigation or under regulatory investigation: Preserve all records. So as crisis manager, no matter what the facts were, I knew we had to prepare for "bad optics" if and when the shredding issue became public.

Ultimately, Hal Hirsch made the wise decision to send the separate report on the shredding to the SEC, and let them determine whether additional investigation was required or even whether there should be a referral to the U.S. attorney. I said nothing. I knew I shouldn't agree or disagree, since the Fulbright investigation had to be in fact and in spirit completely independent. But inwardly, I agreed with Hirsch's decision—and even happier that I had recommended hiring him and Fulbright. (P.S.: Ultimately, the SEC received the Fulbright shredding report and we never heard back from them on the subject—inferring that they had looked into it and verified Scrushy's explanation that it was in the ordinary course regarding medical records and patient privacy rights.)

I hung up the phone, head pounding. What next? I thought.

WHAT'S THE DEFINITION OF THE WORD "CLEARED"?

The linchpin of the strategy that Mike Deaver, Jody Powell, and I had devised was the conduct of a credible independent investigation by an outstanding law firm, and if the investigation backed up Scrushy's version of what happened, to release a summary publicly, with the detailed report turned over to the SEC voluntarily for review.

After several months and complete access given to the Fulbright & Jaworski legal team under the skilled leadership of Hal Hirsch, a rough draft of the report had been completed. Hirsch had agreed that I could read the report just before its public release in summary form so that I could begin to prepare a press release.

It was explicitly agreed between Hirsch and me and the legal team that I would have no right (or desire) to make substantive comments on the report; if I did, even if my comments were rejected, there could be a perception I was trying to influence the inquiry's conclusions.

I never considered, nor did Hirsch, that if we kept to our agreement and I offered no substantive comments, especially about conclusions, someone could accuse me of attempting to influence Hirsch because of his reading me the report before its release.

On Sunday, October 27, Hirsch read me the conclusions and various sections of the report supporting those conclusions, and we discussed the timing of the press release and other related matters.

The key conclusion of the report read to me on the phone, in paraphrase: Before the sale of his stock, the Fulbright/Hirsch legal team had found, there was no evidence that Mr. Scrushy had foreknowledge of a Medicare rule change that he knew would significantly harm the financial status of HealthSouth. The key legal issue, of course, was whether he knew that the rule change would harm the company and, thus, cause a depression in its share value and that he had therefore sold before the rest of the market. He said he didn't—and the Hirsch team had concluded there was *no evidence* that he did.

When I received a copy of the report the next day, I pondered how I could avoid writing a press release leading with a negative statement, that is, that the Fulbright team had found "no evidence of wrongdoing," and instead find a positive way of expressing that.

So the headline and lead in the press release I wrote started by saying that the independent legal inquiry had "cleared" Scrushy of having knowledge that the rule change would be significantly harmful to HealthSouth. I thought that was consistent with the phrase "found no evidence." To be sure there was no misinterpretation, however, I also included the direct quotation from the Fulbright report—that the Fulbright attorneys had found "no evidence of wrongdoing," or illegal insider trading, by Scrushy.

I sent the draft of the release to Hirsch on Tuesday, October 29, and, together with a few colleagues in my office, we called him to be sure he and his colleagues had no issues with the press release. The conversation was rushed and didn't deal with specific words used in the release. When we hung up the phone we had the impression that Hirsch and his colleagues at Fulbright had no problem with our interpreting the phrase "no evidence" as "cleared."

We were wrong. A huge mistake—a lesson learned the hard way.

We sent the press release out on Wednesday afternoon, October 30. The *Times* reporters were also sent the full copy of the Fulbright report, with the key sentence regarding finding "no evidence" that Scrushy had inside knowledge before he sold his stock.

On Thursday morning, the *New York Times* ran a front-page business section article with the headline STOCK SALE INQUIRY EXONERATES CHAIRMAN OF HEALTHSOUTH. When I saw that the *Times* had chosen the word "Exonerates" in the headline to characterize the phrase "no evidence" that they had seen in the full report, I was strengthened in my belief that the word "cleared" in the press release was appropriate. Moreover, the lead paragraph of the story actually used the word "cleared" in referring to the Fulbright report. Here was the full lead paragraph in the *Times* story on the report:

> HealthSouth said yesterday that an investigation by an outside law firm into the recent stock sales of its chairman, Richard M. Scrushy, had found no evidence of wrongdoing and had cleared Mr. Scrushy of having insider information before he sold nearly $100 million in stock.

The article also noted in the third paragraph that the full report had been sent to the Securities and Exchange Commission—also confirming our strategy of commissioning an outside independent investigation.

The phone rang shortly after I entered my office at nine that morning. It was Richard Scrushy. He was very happy, congratulating me for the strategy of launching a credible outside investigation, and was relieved that the *New York Times*—which a few months before had headlines implying that he had been guilty of illegal insider trading—had now written the word "exonerates" in its headline.

Our crisis management team of attorneys was satisfied. We had kept our commitment to transparency, to the media and the SEC, and Scrushy had shown he was unafraid of a truly independent investigation by a first-rate law firm, and we had been open with the SEC—the top regulators.

But our celebration was short-lived. The next day, we had the "oops" moment that taught me some valuable lessons. Hal Hirsch called and insisted that he had never approved the word "cleared" and said the management of his law firm wanted to issue a *new revised* press release, stating only that "no evidence" of wrongdoing was found, omitting the word "cleared."

But there is no substantive difference, I argued. I used the word "cleared" and the *Times* used that word in its lead paragraph, as well as the word "exonerates" in its headline. I honestly thought that that word was okay with Hal and his colleagues at Fulbright.

Obviously, I said, there was an honest misunderstanding. What could we do to fix this? Hirsch, to his credit, didn't want to do anything that would hurt the client, but believed it was necessary to issue a clarifying statement publishing the full "no evidence" sentence that was the only conclusion in the Fulbright report, and not using the affirmative word "cleared." I recognized if that is what Hal and Fulbright wanted to do, then they were independent actors here, and of course that is what had to be done. I called Scrushy and told him the situation. He wasn't happy with the idea of a second statement from Fulbright but ultimately agreed with me that this was not a big deal. Embarrassing, maybe, but it wouldn't change the facts.

As it turned out, it wasn't a big deal, thank goodness. The next day, in conjunction with Fulbright and Hal, we issued a new release, omitting the word "cleared." As I expected, the media calls asked me whether this reflected a retreat from the word "cleared." I simply stated that it was what it was—"no evidence" was what the independent report of Fulbright had said, and how that can be fairly characterized is up to others to decide.

In retrospect, I learned an important lesson. To lawyers, words and nuances matter, and I should have been 100 percent certain that converting "no evidence" to "cleared" was acceptable to Fulbright. I had put Hirsch in a difficult position about using a characterizing word, "cleared," in the headline and the lead paragraph, even though I thought he was okay with that. But what I missed—and a lesson I learned the hard way—was that in this kind of high-profile legal crisis, with regulators and possibly criminal authorities reviewing every word, it was much safer to stick to the actual words and avoid all adjectives, adverbs, and characterizations.

THE CONGRESSIONAL HEARING

Whoever said crisis management was an easy business?

A congressional oversight committee took interest in Scrushy and HealthSouth after I had completed my work at the end of 2002 and no longer represented Scrushy or HealthSouth. In April 2003, a new accounting scandal had broken out for HealthSouth, this one accusing Scrushy and his top managers of manipulating the financial statements to increase earnings fraudulently, leading to artificially inflated stock values.

It was perhaps inevitable that the congressional hearing triggered by the latest accusations against Scrushy for accounting fraud would be conflated with the insider trading allegations that I had handled together with Hal Hirsch the previous year. But they were completely unrelated. Our team and Hirsch's team had no inkling of accounting fraud.

The focus was on the two issues for which, in retrospect, I blamed myself and not Hirsch. The first led to members of Congress questioning my motives for asking Hirsch to read the draft report on Scrushy's stock sales before the announcement of the Medicare rules change. I explained, and the email traffic in the hands of the congressional committee confirmed, that there was no intent to influence the report, I had not done so, and the purpose was to prepare for the issuance of a press release.

But in politics, especially in a political hearing, innuendo can effectively be used, even though the facts trump the suggestion of wrongdoing.

Rep. Cliff Stearns (R-FL) showed the political "courage" to make a speech accusing me of wrongdoing, suggesting through innuendo (and falsely) that I had tried to influence the contents of the Fulbright report. Then, as I tried to answer, he left the room. I called after him to at least wait for my answer, but he didn't wait and left with a wave of his hand. I remember thinking, What a cheap-shot artist!

Now I knew why some members of Congress are held in such low esteem. Here's a guy playing to the galleries, making an accusation attacking my integrity, and then he walks out of the room without the courtesy of allowing me a response. (As noted in the introduction to this book, this is the same Representative Stearns who, nine years later in 2011, announced an "investigation" of Planned Parenthood, which contributed to the decision by the Susan Komen Foundation to cut off funding, at least temporarily, of Planned Parenthood; and the same Representative Stearns whose own Republican Party voters in August 2012 denied him renomination to run again as their congressman.)

After Stearns left the room before I could answer, I still tried to answer the accusation, explaining that it took almost an hour for Hirsch to read the full report to me, and I had made no effort to influence the conclusions, and Hirsch, sitting at the end of the panel table, would confirm that. I knew that if there was a recess, the reporters in the room would run to file their stories before hearing my answer. However, the Republican committee chair called a recess before allowing me to answer, which I knew would result in most of the press leaving to return to their offices to make deadlines.

So it goes for fairness at congressional hearings, and for politicians who have the dais and get to make cheap shots without being held accountable. Shocking!

On the other hand, I had advised my clients never to expect fairness from members of Congress using a hearing platform to make a political point, rather than to seek the facts. Ironically, I was expecting something that I advised my clients never to expect.

After the recess, to a virtually empty hearing room, I stated the undisputed fact that I had never tried to influence the conclusions of the report. I did follow the crisis management rule to get to reporters to correct misinformation before they filed and called several reporters to give them my response and gave them Hirsch's cell phone number to confirm the truth of what I was saying. I managed to reach the *Wall Street Journal* reporter and a few others to tell them my response and succeeded in getting the truth into most of the mainstream media published reports the next day.

The other issue raised, for which I had a good answer but about which I still knew I had made a mistake of judgment, was the use of the characterization "cleared." To his credit, Hirsch left open the possibility that there was a misunderstanding between us, which I then confirmed when it was my turn to respond to questions from a congressman on the panel. Months later, Hal Hirsch and I had a "make up" dinner together. We both agreed that we could have been more precise in what had been agreed for the contents of the press release.

LESSONS LEARNED

First and foremost, my experience with the Richard Scrushy/HealthSouth crisis representation reinforced the notion that being a practicing attorney, enjoying the attorney-client privilege was critical to my doing crisis management in a complicated and dangerous legal situation. As Jody Powell and Mike Deaver themselves pointed out, they could not have conducted the initial interviews of Scrushy and other HealthSouth managers on the facts of their understanding of the Medicare rule change and its effects on the company's finances. I was able to do my best to get to the bottom of what had happened and why, without fear of being subject to a subpoena to compel my testimony, and then kept my word and turned over the results of the investigation on the shredding (as well as the insider trading allegations) to the SEC.

But once I gathered all the facts, I was able to communicate enough to them to develop the basic strategy we decided on—to seek an outside independent investigation and to tell the regulators ahead of time and to tell the press we would publish the results, at least in summary form.

But I also learned the hard way—and not for the first time—how dangerous the profession I had invented was.

In gaining access to all the facts as an attorney with privilege and then crossing over and developing media strategy, I had to be careful about waiving my privilege and becoming part of the media/political story.

On the good-lessons-learned side, I found my effectiveness was greatly enhanced by the friendship and trust I had developed with Hal Hirsch, and in the final analysis, he conducted a totally independent and credible investigation. What a contrast, I thought, between his attitude of professional courtesy and collegiality and the hang-up by Ms. Stewart's attorney, the late Robert Morvillo, without even giving me a chance to explain my overall strategy and hear his viewpoint.

And of course, with the wisdom of twenty-twenty hindsight, I should have practiced what I preached to my crisis management team at my law firm—no adjectives or adverbs or characterizations, just facts. "No evidence" should have been enough—using the characterization "cleared" wasn't necessary.

In the final analysis, with the knowledge that words matter, and even one characterizing word can get you into trouble, it is still critical for effective crisis management that facts be boiled down to a few simple—but accurate—messages.

PUT THE FACTS INTO SIMPLE MESSAGES

3.

PAKISTAN

"The Money or the Planes—What's Fair Is Fair"

On April 11, 1995, a beautiful pre-spring morning in Washington, D.C., I was at the Blair House, the historic guesthouse for heads of state just across from the White House on Pennsylvania Avenue. I was there, along with my old friend Mark Siegel, to help prepare then prime minister Benazir Bhutto for a noon summit meeting with President Bill Clinton. Mark had been a close friend of Prime Minister Bhutto for more than a decade and had served as her speechwriter and American advisor for many years.

He had recommended that I be hired in the fall of 1994 by the then Pakistani ambassador to the United States, Dr. Maleeha Lodhi, a brilliant editor and journalist of Pakistan's biggest English-speaking newspaper. The main reason for my engagement was to work with Mark Siegel to devise a strategy—legal, media, or political, or all three—to convince the U.S. government to deliver twenty-eight F-16 fighter jet aircraft and equipment to Pakistan for which Pakistan had already paid the United States more than $600 million in cash some years before.

The planes were already manufactured and ready for delivery. Or, if the United States would not permit delivery to Pakistan of the paid-for planes, then I was tasked with finding a way to persuade the U.S. government to repay the $600 million to Pakistan, a cash-starved nation.

There were many purposes of this April 1995 summit meeting between President Clinton and Prime Minister Bhutto. She had not visited the White House since 1989, when she was first elected prime minister. Now she was back with much on her agenda—Pakistan had helped the United States in training insurgents to oust the Soviets from Afghanistan and now they needed more economic aid and support. But the most important reason for her visit was for the prime minister to convince President Clinton to permit delivery of the twenty-eight F-16s that had been paid for or to return the $600 million to Pakistan.

When the prime minister arrived, I met her for the first time with Mr. Siegel and Ambassador Lodhi, and we went into a small, sunshine-drenched living room, with a clear view of the White House across Pennsylvania Avenue.

"Well, Mr. Davis," the prime minister said to me, "please tell me how I can convince your friend President Clinton to send us our planes or give us our money back."

I gulped.

"You have to start with nine words," I said, "and repeat them personally to President Clinton at least five times in the ten minutes you can spend with him in a one-on-one conversation, which you must insist on."

"Nine words five times?" she asked with a smile. "That easy?"

First some background.

THE PRESSLER AMENDMENT

The problem was getting around something called the Pressler Amendment, which was enacted in 1985. Named after former South Dakota

Republican senator Larry Pressler, the law singled out only Pakistan for a ban on any sale or transfer of military equipment if it ever developed a nuclear bomb or "capability." The law required the president of the United States each year to certify that Pakistan did *not* have nuclear capability. In the event the president failed to make that certification, then all military weapons and equipment transfers from the United States to Pakistan were banned.

But what if the money had already been paid, the military equipment manufactured and ready for delivery—but in between, Pakistan developed the Bomb? That was exactly the situation facing the United States and Pakistan on the April 1995 morning when Prime Minister Bhutto prepared to see President Clinton.

The Pressler Amendment caused great resentment and anger in Pakistan down to the street level. After all, it was patently discriminatory—it singled out Pakistan and ignored the fact that Pakistan's geopolitical and historical adversary in South Asia, India, had for many years had an atomic weapon, and yet India was not subject to such a ban on military equipment transfers. Thus the law typified for many Pakistanis and other Muslims in South Asia and the Middle East an anti-Islamic, prejudiced U.S. attitude—presaging the perception that led up to and was accelerated after 9/11. Pakistani ambassador Lodhi once told me that the name Pressler was better known in the streets of Pakistan than that of the president of the United States.

She was right. Some months later, on my first trip to Islamabad, the cab driver who picked me up at the airport to take me to my hotel turned around and told me, in broken English, recognizing me as an American, "You need to do something about that bad man Pressler."

In the late 1980s, when Pakistan contracted to purchase the F-16s, it didn't pay the manufacturer—Lockheed Martin—directly. The U.S. Defense Department was the third-party intermediary, under a program called the Foreign Military Sales or FMS program. This was established so the United States could facilitate the sale of U.S. military weapons by U.S. companies to foreign governments by acting as a buyer-reseller go-between. So on the F-16 contract, the United States collected the $600 million, paid it to Lockheed Martin for the twenty-eight F-16s, and then in the early 1990s took delivery and title of the planes and put them in storage, unable to ship them thanks to the explicit language of the Pressler Amendment.

In the late 1980s, U.S. intelligence agencies were reporting that Pakistan was actively working on developing a nuclear bomb to rival India's. Yet President George H. W. Bush, in 1989, his first year as president, certified that Pakistan did not have nuclear capability. This was the time when the United States was working closely with Pakistan to oust the Soviet Union from Afghanistan, after the Soviets had invaded that country in 1980. So President Bush and his anti-Soviet advisors chose to look the other way on Pakistan's evident nuclear capability.

But by 1990, President Bush found he had no choice—U.S. intelligence had verified the possession by Pakistan of the functional equivalent of the Bomb. All the component parts and technology were fully developed. The only thing remaining was final assembly, which intelligence reports stated could be done quickly and easily. (As some said at the time, Pakistan was a "turned screw" away from the Bomb—a similar expression is used today by many experts regarding Iran's "almost" nuclear weapon capability.) So in 1990, President Bush was no longer able to make the negative certification required under the Pressler Amendment. That triggered the applicability of the law, meaning that the twenty-eight F-16s, which were just about to be completed and ready for shipment, could not be shipped to Pakistan.

To add insult to injury, the United States was reportedly charging Pakistan about fifty thousand dollars per month to store the planes in hangars in the desert in a southwestern state, while neither shipping the planes nor sending back the money.

Meanwhile, the U.S. government did not have the $600 million in a bank account somewhere to return to Pakistan even if it wanted to. That money had already been paid to the manufacturer, Lockheed

Martin. And the only way to pay back Pakistan $600 million was to go to Congress and ask it to appropriate an *additional* $600 million especially for Pakistan—instead of spending that money on such projects as roads, post offices, and bridges (to nowhere?). Fat chance.

THE POWER OF A PHRASE

A few weeks before we met with the prime minister at Blair House, as she prepared to cross the street to see President Clinton, Mark Siegel and I met to come up with a strategy—and a message—to maximize the chance President Clinton would see the light and do the right thing for Pakistan on the F-16 issue.

We knew that President Clinton was boxed in by the black letter of the Pressler law—he couldn't authorize shipment of the planes. His White House national security advisor team also did not want him to discuss with the prime minister, much less make any commitments about returning, the $600 million in F-16 money.

Mark and I were determined to overcome this staff opposition to a Pakistani position on the F-16s that seemed overwhelmingly right on the merits. We both believed that if Prime Minister Bhutto could spend a few minutes one-on-one with President Clinton and appeal to his sense of fairness, he would override advice from his senior advisors and do and say what he thought was right.

But what should Madame Bhutto say? In a short phrase, maybe having only a minute or two with the president, what simple message could she communicate that would be effective?

Mark and I didn't exactly originate the essence of the key nine-word phrase. It was derived from the politically savvy, former journalist Pakistani ambassador Dr. Lodhi, who had a good instinct for a headline, since she was a former outstanding journalist and editor in Pakistan.

"I don't know," she answered, "but it just seems obvious that if you pay for planes and you don't get the planes, you should either get the planes or get your money back. That is only fair."

That thought stuck in our minds somewhere, ready to be called up when needed. Mark and I knew that there was a headline, a simple message, somewhere in that sentence.

Before our meeting with Prime Minister Bhutto, Mark and I tried to whittle it down to a few words that would resonate most with President Clinton.

We tried lots of formulations—

"Pressler isn't worth ruining Pakistani-American relations. . . ."

No.

"America should return the $600 million it owes to Pakistan. It can't have it both ways."

Getting there, but still no.

Then almost at the same time, the two of us remembered Ambassador Lodhi's formulation.

Siegel said, "It's not right for Pakistan to pay the money for the planes and then not get the planes or the money back."

Getting closer.

"We need to remind the president that this just isn't fair," Mark said. "Fairness is an important word to him."

I knew we needed fewer words to make a headline. Then I thought I had it: "The money or the planes. You can't have both."

Mark said, "No . . . 'you can't have both' is disrespectful. How about adding what Bill Clinton would most respond to: " 'It's not fair.' "

"I like it!" I exclaimed. Then I changed it slightly. "What's fair is fair."

"The money or the planes—what's fair is fair."

We had our two sentences. Nine words. Simple. We knew it was right as soon as we said it.

"That's it!" I said, and we high-fived.

PRESIDENT CLINTON'S PRESS CONFERENCE

So on that April morning at Blair House, with a beautiful sunlit White House visible through the window across the street, Mark and I spent the last few minutes with Prime Minister Bhutto imploring her to repeat our newly minted phrase to President Clinton—"The money or the planes—what's fair is fair"—especially if she could get a few minutes with him one-on-one. We suspected that his senior advisors would oppose a meeting at which they were not present and couldn't block discussion of the F-16s. But we thought there was a good chance, if Prime Minister Bhutto could use that phrase in a personal meeting with him without the interference of his outside advisors, that President Clinton would come around. We just had faith that his strong sense of right and wrong and fairness would cause him to agree with Pakistan's position after all these years. We worried only that staff, for understandable reasons, would not want President Clinton to go public about the controversial subject of the F-16s, nuclear proliferation, and the return of hundreds of millions of dollars to Pakistan.

As the prime minister walked out the door to cross the street to enter the White House, I said: "Remember—'The money or the planes—what's fair is fair.'" And Mark said: "And remember, too—ask to talk with him alone in the Oval Office, without his advisors around."

The prime minister turned and smiled. "I know what you two are up to—you want me to repeat that phrase over and over like a broken record."

"Yessss!" we exclaimed. She shook her head with amusement, nodded, and left.

Mark and I paced nervously, with the TV set tuned to C-SPAN. We weren't sure whether there would be any joint televised appearance of the president and the prime minister, but were hoping there would be.

Then it happened . . . far more than we could have hoped.

At about 1:50 p.m., President Clinton and Prime Minister Bhutto suddenly appeared on C-SPAN walking into the White House Press Room. Both took the podium and made brief remarks.

Then a reporter from the Associated Press asked the first question—on the F-16s! (We had talked to several White House reporters, including a couple from the Associated Press, and suggested they ask about the F-16s. It worked. We had no idea it would be the *first* question asked. *Amazing!*)

When we heard President Clinton's answer, we knew that Prime Minister Bhutto had somehow delivered the nine-word message.

"As you know, under the law as it now exists [referring to the Pressler Amendment] we cannot release the equipment . . . ," President Clinton said. "However, Pakistan made payments. The sellers of the equipment give up title and received the money, and now it's in storage. I don't know if what happened was fair to Pakistan in terms of the money."

"Did he just use the word 'fair'?" Mark asked rhetorically, as we high-fived.

Then it got better. The president made reference to the F-16 issue several times, and each time he spoke about finding a solution based on fairness principles. He referred to the situation Pakistan faced as a "catch-22," and then said: "This [Pressler Amendment] puts Pakistan in no-man's-land where you didn't have the equipment and you'd given up the money."

And then, best of all, President Clinton said: "I don't think it is right for us to keep the money and the equipment."

Not "right"!

This was the Bill Clinton Mark and I had known for many years—a man whose instincts went beyond diplomatic niceties and complicated geopolitics and were grounded on basic questions of right and wrong.

About a half hour or so after the press briefing ended, Prime Minister Bhutto returned to Blair House, a big smile on her face.

"Well, Lanny and Mark, it looks like you were right—President

Clinton believes what's fair is fair—the money or the planes!" We were beaming. She continued: "I don't think they are going to repeal Pressler, but I think we have a chance of getting our money back."

But, as it turned out, it wasn't that simple.

"YOU EXPECT ME TO SUE BILL CLINTON?"

Despite the clear expression of what was right and wrong by the president of the United States, that isn't always enough to move the U.S. government—certainly not to move the U.S. Congress to appropriate $600 million specially for Pakistan or to enact a waiver of the Pressler Amendment. And within the White House staff, we were told, there was a decision immediately at the senior levels of the foreign policy/national security advisors to dampen anyone's hopes that the president's words could be taken too seriously.

The president's press secretary, Michael McCurry, was quoted in the same Associated Press article that day, after the press conference, obviously reflecting caution from the president's senior national security advisory staff, as saying, "[Pakistan] is not going to get money or planes anytime soon."

McCurry, as usual, was right. Nothing happened for more than three years. When we went to the leadership of Congress on both sides of the aisle, we almost got laughed out of the room when we asked about the chance of a separate $600 million appropriation for Pakistan. Plus, there was substantial ideological congressional opposition, most from liberal, anti-nuclear-proliferation Democrats, who were angry at Pakistan for building the Bomb and then expecting the Pressler Amendment to be ignored after they did it.

For the next year, we continued to visit members of Congress to solicit their support for some compromise—such as that Congress would appropriate part of the $600 million and Pakistan would find a way to sell the compromise to its people, or perhaps some of the

F-16s could be sold to other nations, with the proceeds turned over to Pakistan.

Ambassador Lodhi was skeptical: "So I see—we tell the Pakistani people, 'You see, we paid $600 million, can't get the planes, and we tell everyone that the reason we can't get our money back is because some guy named Larry Pressler picked out Pakistan alone to sanction if we developed the Bomb, but forgot about India.' Can you imagine an American president selling to the American people: 'America is sanctioned by the rest of the world for developing the Bomb, but the Soviet Union isn't'? Come on!"

We thought this contradiction would ring true with many congressional leaders who realized the vital role Pakistan played in training and financing guerillas in Afghanistan to force the Soviet Union to withdraw its occupation. Mark Siegel and I visited Sen. Paul Sarbanes (D-MD), who was also a good friend of both of ours for many years.

Before we could get the second sentence out—the first one suggesting the "fairness" issue and the double standard applied to Pakistan—Sarbanes cut us off.

"The Pakistanis are dangerous people and they thought they could fool us by developing the Bomb and escaping Pressler," he said. "Well, they didn't."

That was that. Opposition within the White House national security staff structure—forget about the opposite feelings of the president of the United States. Opposition in the Congress to appropriating any money, even partial repayment. We had hit a stone wall.

The message strategy hadn't worked . . . yet. The political strategy hadn't worked . . . yet. So now we turned to another tactic, often the one chosen in desperation: We put our legal hats on and considered the question, "How about Pakistan suing the United States for breach of contract?"

It seemed like a crazy idea, but my law partner, Steven Schneebaum, one of the world's leading experts on international law and litigation, shocked me by saying, simply: "Pakistan can sue the U.S.

government in the U.S. Court of Claims." That is a special court in Washington, D.C., where a private party or another government can sue the U.S. government for breach of contract and get jurisdiction under international law. Then Schneebaum said something even more shocking: "And we will win."

One thing Steven Schneebaum did not lack was confidence.

So in April 1996, Schneebaum and I and Mark Siegel traveled to Islamabad, the capital of Pakistan, to meet with Prime Minister Bhutto to make the recommendation that we file the lawsuit against the U.S. government . . . or at least threaten to.

We arrived in the early morning in a large conference room with a long conference table. Prime Minister Bhutto sat at one end, and we were seated way down at the other end. Surrounding the table and filling the room were what seemed like more than a hundred men and only a few women, most of her cabinet and a lot of uniformed, full-braided military officials, together with a number of super-serious dark-suited men who we were told later were the senior officials of the ISI, Pakistan's intelligence agency.

Schneebaum explained the straightforward legal case for breach of contract that Pakistan could file against the U.S. government. Uncle Sam, after all, was the holder of the title of the F-16s purchased by Pakistan and was the receiver of the $600 million. He explained the case and the law simply. If A promises to deliver merchandise to B, and B pays A for delivery, and A doesn't deliver, the law holds that B can sue A for breach of contract and collect money damages equal to the price paid for the undelivered merchandise.

There was dead silence in the crowded room.

I could hear my heart beating as Prime Minister Bhutto, sitting at the far end of the long, long conference table stared at me, with a look of obvious incredulity.

"You mean, Mr. Davis," she said, "you expect me to sue your friend Bill Clinton?"

I took a breath.

"Well, not really, Madame Prime Minister," I answered. "You are not really suing President Clinton—you are suing the U.S. government as the named defendant."

She looked at me with even more skepticism.

"And who is the head of the U.S. government, Mr. Davis?" she asked.

"Well, technically, President Clinton is, but you see . . ."

I stopped. I knew adding the word "technically" was . . . well . . . dumb.

The prime minister smiled.

"Oh, 'technically'? I hope the next time you see him you will tell President Clinton that he is only technically the president," she said.

Ouch.

"Mr. Davis," she continued, "we will take your presentation under advisement. I also expect you to be more creative and come up with a solution other than expecting me and my government to sue the United States of America and President Bill Clinton."

The meeting seemed to be over, as she closed her folders and the room quickly emptied. She motioned me into a private room.

I was struck by her beauty and her sharp eyes and intelligence.

"So, Mr. Davis, you are a friend of President Clinton, yes?"

"Yes, Madame Prime Minister, for many years."

"So I have a feeling that you don't want to sue President Clinton either. I certainly don't and won't. So why don't you come up with another idea?"

When we returned to the United States, we again went back to Congress and the White House to try to get some money or a waiver under Pressler, but we got nowhere.

But we couldn't figure out anything short of filing a lawsuit against the U.S. government, and we pressed our case again with Ambassador Lodhi. She was sympathetic, understanding that this was truly our only option, since as a former journalist and politically savvy expert at U.S. politics, she saw the political realities.

But after checking back home, she again repeated instructions from her boss, the prime minister: no lawsuit. So we were stuck against a wall, with nowhere to go to solve the problem.

Several months later, in December 1996, I received the call from Clinton White House counsel Jack Quinn, and I left my law firm to join the White House as special counsel to speak for the White House on all "scandal" questions.

I knew, and I religiously followed the restriction, that I was not allowed to mention to anyone at the White House any client matter I had worked on as a private attorney, so I never mentioned Pakistan during my fourteen-month tenure at the White House. Nor did anyone—Mark Siegel or Steven Schneebaum, Ambassador Lodhi or anyone—ever call me or discuss the subject with me.

A WIN-WIN SOLUTION—SUING BUT NOT SUING

When I left the White House in February 1998 and returned to my law firm shortly thereafter, I agreed to represent Pakistan once again on the F-16 matter. There was, however, a new prime minister who had defeated Madame Bhutto in February 1997 elections, Nawaz Sharif, and a new Pakistani ambassador to the United States, Riaz Khokhar, a foreign service professional with experience in high-level and difficult negotiations—just what we needed.

I told Ambassador Khokhar that as a condition of my agreeing to resume my efforts to find a solution on the F-16 issue, I would not talk to anyone at the White House about the matter—not staff, not anyone. Regardless of legal restrictions on doing so, I wouldn't have lobbied the White House so soon after leaving it—it would not have felt right to me.

But I was free to act as an attorney and to resume the research on filing a lawsuit for breach of contract against the United States. With a new prime minister and new ambassador, we found a more receptive audience to doing so. And I was free to have communications with legal officers in the Justice Department and the Department of Defense about possible legal claims by Pakistan—acting as an attorney, not as a lobbyist.

After some research and conversations with Justice Department attorneys, we almost accidentally fell upon a novel twist in the legal options: We might be able to obtain all or a good portion of the $600 million without having to go to Congress and without actually having to file a lawsuit.

"And how do you perform this miracle?" Ambassador Khokhar asked after we told him the new idea.

"We draft the complaint, but we send copies to the U.S. Justice Department lawyers and the Defense Department *before* we actually ever file the suit," I explained.

"We have found that there is something called the 'judgment fund' or some name like that at the Justice Department. It can be used to settle cases, with the attorney general having total discretion. And here is what is unusual: If the attorney general determines that the case filed against the government cannot be successfully defended and the government will end up paying damages, the AG can decide to use the judgment fund to settle the case before it is filed."

When we met with the Defense and Justice Department lawyers, there were more than twenty government lawyers in a small conference room at the Pentagon. We had a long discussion about the pros and the cons of the breach-of-contract case. They pointed out there was some legal defense to the case—that Pakistan "assumed the risk" of paying for the F-16s at a time when it knew it would be developing a nuclear weapon and thus would be barred from receiving the planes under the Pressler Amendment.

But I reminded them that our nine words, "the money or the planes—what's fair is fair," would be seen by the court (and the media) as about the fundamental principle of fairness. I made that point after noticing that several of the lawyers in the room had highlighted or underlined the same section in the introduction section of the complaint that Steven and I had drafted: "This is more than a case about the law of contracts and recovery of damages for a clear breach of contract. It is a case about the law of fairness, about what is right and what is wrong."

I wrote that sentence with the knowledge that it would have media appeal as well as "equitable" appeal—the word used by judges when they decide a case based on fairness principles, even though strictly speaking a breach-of-contract case is supposed to be decided purely on the basis of the law of contracts.

From this point on, the successful end result should be credited to the negotiating skills of Pakistani ambassador Khokhar. In December 1998, the final deal was announced: Some of the $600 million would be paid after sale of the F-16s to a third country, with the proceeds going to Pakistan; another portion would come from the Department of Justice's "judgment fund," a decision ultimately made by the attorney general, Janet Reno; and the balance would be "paid" through the shipments of wheat to Pakistan, which Pakistan would not have to pay for (the U.S. government would pay U.S. wheat farmers, we were told, from existing agriculture subsidy programs).

Voilà!

A solution after all these years. Everyone's happy—Pakistan, the U.S. government for getting rid of a thorny problem seriously impeding U.S.-Pakistan relations, and don't forget U.S. wheat farmers, happy to sell more wheat.

LESSONS LEARNED—A SIMPLE MESSAGE AND A COMPLICATED SOLUTION

The final outcome on Pakistan was a lesson in aligning law, facts, and media into a focused strategy. But ultimately, the final outcome needed a pivot—a message—that summed it all up, to trigger the multipronged strategy leading to a win-win solution for all.

But what made our message most effective was our decision to ask Prime Minister Bhutto to deliver it personally to President Clinton, because we all knew that Mr. Clinton has a strong and intuitive sense of right and wrong, and this was a pure question of right and wrong.

We knew that if international or foreign policy or political considerations were allowed to be interjected into the conversation with President Clinton, the pressures might get him off the core issue of right versus wrong.

Then there was the subsequent legal strategy to give the administration solid reasons for settling the case—meaning we needed to bring to bear legal expertise and litigation skills that would open the door to payment of a settlement without having to go to Congress. Without a strong legal case, the "judgment fund" would not have been available.

Sometimes a successful outcome to a crisis management challenge mixes professional disciplines with personal interactions, political judgments, and just plain luck in timing and personalities. In other words, it's lucky there was Bill Clinton, whose fairness instincts were ready to be triggered by the brilliant and persuasive charm of Benazir Bhutto.

4.

ROYAL CARIBBEAN

"We're a Cruise Ship—Not CSI*"*

The cell phone rang and I had a hard time hearing the voice.

It was my good friend Richard Fain, the CEO and chair of Royal Caribbean Cruise Lines. Several weeks before, in early December, I had seen nightly cable news shows about a young man who had gone missing on a Royal Caribbean multitiered cruise ship the early morning of July 5, 2005. George Allen Smith IV, a twenty-six-year-old Connecticut resident, was on his honeymoon with his new wife, Jennifer Hagel Smith. By the middle of the day, with blood found on a lifeboat's canopy four levels under Mr. Smith's room, the conclusion was inevitable that Mr. Smith had been lost at sea some time early on the morning of July 5, somewhere in the Mediterranean between the Greek island of Mykonos in the Aegean Sea and the ship's next port, Kusadasi, Turkey. The newlyweds had boarded the ship on June 25 in Barcelona, Spain.

Night after night throughout December, cable shows hosted by Greta Van Susteren on Fox News, Rita Cosby and Joe Scarborough on

MSNBC, and Larry King and Nancy Grace on CNN broadcast interviews of attorneys for the Smith family and Mrs. Smith. The attorneys were accusing Royal Caribbean for allegedly botching the investigation of the missing young man, who was declared lost at sea later that morning. There were even dark suggestions that the young man had been murdered. And the blood found on the canopy, they said, had been hosed off by the ship's officers, with the not-too-subtle suggestion that there might have been a cover-up of what really happened. The questions posed to Royal Caribbean regarding all these allegations, however, had gone unanswered, except for a sympathetic statement about Mr. Smith's tragic loss and expressions of condolences to Mrs. Smith. And the clamor of criticism in the face of the cruise ship's silence increased.

When I received the call from Mr. Fain a few days before Christmas 2005, I was on a family holiday with my wife and children in Charleston, South Carolina—the "Renaissance Weekend," in which a few thousand intimate friends and political junkies get together and party by attending seminars with such scintillating titles as "What Is Most Important in Life" and "Ten Reasons to Hate Politics."

We discussed what to do. I understood the company's concern about appearing to be insensitive to the heartfelt grief of the parents and Mrs. Smith. There were also concerns that with a criminal investigation ongoing, and civil attorneys threatening lawsuits, it was prudent to say as little as possible about what happened on the ship.

What to do? Whether to go to the media and what to say, of course, depended on the facts. And only Royal Caribbean's lawyers who conducted the man-overboard investigation on the ship, including interviews of passengers on the ship at the time of the tragedy, could help me get the facts about what probably happened that night and why.

Mr. Fain asked me when I could get started assisting Royal Caribbean to get the facts out and move on beyond the media crisis. I told him I was on a family holiday and was planning on going to a big New

Year's Eve party at Renaissance Weekend. How about waiting until after the New Year and until I get home, and then I could get started helping Royal Caribbean on this crisis?

"Happy New Year," Mr. Fain said. "Now, I need you to get to work . . . immediately."

THE GROOM-OVERBOARD STORY

I immediately got members of my crisis management team in Washington to gather as many facts as were publicly available in the media and to respond to the most damaging unanswered charges. The worst charge involved the bloodstains on the canopy that were hosed off and led to the charge of a cover-up. The photograph of blood on the canopy of a lifeboat below the balcony of the Smiths' cabin was broadcast virtually every night on cable TV and broadcast news programs and featured in the nation's newspapers and on the Internet. It was widely reported that the blood was removed within a day of the tragic loss of Mr. Smith. The ship's captain, Michael Lachtaridis, had admitted to ordering that it be removed by water hoses.

The questions were asked again and again: Why? Why not preserve the blood, which might be important evidence? Why would the captain order the blood hosed off before the FBI had a chance to board the ship to do its own sampling of the blood and other forensic work, which wouldn't take place until the ship reached its next port in Greece? Royal Caribbean was not responding to these questions.

Another harmful unanswered allegation first published in the influential *New York Times* was that the cruise ship had left Mrs. Smith after the tragedy on the dock with bags packed as the ship sailed off to the next port.

The company, on advice of counsel, understandably declined to comment on unknown details about what happened and why on

TV cable shows. But they did put out statements of sympathy for Mrs. Smith's and Mr. Smith's parents.

COMPLETING THE FACT-FINDING

Royal Caribbean Cruise Lines was (and is) a public company listed on the New York Stock Exchange. The attorneys for the company were understandably concerned about any public statements about the facts made by the company until a full investigation of what happened and why could be completed, not only because of the threatened civil action by the parents and Mrs. Smith but in light of a continuing criminal investigation that had been announced.

Better "no comment," the attorneys believed, as most do, at least when all the facts are not known—and the key fact, how and under what circumstances Mr. Smith went overboard, was certainly still unknown. But the result of not responding was an increasing cloud over Royal Caribbean's sterling reputation as a class cruise ship company with first-rate facilities, and well known for its hospitality and the caring staff on board its ships.

On this occasion, unlike my experience with Martha Stewart, the cruise ship's attorneys were cooperative. We also assembled facts that had already been published in various places but not compiled in an easy-to-understand chronology. For example, on the key issue of why the blood was hosed down off the canopy, we learned that the ship's captain, Michael Lachtaridis, had decided at the end of the day of the tragedy that he was concerned about passenger safety due to the many people who were leaning over the rails to take photos of the bloodstain. We also learned that the blood was not hosed down until permission had been obtained by the Turkish police after they had taken blood samples and had finished their onboard investigation.

By mid-January, piecing together all the sources—attorneys' interviews, interviews with the ship's officials, key records, and so on—our crisis management team drafted a detailed, hourly, even minute-by-minute factual chronology, with documented sources for all facts listed, focusing on answers to the major questions being asked by the media that had remained unanswered or whose answers were unclear.

We had the feeling we were in a *Columbo* TV episode, where the famous detective played by Peter Falk starts out knowing that someone had died tragically and goes back to try to piece together what had happened and, ultimately, who the perpetrator was. Once we had the key answers from documented facts and observations from passengers, we circulated the draft chronology to the attorneys and company management, who reviewed, edited, and finally approved it for posting on the company's Internet website. We made multiple calls to key reporters that we had done so—and the word rapidly got out.

Included on the website were the following key points in the narrative:

- George and Jennifer Smith were seen drinking late into the early-morning hours.
- Sometime after 4 a.m. on July 5, George Smith was seen walking shakily alone back to his room, assisted by young men who had been with him and Mrs. Smith at the bar.
- After 4 a.m., passengers in the cabins next door to the Smiths' who reported hearing sounds of furniture moving and raised voices, as if there was an argument, made at least one phone call to complain to the ship's security services.
- Security officials responded to the call sometime near 5 a.m., and heard only silence in the room, and therefore did not knock or break into the room.
- Regarding treatment of Jennifer Smith by Royal Caribbean personnel after the tragedy, the chief of customer relations, a young, female French merchant marine officer named Marie Breheret, stayed with Mrs. Smith throughout

the day, and was with her off the ship when she was examined by police at the Turkish port, taken to police headquarters for further questioning, and then to a hospital for personal examination. She had helped Mrs. Smith place a call to her parents, packed her bags for her, and helped provide for arrangements for her to stay overnight and fly home the next day—all facts that had not been reported.

- On the morning of July 5, after breakfast, the housekeeping staff knocked repeatedly on the door and there was no answer. When they finally entered, they found the room disordered, the furniture askew, and, apparently, a still-made bed that seemed not to have been slept in. The staff also found minor bloodstains on towels in the bathroom and on the exposed sheets. They reported what they observed to security, which immediately put out a public announcement asking either Mr. or Mrs. Smith to call guest services immediately.

- Someone in the ship's spa heard the public address announcement and called guest services to say that Mrs. Smith was there. When security officials showed up to ask her where her husband was, she said she did not know, had been briefly back to the room at about 5 a.m., found that he wasn't there, slept a few hours, and then went to the spa a little after 8 a.m.

As to the ultimate question—what happened to Mr. Smith and how he fell overboard—we had no answer. What was most troublesome was that the railing on the balcony was so high—chest level—it was hard to imagine that George Smith had tumbled over the railing accidentally.

Whether one or more of the young men who had been with him, who were from a Russian family on board the ship, had played any role in pushing him over, and what their motive might have been, was up to law enforcement to decide. Still, it was the subject of broad and irresponsible speculation by the tabloid papers and on the nightly cable shows, but it was nothing but that—pure speculation. In any event, the ultimate question was being investigated by the FBI, under the supervision of the Connecticut U.S. attorney.

One of the security officials who searched the room reported that he had found a chair on the balcony next to the rail and ashes that closely resembled thick cigar ashes, the inference being that someone was on the balcony that morning smoking a cigar, perhaps sitting in the chair.

That certainly suggested that Mr. Smith, who we were told had been observed by other passengers during the voyage smoking cigars, might have been on the balcony smoking a cigar sometime just before his disappearance, since the ashes were still there and hadn't yet been blown away. But the cigar might have been smoked by one of the young Russians, for all we knew.

Now, before posting the chronology on the company's website with all the facts of highest interest and circulating it widely to the media, we needed to develop one or more simple core messages that accurately reflected all the facts—in Clinton press secretary Mike McCurry's words, we needed to put "the waterfall of facts through a garden hose."

THE CORE MESSAGE—FINDING THE SOUND BITE

The cruise ship had been accused falsely of a lot of bad things, but the worst was that it had been involved in a cover-up—by actions such as hosing down the blood on the canopy, or allowing housekeepers and its own security people to search the room before law enforcement officials had access to it. That charge was false and unfair. We needed to sum up the response in a few simple words or sentences.

Our first thought was a simple sentence: Royal Caribbean did its best under difficult circumstances.

But "we did our best" wasn't exactly a bell-ringer of a message.

Then we sorted out all the criticisms, especially the one about treating Mrs. Smith insensitively, which we knew was false, and we came up with the notion that "Royal Caribbean cares. . . ." But that, too, didn't exactly connect with the specific situation at hand and was pretty trite.

Finally, someone—I recall it was one of the attorneys in charge of the litigation—complained that the nightly cable critics who criticized the captain for his decision to wash off the blood from the lifeboat canopy were watching too many TV police-detective programs. After all, "We're a cruise ship," she said.

"Wait a minute," I immediately jumped in. "That's it. 'We're a cruise ship—not the FBI.'"

"No," someone else said, "let's stick in the name from the TV series—'We're a cruise ship—not *CSI*.'" I knew we almost had it. I suggested, "Let's add a second sentence: 'We did our best.'"

"Best at what?" someone asked.

"Cooperating with police authorities," I answered.

We were close.

"We're a cruise ship—not *CSI*. We did our best. We cooperated with police authorities."

Almost there.

"Doing your best" showed there were limitations we couldn't do anything about—a cruise ship in a foreign port, with no direct evidence of what exactly happened to George Smith. The phrase also contradicted the accusation of negligence, which we knew the attorneys for Mr. Smith's parents and for Jennifer Smith were alleging as a basis for a possible "wrongful death" suit seeking damages from Royal Caribbean.

We also needed to convey that from the beginning the cruise ship cooperated with law enforcement authorities—I liked the phrase "law enforcement" better than "police." And that cooperation was "continuing," since we knew there was a continuing criminal investigation by the Connecticut U.S. attorney and the FBI.

Okay, I said, I think we're there.

"We're a cruise ship—not CSI.

"We did our best under the circumstances. We immediately cooperated with all law enforcement authorities, and continue to do so."

Done. We all liked it.

And that became the core message—to be repeated over and over again: on the record.

This message was the truth in the fewest words possible, based on the provable facts: It stated that Royal Caribbean acted responsibly, did its best under difficult circumstances, with one good punch line that we believed would be the linchpin message: "We're a cruise ship—not *CSI.*"

The message was approved after circulation among Royal Caribbean's chief management, attorneys, and public relations consultants. It constituted the best marriage of legal necessities (denying any claim of negligence in causing Mr. Smith's death) and media-message simplicity.

We had no problem getting this message out once the chronology was posted on the website. All the reporters who called were referred to the website to get their questions answered, and we gave them the core message as a quotation from a company spokesman. Also, the cruise ship company management made the decision to encourage cable TV show producers to invite me to appear on their shows to counter what they were hearing from the Smiths' attorneys, and I did—sticking, of course, to the facts that were in the chronology posted on the website.

We also arranged for a leading TV cable show host, Greta Van Susteren, who was also an experienced attorney and former prosecutor, to go onto the cruise ship and get a walk-through by a senior ship's officer of the scene, including the bar, the hallway where George Smith had been helped to his room, the room itself, and, of course, the balcony and a shot of the canopy of the lifeboat immediately below the balcony where the blood was found.

Van Susteren did her usual complete and professional job as a former prosecutor to describe the scene factually, but leaving a strong inference that the tragedy was an accident, with George Smith somehow falling over the high railing of the balcony to the lifeboat below. Her perspective was clear—the cruise ship had acted responsibly.

ANSWERING THE WHODUNIT QUESTION

We talked to lots of reporters and got the factual chronology published, in large part, by many newspapers and into the conversation on the cable TV shows. But we still didn't have one comprehensive version of the entire story and certainly still didn't have an answer to the whodunit question about what happened to Mr. Smith, nor did we believe we would ever get the answer.

Then one day in February 2006 I received a phone call from a reporter I didn't know personally but knew of as a great reporter—Bryan Burrough, who was an investigative reporter for *Vanity Fair*, a well-respected, nationally circulated magazine that often allowed substantial space, in the thousands of words, to tell the full story.

"I read the company's chronology online, and that is a great starting point," he told me. "Now I need to talk to key witnesses on board the ship who can tell me everything they know and saw."

And so began the classic process that I had come to know from my days in the Clinton White House: back-and-forth, back-and-forth, questions and answers, prodding and responding, pushing the reporter away from false or misleading information, suggesting ways he could find the facts for himself—just like my days, hours, and minutes virtually every day at the White House for fourteen months, until the reporter had all he or she needed to write an accurate story.

During these conversations, as usually happened, a fragile and then strengthening fabric of trust was created.

I said I would recommend to management that they cooperate with him. "Do you want to know the ultimate on-record comment here that we are working on?" I asked so he could gain insight into what we regarded as the core message of the role Royal Caribbean had played in this controversial and tragic incident.

"Sure," he responded.

Our sound-bite message was now ready for delivery:

"We're a cruise ship—not *CSI*.

"We did our best under the circumstances. We immediately cooperated with all law enforcement authorities, and continue to do so."

After nearly a week of multiple conversations between us, Burrough called and told me he was done and the story would be in the April 2006 issue. He was able to do independent reporting by talking to a number of passengers. He was able to verify for himself most aspects of the timeline we had put together months before.

SO "WHO DUNNIT?"

At the end of Burrough's reporting process, which took several weeks and perhaps a dozen or more calls between the two of us, he called me to review all the factual assertions and quotations (paraphrasing, in effect, the entire story). It was accurate, fair, and, I thought, would therefore put Royal Caribbean in a framework consistent with our overall message.

The result: a lengthy, detailed story published in the April issue of *Vanity Fair*, mostly confirming the story we had told in the "tick-tock" chronology on the website, as well as a list of the "Top Ten Myths" about the incident, but now being read by the large audience of *Vanity Fair* readers and the millions more who would rewrite it and read it on the Internet at various websites and in news stories.

Burrough credited in his story the chronology our legal crisis management team had prepared and posted. "The mystery began to clear up in January when Royal Caribbean issued its time line," he wrote. "Overall Royal Caribbean has succeeded in countering the most damning claims." And Burrough found a passenger who repeated our core factual message that Royal Caribbean was being unfairly blamed: "Watching all this stuff in the press, I just started feeling very, very sorry for Royal Caribbean . . . so different from the way Royal Caribbean has been portrayed. I mean, since when does a cruise line have an obligation to become a CSI unit and solve crimes?"

And finally, the Big Question—what really happened to George Allen Smith on the early morning of July 5?—was at least given a strong suggestive answer by Burrough at the end of his story.

Burrough had asked me about why the ship's captain had described Mr. Smith's loss as an "accident" in various news reports shortly after the July incident. That word "accident" from the captain stirred up quite a firestorm in the tabloids and on cable TV evening shows. Some lawyers went on cable TV to suggest that this was further evidence the captain was in on a cover-up. They reminded people of the fact that the railing on the balcony was chest high and that it was highly unlikely that anyone could "accidentally" fall over that railing, no matter how much alcohol he had ingested. And, they pointed out, this was the same captain who had ordered the blood on the balcony hosed off!

I never knew exactly how Burrough got the answer confirmed until I read the complete *Vanity Fair* story. Here is what he wrote—he waited until the last paragraph of his long story to suggest the answer to the mystery:

"The ship's captain, Michael Lachtaridis, later told Royal Caribbean executives he saw what he called a 'butt print' on the balcony railing—the outline of a derriere in the dew the next morning. . . . 'The boat was rocking pretty good that night,' one passenger told me, 'if he sat up on that railing, it wouldn't be hard to fall off—especially if he was really really drunk.'"

And so far, that theory—that poor George Smith had used the chair to sit on the railing on his butt, smoking his cigar, and during a pitch and roll of the boat in what we knew that night was relatively rough seas, he had lost his balance and fallen down, down, down to the lifeboat with the canopy several decks below the Smiths' room, and after hitting the canopy and leaving blood behind, he either remained there before another pitch and roll caused him to fall overboard, or immediately was lost at sea after the impact. A sad and horrible tragic accident.

There was no direct proof. But this seemed to many at least a logical possibility.

PUTTING THE CEO AND THE HUMAN FACE
OF ROYAL CARIBBEAN ON TV

But our task was not over, as good and complete as the Burrough story in *Vanity Fair* was. We still had the charge of callousness toward Mrs. Smith and about the tragic death of Mr. Smith leveled at Royal Caribbean senior management and staff, and unfortunately it had lingered on, despite the contrary facts posted on the website in the chronology.

We realized the best and most persuasive answer would be to put someone from Royal Caribbean on a widely watched TV interview—someone whose style and demeanor would reinforce empathy far better than actual words or cold facts published on a website.

We all knew that there was only one person who could do this best—Richard Fain, the chairman and CEO of the company. Mr. Fain was, to put it simply, a kind and gracious man. It came from within him—and everyone who met him and knew him saw that about Mr. Fain. He was the real deal.

And we were equally unanimous that the best TV interview program on which for him to do so was *Larry King Live*, on CNN. While the audience of Larry King's show was smaller than that of a broadcast TV show such as *20/20* or *60 Minutes*, we believed the interview on CNN would be picked up by all the major media and, especially, would influence other cable TV nightly shows that had proven so damaging to Royal Caribbean over these many months.

We also regarded King as the ultimate professional—someone who asked all the questions, including the tough ones, that average people wanted to ask, in an unbiased fashion, leaving the guest the opportunity to answer in full.

We spent several hours giving Mr. Fain some tips about TV demeanor and style, but knew he was a sympathetic person, one who would convey sincerity and empathy, and that he had full knowledge of the facts, more so than anyone else, as a hands-on executive and leader of the company. In other words, he didn't need media training. He just needed to be himself.

We also decided to have on the Larry King set with him the ship's officer in charge of passenger services, Ms. Marie Breheret, who had stayed with Mrs. Smith through the day and into the evening before the ship departed. She could refute, once and for all, the false charges that the cruise ship had treated the widow callously and had virtually "abandoned" her. And her French accent was winning and gave her an authenticity to add to her obvious empathy and feelings toward Mrs. Smith as she experienced this horrific tragedy on her honeymoon.

Richard Fain did what we expected him to do—he left a strong, positive, and humane impression on viewers and left them with the ultimate message we had crafted from the beginning: Royal Caribbean tried its best, but it was not *CSI*—it could only cooperate with law enforcement authorities, not solve the mystery. And he showed his kindness and caring qualities in speaking about what George Smith's parents and Jennifer Smith had gone through.

Ms. Breheret also proved very effective. She was wearing her white merchant-marine officer's uniform. And we were right that her soft

French accent and her demeanor were positive—to women as well as men. Certainly seeing her and listening to her made it completely implausible that Royal Caribbean was "callous" toward Mrs. Smith.

Ms. Breheret described in detail how she had stayed with Mrs. Smith all day during police questioning and medical examination, a fact that had been omitted from almost all reporting. And she finally put to rest the false impression created by Jennifer Smith's attorneys that she had been cruelly left on the Turkish dock with packed bags to fend for herself, as the cruise ship sailed on to other Mediterranean ports.

No, she said, that's not true. I asked Mrs. Smith whether she wanted to go on with the cruise, and understandably she said no, she wanted to go home. Ms. Breheret explained that she packed up Mrs. Smith's belongings to save her the pain of having to go back into the room, brought them to Mrs. Smith, who waited on the pier, and then made arrangements for her overnight stay and flight home.

Larry King appeared impressed with both Mr. Fain's and Ms. Breheret's truthfulness and authenticity and said so at the end of the interview.

Mission accomplished. End of story.

Or so we thought.

MANAGING OPRAH

Shortly after the Larry King interview, we heard that *Oprah* had scheduled in the near future an interview of Mrs. Jennifer Hagel Smith alone, without anyone from Royal Caribbean allowed to join her.

We were concerned that with *Oprah*'s tens of millions of female viewers, Royal Caribbean's sensitive treatment of Mrs. Smith would not be fully conveyed. My first call with one of *Oprah*'s producers was unproductive. I was told in no uncertain terms that the show was "about Jennifer and her feelings"—not about the facts or the investigation. I tried to persuade the producer that the show would be better if it told the full story from the cruise ship's perspective and its support for Mrs. Smith throughout her crisis.

"Let me get back to you," the senior producer said.

The resolution was typical Oprah—why, I realized, she is such a genius and why her show was such a success. She didn't change her approach—this was to be a show about feelings, not facts, with only Jennifer on the stage with her. But she offered to permit a Royal Caribbean executive to be in the audience, with the expectation that he would be allowed to say something, or be asked by Oprah to say something, and in so doing, would talk to Mrs. Smith directly and personally.

With Richard Fain out of town, it was the company's president, Adam Goldstein, who was willing to appear. Mr. Goldstein, in addition to being an effective executive with full knowledge of this entire matter, was also a kind and thoughtful man, just like Mr. Fain. During the weeks after the tragedy, he had the opportunity to talk to Jennifer in assisting on her personal arrangements after Mr. Smith's death. He felt he had developed a good relationship with her. I was confident that his demeanor and people skills would come through on TV—and I was right.

"We can't promise Mr. Goldstein will be on the air," the producer said to me, "but maybe there will be an opportunity for him to raise his hand and get recognized by Oprah to say a word or two to Jennifer."

So the story ended with a magical moment on *Oprah*.

Jennifer told her heartfelt story about the trauma and grief of losing her newlywed husband overboard on a cruise ship honeymoon, with tears shed by Oprah and Jennifer as well as most people in the studio audience and, I am sure, many viewers. But Mrs. Smith did not repeat her assertion about being treated callously or the erroneous assertion that she had been left stranded on the dock, uncared for by Royal Caribbean staff during the day.

And then Mr. Goldstein raised his hand. Oprah recognized him—it was obvious she knew about the proposed scenario—and Mr. Goldstein identified himself as president of Royal Caribbean. He simply expressed his deep sorrow and condolences to Mrs. Smith and to Mr. Smith's parents and did so with an intensity that could not have been made up.

At that point Oprah—surprise!—invited Mr. Goldstein onto the stage. And—further surprise!—Oprah hugged him, and he hugged Jennifer, and Jennifer hugged him, and Oprah hugged them both, and everyone at home, I am now imagining, hugged each other.

Now I knew with certainty as I watched the show: The crisis was over. Finally.

Not necessarily a happy ending, of course, given the tragedy. But an ending . . . which is happiness for any good crisis manager. But the tragedy of the loss of Mr. Smith for his parents and for Jennifer Hagel Smith, of course, continues and could never be forgotten. And all involved in this crisis tale felt sadness then . . . and now . . . for them.

LESSONS LEARNED: FACTS + MESSAGE SIMPLICITY + HUMAN DIMENSION = SUCCESS

We knew that facts plus simple messages were key to effective legal crisis management. But the Royal Caribbean tale taught us that sometimes only a human face, with genuine emotion and empathy, can truly bring closure to the tragic human situation that triggered the crisis.

Sometimes crisis management rules can get you only so far. Sometimes, it's also nice to have some luck. Even a stopped clock is right twice a day. And Bryan Burrough's deciding to write a story and being a great reporter to find his own sources to verify the information and write a comprehensive story were especially helpful.

And of course, the efficacy of the simple message "We're a cruise ship—not *CSI*" proved to be the key crisis management tool to put a major media crisis behind the cruise ship company and its senior officials on the ship.

The final takeaway from all our work was the general understanding by the public and in the media, as the crisis receded, that Royal Caribbean was a good company led by good people who had tried to do the best they could under difficult circumstances—which was the truth.

GET AHEAD OF THE STORY

5.

MACY'S

Don't Make It About Race . . . or Handcuffs

"The *New York Times* says it is publishing the story in the next several days accusing Macy's of racial discrimination in apprehending shoplifters," the voice on the phone told me. "What should we do?"

The call was from James Zimmerman, then chairman of the board of Federated Department Stores, the owner of Macy's, in early June 2003.

The story the *Times* reporters were working on concerned the most famous Macy's department store in America—Macy's flagship store, Herald Square, the Macy's on Thirty-fourth Street in Midtown Manhattan that is the setting of the famous Macy's Thanksgiving Day Parade, televised every year and watched by tens of millions of Americans.

The situation faced by Macy's famous department store tested whether the third, somewhat counterintuitive rule of crisis management really works—to volunteer proactively all facts, good and bad—*especially bad*—to get a complete predicate story written and, thus, to get the story over with as quickly as possible.

By the time I received the call from Mr. Zimmerman, Macy's had already been sued several weeks before in a class-action case for a policy of racial profiling and discrimination in apprehending and arresting customers, with a disproportionate number allegedly selected because they were people of color.

The suit was triggered when, on December 17, 2002, an African-American lady, Sharon Simmons-Thomas, a single mother from the Bronx, who worked as a legal secretary at a major Manhattan law firm, was apprehended and taken into custody for allegedly shoplifting at the Macy's Herald Square store. Ms. Simmons-Thomas claimed she was shopping for Christmas gifts and was planning to return some items she had bought three days earlier, all in the cookware department. She said that after she had returned three pots and bought two pans and a bakeware set, two plainclothes security guards surrounded her and accused her of shoplifting. She said she showed the guards her receipts but they still forced her to accompany them to the store's detention center on the balcony level.

She said she was taken to a holding cell, was subject to a pat-down search of her body, and was handcuffed to a bench for over an hour. She claimed she was denied the right to leave to pick up her nine-year-old daughter from a babysitter and was forced to sign a false confession, which she said she refused to do. Finally, she says, the guards let her go, after retaining the pots and bakeware, worth forty dollars, and told she could not return to the store for seven years.

On May 20, 2003, her attorney—a media-savvy young African-American, Kenneth Thompson, who used to work at the law firm where Ms. Simmons-Thomas had worked —filed a lawsuit on her behalf, alleging that she had been apprehended based on her race. (Coincidentally, this was the same attorney and former prosecutor who would represent Ms. Diallo eight years later in the DSK case.)

But the suit wasn't just about harm and injuries allegedly suffered by Ms. Simmons-Thomas in this particular incident as a result of her race. The suit also sought class-action status. To qualify for class-action status, Ms. Simmons and her attorneys would have to prove that the apprehension of Ms. Thomas was part of a "pattern of practice" of racial profiling of people of color by Macy's storewide or company-wide, and not an aberrational incident contrary to company policy. If they could prove that, then the damages recoverable were not just those owed to Ms. Simmons-Thomas for the harm and trauma she had suffered, but for all members of the "class"—that is, all people of color who had shopped at Macy's (companywide or in the Herald Square store) who had been falsely apprehended for shoplifting based on their race. Thus the liabilities in a class-action case can be huge—in the tens of millions, even hundreds of millions, of dollars, depending on the number of people of color who come forward after the class is "certified" to claim the same thing happened to them.

The suit filed by Thompson asked for $100 million in "compensa-tory" (for losses) and "punitive" (to punish Macy's if racial discrimi-natory policies were proven) damages. The headline story in the *New York Post* on May 21, 2003, the day after the suit was filed in federal court in lower Manhattan, splashed across the front page: OUTRAGE ON 34TH STREET: "MACY'S CALLED ME SHOPLIFTER BECAUSE I'M BLACK." No subtlety there.

The *New York Times* headline was more restrained, but still hurtful to Macy's reputation: SUIT ACCUSES MACY'S OF BIAS AGAINST MINOR-ITY SHOPPERS.

Two weeks later, on June 3, an amended version of the suit was filed by Thompson, this time for $500 million in damages, as opposed to the original amount two weeks before of $100 million in damages. It appeared that Thompson had picked up additional individuals who were prepared to testify that they had been falsely apprehended by store security officials because of their race. The headline in the *New York Post* read: TROUBLE IN STORE—EXPANDED RACE SUIT HITS MACY'S. The story reported that Thompson now had data that proved the shoplifting apprehensions couldn't have just been aberrations or anecdotal, rather, must have been part of a storewide and company-wide pattern and practice of racial profiling.

The new data that Thompson had allegedly obtained, apparently from someone working at Macy's Herald Square or who used to work there, showed that of the sixteen hundred people apprehended for shoplifting in the previous year, *92 percent* were people of color and *8 percent* were white.

That 92 percent to 8 percent ratio of nonwhites to whites in shoplifting apprehensions over the previous year was compared to the ratio of nonwhites to whites among all customers, which Thompson claimed was 20 percent nonwhites to 80 percent whites. If he was correct in both ratios, it certainly seemed that a disproportionate number of shoplifting apprehensions were nonwhites—92 percent nonwhite apprehensions, while nonwhites were only 20 percent of store customers. Those numbers, if true, certainly seemed suspect. How could such a disparity between racial characteristics of those apprehended and customer population be so great unless it was the result of intentional discrimination or reckless disregard, the latter treated virtually the same, under the law, as intentional policy?

"The statistics don't lie," Thompson told the *New York Post*.

When Zimmerman and his public relations/media senior official sent me the *Post* article with the data on apprehensions of customers, I thought of the line from *Apollo 13* after the astronauts reported an explosion aboard their moon-bound rocket. Houston, we have a problem, I thought. How to explain that this substantial racial disparity between shoplifting apprehensions and customer population was not due to company policy or indifference, but to pure accident?

I was impressed by attorney Thompson's ability to get major media attention just for the filing of a lawsuit with unproven allegations—not only in the tabloids, but also in the august *New York Times*. And I was also impressed, and concerned, that Thompson had already obtained inside information from one or more "moles" who had access to the annual racial breakdown of shoplifting apprehensions.

This isn't going to be easy, I thought. I faced not only some bad facts that appeared to be true (at least I assumed that at the outset), but also a media-savvy lawyer who had already succeeded in harming Macy's reputation and share value (its parent company, Federated Department Stores, was a New York Stock Exchange public company) and had gotten significant media attention to potentially prejudice the jury pool if the case ever went to trial.

I knew that for Macy's more than many other department stores, the headline suggesting a company policy of racial discrimination in shoplifting apprehensions could be especially harmful. Macy's retained many locations in urban areas across the country where there was a large population of nonwhite minorities. They were credited for this in the African-American urban community—here was a department store chain that didn't flee to the mostly white suburbs but stayed in the inner cities, developing good customer and community relations with minority community civic and church leaders. This was especially the case for Macy's Herald Square, which prided itself on having a racially diverse population of employees as well as customers. But that meant its business would be more vulnerable to blaring headlines accusing it of intentional racial profiling.

So when I heard that the *New York Times* was doing a substantial follow-up story on the case, I knew there was a significant likelihood it was going to be harmful to Macy's. I checked out the reporter who wrote the first May 21 story on the filing of the case, Andrea Elliott, and knew that she had worked as an investigative reporter for the *Miami Herald* and had a very good reputation as a tough but fair reporter. Again I had to admire the work that Ms. Simmons-Thomas's attorney, Ken Thompson, had done here—not only attracting a major *New York Times* story when the case was filed, but now succeeding in getting the *Times* reporter committed to a major investigative piece that would likely be well played in the *Times*, probably on page one.

Not good.

And, as Zimmerman and his PR senior executive had told me, the reporter, Ms. Elliott, had indicated the story was virtually written and she was calling only for a comment from Macy's to be included in the story, meaning there was little time before the story would be published. I knew that sticking a defensive quotation in a virtually already-written story was not exactly the best way to implement an effective crisis management plan. Indeed, it was the worst way, since there was no way to counter a story filled with negative facts and personal anecdotes, as I suspected would be the case with the story Elliott had already written, with a self-serving denial quotation that would have little credibility.

So one strategic crisis management question we faced in advising Macy's was: How do we delay the *Times* reporter until we had time to gather facts and convince her to take another look at the question of whether Macy's had a companywide policy or whether these apprehensions, if they were in fact mistaken, were aberrations and not storewide policy?

Should we cooperate with the reporter or not? Should we answer all questions or only some? How much access should we give the reporter to the company's premises and records?

It didn't take much thinking for me to come up with the answers. I knew the best, indeed the only, choice was to follow the third rule of crisis management—give the reporter all the facts and get out in front of the story, rather than sit in a defensive position with one or two self-serving "spin" comments or, worst of all, "no comment."

So our answer was to recommend to Macy's management that we had no choice but to go transparent and give the reporter total access and answer all her questions. I called her to offer her complete access to interview employees, review records, and observe training sessions of store detectives designed to avoid racial discriminatory practices, and even access to the holding cells. The only two things I asked for, in return, were more time, so she could visit and gather all the facts we had available for her, and her commitment to be fair and not to start out with any predisposition based on the version of the facts that came from the plaintiff's attorney.

Ms. Elliott was dubious about giving us more time. She reminded me of the trick that some PR firms use—while they delay a bad story, they go to another news organization and get a favorable story written that attempts to preemptively refute the story that was about to be published, before it was delayed.

I told her that I would never do that—Mike McCurry, my mentor during my days at the Clinton White House, had taught me the ethical rules as well as the "tell it all/early/yourself" crisis management rules. And the one ethical rule he said was most important of all is never burn a reporter by taking advantage or compromising the reporter's work product before publication, such as by leaking it to another reporter. "You do that once, Davis," McCurry said, "and you're out of business. Burn a reporter once and that reporter will never trust you again—and, I promise you, the word will spread and no reporter will trust you, and you become useless to help your client mitigate or turn around a bad story."

I never forgot those words, and I told Elliott that story to convince her that I meant what I said and said what I meant. To further convince her, I asked her to put her editor on the phone so I could repeat my words and commitment with the editor listening.

She called me back and said it wouldn't be necessary for me to talk to her editor. They had checked me out (too!) and apparently I had a reputation for not burning reporters and for being straight in keeping my commitments. And she was fascinated, although still skeptical, that I was going to give her total access, including access to possibly negative facts and scenes in the holding cell area, which, she imagined, would be somewhat frightening and might, just might, lend credence to the Simmons-Thomas case by having, not so coincidentally, mostly all people of color in detention.

I knew I was risking exactly that, and we debated the strategy and whether that risk was worth taking. Resisting the strategy were some of the outside attorneys who were understandably concerned about defending the Macy's store in the litigation filed by Thompson. But I won the argument with the usually decisive comment—"This is going to be a terrible story if we do nothing, and if we grant the access and it doesn't turn out well, it could be a more terrible story. But if we have the facts on our side and we really do train detectives and store personnel not to racially profile, and can convince the reporter of those facts, we have a chance of making it a 'less bad' story."

Not exactly a compelling argument for taking the risk of transparency—from "terrible" to "less bad." But I won the argument because the CEO of the parent company, Federated Department Stores, Jim Zimmerman, and its general counsel, Dennis Broderick, were good and decent people who were confident that, in fact, if the reporter wrote the facts accurately, she would conclude that Macy's did its best to train and teach against any form of racial discrimination. Apart from right versus wrong, and moral versus immoral choices, Zimmerman pointed out, it would be totally self-destructive for Macy's to engage in racial discrimination when so many of its customers were people of color.

I and a few colleagues spent several days at the Macy's Herald Square store, interviewing employees, observing in the closed-circuit TV monitoring room store detectives watching suspicious individuals and determining who should be apprehended, reading the training materials, and attending actual training seminars where store security personnel and detectives were instructed on conduct to look for suggesting a possible shoplifter—such as a customer wearing a heavy overcoat on a summer day, or customers looking around in an isolated part of the store to be sure no one was watching and then putting merchandise in their pockets and heading out the door—conduct that had nothing to do with the color of the customer's skin.

We also stood on the floor of the store over several days and did an unscientific count of the racial demographic of customers in the store, counting whites and nonwhites for hours at various times during the day, and we reached the conclusion—although we knew it wasn't a professional poll or cross-section—that the ratio of whites to nonwhites was closer to 50–50 than 80–20. So several days later, we greeted Andrea Elliott when she arrived, taking the plunge in allowing her 100 percent access so she could write what we hoped would be the "predicate" story—with the goal of one complete story, with all the facts, good and bad, by the *New York Times*, which is seen as the newspaper of record by many reporters.

An effective predicate story, therefore, should then become the basis for future inquiries and dampen any follow-up stories because of the lack of new information. And if we were lucky, the good facts about the store's efforts to prevent racial profiling would be accurately reported, and thus would contradict the necessary fact for the case to qualify for class-action certification—that Macy's implemented a policy of racial profiling, as opposed to exceptions and mistakes that were contrary to company policy.

We also decided on a political strategy involving outreach to the New York City minority community. I had come to respect the plaintiff's attorney, Ken Thompson, and assumed he would also be using a political strategy of finding minority community leaders and protesters to picket or try to embarrass Macy's, attracting media and TV cameras, further harming Macy's reputation. So we formulated a preemptive "immunization" strategy of contacting New York City civic and church minority leaders. Fortunately, that wasn't very hard to do, because Macy's had already done a great job of participating in urban community events, supporting charitable and community organizations, and developing personal relationships with leaders of the African-American and Hispanic communities, as well as leading local and congressional elected officials.

Moreover, Macy's had a positive reputation among minority community leaders in New York and other urban areas, since it was one of the few national department store chains that remained in its urban locations and had not fled to the suburbs—creating jobs and shopping opportunities, as well as regentrification momentum.

We enlisted African-American community leaders in New York and members of Congress from Harlem and Hispanic neighborhoods from various New York City congressional districts, to talk to the *New York Times* reporter and other reporters to confirm that Macy's was the last company that would be guilty of racial discrimination and profiling in shoplifting apprehensions.

Our message to the reporter: If this particular apprehension was a mistake, that did not mean there was intentional and discriminatory racial profiling as a matter of corporate policy—the charge the attorneys had made in their complaint. They would have to prove that to justify representing a broad "class" of all people of color apprehended by Macy's.

Our decision to provide total and unfettered access to the reporter seemed to work out well. She attended training meetings where store detectives and security monitoring personnel were instructed on avoiding racial profiling in any way whatsoever—taught to focus on suspicious *conduct*, not the color of someone's skin.

We also agreed, on the reporter's request, to allow her to interview detectives in the TV monitoring room on the top floor of Macy's— those who, during store hours, were able to monitor TV screens from various live cameras throughout the store to detect suspicious conduct that might mean an individual was shoplifting, looking for shoppers who entered the store on a hot summer day wearing a heavy overcoat under which merchandise could be stuffed and hidden, or shoppers who were wandering the aisles and seemed more intent on looking over their shoulder for someone watching them, or cameras that might be pointed at them, than actually shopping.

When we took the reporter into the detective/TV monitoring room, we were obviously nervous, not knowing whether it might lead her to conclude that African-Americans and Hispanics were being monitored more than whites. We also didn't know what any of the security personnel in the room might say to her, since she would be free to interview them. It was a risk. But if we said no, you can't go there, would she suspect that something wrong was going on? We discussed the issue, and all of us—the crisis managers and the senior Macy's management—decided it was important for her to see exactly how it worked and the view from the top floor and on the TV monitors.

The *Times* reporter looked around, and then picked out one lady monitoring several TV sets and asked her a bunch of questions. The lady being interviewed was Latino—and the person she was watching on the TV, who she pointed out to the reporter was acting quite suspiciously, was an elderly white woman. (I thought to myself: There is a God in heaven, even protecting crisis managers!)

At the end of a long day, the reporter seemed to be satisfied and went back to the *Times* to begin writing her story—much more extensive, with greater space, she explained, than had originally been planned. "My editors thought that given the access you've given me, this could be a longer story explaining the difficult challenge department stores face in reducing losses from shoplifting," she said.

For the next couple of days, we talked on many occasions, she asking various questions, and I continuing to call Macy's corporate officials in New York and in Cincinnati to get factual answers. I sent the reporter all of Macy's training materials and its express, written "zero tolerance" policy against any racial profiling or presumption. I kept reporting back to Macy's that she seemed to be moving in the right direction.

Nevertheless, the reporter still asked for our answer to the central, still unanswered, negative fact that we faced at the beginning of our inquiry and still faced (proving my McCurry-repeated rule, "You can't delete a bad fact—it won't go away—you have to deal with it"): 92 percent of the apprehensions were of people of color, while only 20 percent (according to Ken Thompson) of customers were nonwhite.

What *was* the answer? The inference, of course, is that the disparity between the number of people of color who were apprehended and the percentage of customers who were nonwhite constituted strong evidence, if not proof, of racial discrimination, of focusing too much on people of color as presumptive shoplifters. How else to explain it?

We knew that Macy's trained employees against making shoplifting apprehensions based on the color of someone's skin or other ethnic or racial reasons. But how could we prove the negative—that there was not an unconscious assumption, even on the part of store detectives who were black or Latino, that members of such racial groups were more likely to be shoplifters than whites.

One possible answer we could derive was the obvious, but ugly, socioeconomic one: People of color in urban areas are more likely to be on the lower rung of the social, educational, and economic ladder; more in need of clothes and basics that they can't afford; and thus, more likely to be tempted to shoplift. But even stating what we perceived to be that demographic reality, which was not about race, but about class, still seemed dangerous. We knew, for example, there were also many affluent suburban whites, especially younger ones, who were apprehended for shoplifting, not for economic reasons but for many others—including the thrill of "getting away with it" or some kleptomaniacal compulsion to steal.

Finally, a local New York City law enforcement expert suggested that we check with local police precincts and find out what their data were regarding "stop and frisk" arrests in local police precincts around Macy's Herald Square, which was predominantly white, as well as those from predominantly minority lower-income urban neighborhoods elsewhere in New York. He suggested that the lower-income neighborhoods, which are predominantly minority, may have a higher ratio of minority people who are "stopped and frisked" and arrested. Of course sometimes police did racially profile, but I believed that was the exception, not the rule. But at least in many instances it could be shown that crime is correlated with socioeconomic level, among people white or black, and that those who are stopped by police in high-crime neighborhoods in New York are also from mostly minority neighborhoods.

Despite my doubts about this point, since I feared we would be encouraging the racist stereotype that poor black people are more likely to be crime-oriented than wealthier white people, I still was willing to suggest to the reporter that she do her own checking with local police precincts to see whether she, herself, would report that percentages of apprehensions were more about class and income and social deprivation than race.

She seemed at least open to reporting the socioeconomic facts that could explain the 92–8 versus 20–80 disparity, and said she would talk to local police as well as sociologists and urban crime experts.

So here was a classic example of the advantage of working with a reporter on a comprehensive predicate story—having enough time to work with a reporter who is interested in writing a comprehensive, balanced story (not always the case) in creating what we came to call during my Clinton White House crisis management days a "S**T sandwich"—surrounding a really bad fact by good facts, counterpointing the bad fact or at least putting it in context: a key "thread" connecting all the basic rules of crisis management.

During her visit to Macy's, we let the reporter roam throughout the store, observing customers, interviewing customers if she chose, as long as she wasn't too conspicuous, so as to divert attention from shopping by other customers and, especially, store detectives looking for shoplifters.

She requested a chance to see the room where apprehended shoplifters were held, pending investigation and arrest by New York City police, who often took a while before they arrived.

I had observed the room the day before and found it chilling and not very attractive. It was pretty bare, had wire cells for holding people who might be violent or dangerous, and had handcuffs that were obvious on the flat bench tables, with the policy that everyone had to be handcuffed for security and safety purposes until the NYPD arrived to take over and bring the suspects to the police station.

The Macy's managers argued in favor of allowing her to see the room—after all, these were suspected shoplifters, so it wouldn't be expected to have a lot of comforts. After we took her in and she looked around and saw the handcuffs and wire holding cells, she asked the security personnel why they were necessary. They told her that some of the detained individuals become violent and this was for everyone's safety. She seemed to be satisfied by that answer.

But when she asked if her photographer could take photos, I drew the line. "No, I don't think that would leave a fair impression to the average reader," I said, thinking of the handcuffs and the holding cells, which, taken out of context, could look excessive and draconian.

But the reporter made the argument that without a photo, the description could lead to excessive imagining and make it seem worse than it really was. We conferred and, despite my doubts, allowed the photographer to take a few photos.

The next morning, June 17, I was up early, before daylight, waiting for the paper to be thrown onto my driveway. I went down to the curb to get the *Times*. And, to my utter horror—I remember moaning in agony—there was the story on the front page, with a huge photograph of the holding room, handcuffs and all.

What a horrible stupid mistake, I thought, hating myself.

Or was it?

The story itself, aside from the horrible photograph, was as good as I could have expected—indeed, better, since the reporter had included all the facts that we had hoped she would regarding Macy's efforts to avoid racial profiling through training and close monitoring of store security personnel. Elliott also included the statistics on the substantial economic losses, or "shrinkage," as retailers refer to losses from shoplifters and store personnel. She reported that the Macy's Herald Square store lost $15 million to theft in the last year, which we pointed out meant that some prices on store goods could be higher than they needed to be to make up for those losses. She later reported that "$100 million was lost last year to thieves [a word we had used frequently, as opposed to the more benign "shoplifters"] in the 105 stores in the Eastern United States that make up Macy's East."

The more I read, the more I was amazed at how many of the facts that we had wanted to get into the story got into the story. When I saw the subhead in the middle of the story, "A Look Behind the Scenes," I gave out a whoop of joy. Elliott described the "immense security challenge" faced by Macy's. And she wrote:

> Macy's officials said the recent charges against them were reckless, and they ardently defended their security practices as lawful, professional, and exacting in their ability to weed out thieves among innocent shoppers. To counter allegations of unfairness, the store allowed a reporter wide behind-the-scenes access to its Manhattan store, the company's flagship.

"... *The store allowed a reporter wide behind-the-scenes access...*"

Another whoop of joy.

The strategy worked—transparency worked, with all its risks, because it showed the reporter we had nothing to hide and were willing to take the risk of letting her get complete access to all the facts, good and bad.

But my eyes still returned to that awful photograph of the detention center, or "jail," as the group vice president for security at Macy's East had called it, and I winced when I saw that he had used that word. And what about those awful handcuffs in the photo, which we worried so much about? We had prepared ourselves to address the handcuffs issue, had discussed it with this senior Macy's official, and made him available to Elliott precisely to address the question and have his facts ready to do so. So when she was taken to the detention room and saw the handcuffs, she asked, "Why the handcuffs?" just as we expected. And he was ready with the answer and the facts:

> The jail [with the handcuffs] is not excessive . . . given the number of altercations with shoplifting suspects. In the last four months, 25 people have assaulted security officials, 10 of whom required medical attention. . . . In about half of all apprehensions, weapons are recovered, including knives and guns.

So we had done our best to address the issue of excessiveness in the detention center, which we knew would trouble civil libertarians, especially given the data that the preponderance of those apprehended for shoplifting and taken to the detention center were people of color.

But I was still concerned. That awful photograph! All that work down the drain, because I had drunk my own transparency Kool-Aid and couldn't resist saying yes when a reporter challenged me to allow her access to everything, even an ugly holding cell room with handcuffs.

I arrived at my office dreading the phone call from Macy's management. How could I have allowed that *Times* photographer to get into the holding room to take that photo? Why hadn't I, at the very least, hidden the handcuffs, so Macy's wouldn't be depicted as a company using something between the Spanish Inquisition torture chambers and Alcatraz?

When the phone rang, and I noticed the area code was the one for Cincinnati, where Macy's corporate headquarters was located, I swallowed hard, took a deep breath, and answered.

"Hi, Lanny, it's Jim," I heard. James Zimmerman, The Man Himself, the chairman and CEO of Federated Department Stores, the public company conglomerate that owned Macy's, as well as Nordstrom and other well-known department stores.

I immediately burst out: "Gosh, Jim, I am so sorry. How could I let that photographer take that shot? The story should have shown Macy's had done everything to train its people about reasons to suspect shoplifting, and that apprehending people had nothing to do with race. Even honest mistakes sometimes were made by store detectives."

There was silence on the phone. I nervously continued.

"I am talking about that horrible photograph showing the holding room, the cells, and the handcuffs. I should have said no to the *Times* photographer," I responded.

"Excuse me, Lanny," I recall Mr. Zimmerman saying, now with a soothing voice. "You are worried that people who see that photograph will be negative about the consequences of being apprehended by Macy's for shoplifting? The last time I looked, such as last year, Macy's lost over $15 million in stolen goods due to shoplifters in the Herald Square store alone, just as the *Times* story reported. Are you really concerned that the photograph might discourage shoplifting at Macy's?"

"So you didn't mind the photo?" I asked, incredulous.

He reminded me that the story was balanced, contained all the facts, and explained why, unfortunately, handcuffs were sometimes, though rarely, needed in the holding room until the police arrived, since sometimes suspects had been violent.

"Congratulations," he said. "Great job."

I started to protest, and then decided to follow my own rule of personal crisis management—when you can't improve on silence, be quiet.

"Thanks, Jim."

I reread the full story and felt much better.

I realized that we had achieved the predicate story we set out to get written—and then some. The front-page story was long and detailed, with the "flip" to the inside page, covering almost the entire inside page.

It was exactly what the reporter had promised: a comprehensive survey and explanation of what a department store does to try to control "shrinkage."

Of course, also contained in the story were negative accusations and quotations from the suit that had been filed and from the lady who had been apprehended and, as she contended, mistreated in the holding room.

The end result: We had, at the very least, made a bad story better by getting the facts out and getting ahead of the story. (Macy's certainly would have preferred that no such story was written at all, but the lawsuit was a fact and the *Times* had already decided to write a story). And maybe, as Jim Zimmerman reminded me, we had helped Macy's and other department stores by reminding honest consumers that they may end up paying for shoplifting losses, at least indirectly, because stores must spread the losses in pricing products.

Applying this third rule—helping a reporter write a complete predicate story—built upon the first two rules: First, as attorneys with privilege, we were able to get access to all the security records and training materials and interview store personnel; second, establish the simple message that Macy's had acted responsibly and carefully to teach apprehension of possible shoplifters based on conduct, not race.

It was a classic example of the first two rules helping create the predicate story—without attorney-client privilege, the attorneys would never have allowed us to interview store personnel and detectives, see actual apprehension records, and learn "bad" facts from the standpoint of litigation. If we were nonattorney public relations or crisis management consultants, we could have been compelled to testify by the plaintiffs in discovery proceedings without the protection of attorney-client privilege.

Of course, a successful predicate story depends on finding a good reporter, one who was willing to devote the extra time and effort to writing the comprehensive story, good and bad. In the Macy's example, we had inherited a reporter. But we were lucky that she was a conscientious reporter willing to take the extra time to write a complete and balanced story—so long as we kept our word on giving her full and complete access to everyone and everything she needed.

The final product may still be a "bad" story—opening yourself to second-guessing by the client. As someone in the White House once asked me after I had helped a reporter on a pretty negative predicate story, "Whose side are you on?"

Trying to prove the negative to a client is very difficult. The best you can do is to say, "The story would have been worse had we not done the predicate story." But if that story is done as comprehensively as is the goal—containing all major facts, good and bad—the story should be over and done with quickly (except for repetitive rewrites, without anything new). This is the ultimate goal for a good crisis manager, and should prove to the client that the strategy produced the intended results.

The Macy's litigation was ultimately settled on terms not made public. The potential substantial damage to Macy's reputation was avoided by applying my legal crisis management rules. We had made a bad story better . . . and killed it before it spread and got worse.

This is the advantage of having the facts on your side—the singular challenge is getting those facts into the hands of a good reporter ready to write them, even if those facts run counter to an earlier predisposition based on the one-sided facts presented to the reporter by the other side.

6.

REPRESENTATIVE CHARLES RANGEL

No One Believes in an "Honest Mistake"

"They wrote a hatchet job about me and my wife and they don't care about the truth—to hell with them," said my friend Rep. Charles Rangel (D-NY), the congressman from the historic neighborhood of Harlem, New York City, for forty years.

It was Friday, July 11, 2008. Charlie (as his friends called him—rarely "Congressman") was the subject of a lengthy, front-page article in the *New York Times* implying that he and his wife, Alma, had been given favoritism in being allowed to live in several rent-stabilized apartments and may have violated New York state laws.

"Charlie—I want to help," I answered. "But I can't if you refuse to answer questions and attack the press for getting it wrong at the same time."

"They are attack dogs—they are not interested in the truth," Charlie said, in return. He told me he had just been surrounded and attacked by a media gaggle as he emerged from the apartment.

"Did you lose your temper on camera?" I asked, fearing the worst.

"I sure did," he responded.

From that moment on, I worked with Charlie to get him to see that when the press smells blood in the water and is in a feeding frenzy, that of all times is the moment when you have to "feed the beast" and become transparent—unless, of course, there are criminal risks, in which case a criminal lawyer needed to be called in.

But here, it seemed, there was no danger of that—at least so it seemed to me from reading the *Times* story on that Friday morning.

Little did I know, however, that this story would metastasize from breathless questions raised and supporting quotations from "ethics experts"—who had apparently no independent knowledge of the facts but didn't mind offering an uninformed opinion—in this first *Times* story about the rent-stabilized apartments' possibly being unethical "gifts" above the hundred-dollar limit of the House rules (it turned out they weren't); to raising money for a higher-education center to serve Harlem kids interested in public service (allegedly violating House rules on using congressional stationery for such fund-raising); to the embarrassing story that Charlie hadn't paid income taxes for more than twenty years on noncash distributions credited against his mortgage on a small Dominican Republic beachfront condominium unit, amounting to owing the federal government at most an average of less than five hundred dollars per year over a ten-year period, including interest and penalties, and probably zero, if you include the offsetting tax credits under Dominican Republic tax laws; and ultimately, to censure by the House of Representatives a little more than two years later, on December 2, 2010.

Once the *Times* got on the story, it kept going, and of course, as the nation's newspaper of record, it created the fervor and frenzy with which those of us in the crisis management business are unfortunately so familiar—blood in the water, circling media gaggles trying to one-up their competitors and chalk up another politician brought down by scandal, however that word is defined, from the ridiculous to the serious.

"Oh, Charlie," I said, "you are about to go on a roller-coaster ride. Hang on—and let's give the press all the answers and all the information they want, and give them more than they want, and let's kill this story before it spreads like . . . oil on water and kills you politically."

"Why should I?" Charlie asked.

Getting the facts out to get a bad story over with was my profession, I explained, and the only way to do that is to drown reporters with facts, facts, facts, good and bad—and do it first, before they dig them up themselves . . . which they will.

HILLARY FOR SENATE

I had known Representative Rangel only casually for more than thirty years, since I was a young staffer in the presidential campaign of Senator Edmund Muskie. I was visiting the New York City Muskie headquarters in 1971 when, I believe, I went to a meeting in Harlem and met the young and newly elected Charles Rangel, who had ousted the legendary Harlem representative Adam Clayton Powell in 1970. Powell had served in that seat for twenty-five years, since 1945. In 1968, the House voted to expel Powell due to corruption charges, but Powell was reelected in 1968, and the Supreme Court ruled that he was entitled to be reseated in 1969, despite the expulsion decision the year before.

In 1970, the young Charlie Rangel, a hero of the Korean War and well-known Harlem Democratic reform leader in a new generation of Harlem African-American political leaders, had the audacity, as it was described at the time, to challenge Representative Powell in a nationally publicized primary. He won reelection twenty times over the next forty years.

I experienced the reason why one day in Harlem, shortly after the first *New York Times* story, when I visited his office in New York to talk to him and his staff about the facts and allegations in the *Times* story.

At lunchtime, he took me to a famous Harlem restaurant, Sylvia's, where for decades the superstars of Harlem sports and nightlife in the heyday of jazz and New York City entertainers—from Nat King Cole to Frank Sinatra to Willie Mays—would go for dinner or a home-style lunch, with the waitress often the famous Sylvia herself.

It was a short walk from Charlie's office to Sylvia's. Mr. Rangel already had the overhang of media scandal and notoriety as we walked down the street. I knew and felt this because it seemed that every cabdriver, every passerby, white and black, every street vendor and homeless person, and even an apparent drug dealer or two would stop Charlie, shake his hand or hug him or, in the case of cabdrivers, honk their horns at him, and all with just about the same message—"Don't let the bastards get you down," or "Hang in there, Charlie."

Despite the *Times'* implications to the contrary, there was no apparent resentment that Charlie had lived in a rent-stabilized apartment for twenty years. These folks just loved him—unconditionally.

My close friendship with Representative Rangel really began as a result of a chance meeting at a White House party on the evening of February 12, 1999, celebrating the acquittal of President Clinton on the House impeachment resolution.

The talk that night was on the illegitimacy of the House impeachment effort and its repudiation by the Republican-controlled U.S. Senate, that is, the remarkable fact that despite all the partisan furor and intense legal arguments by House managers, neither of the two impeachment counts won a majority of the fifty-five Republican senators—with one count winning only forty-five Republicans, and the other just fifty.

I joined a mesmerized small group of Clinton friends in the main lobby of the North Entrance portal of the White House residence, the one facing Pennsylvania Avenue, with Representative Rangel. Charlie conducted a mini-history class. He reminded a circle of politicos of the close comparison between the virtually all-Republican House vote supporting the two counts of impeachment of Clinton and the similar partisan impeachment vote in 1868 by the antislavery "radical Republicans" to impeach Democratic president Andrew Johnson. And in both instances, a majority-controlled Republican Senate failed to support the House and acquitted both presidents.

"Only Tom DeLay's obsessive hatred of Bill Clinton and raw-power bullying could have pushed through a vote to impeach including members of his own party who had just been defeated in the November elections," Representative Rangel told the group circling him, including his close friend for many years, the First Lady Hillary Rodham Clinton.

Then Representative Rangel turned to Mrs. Clinton. "You've got to come to New York and run for Robert Kennedy's former Senate seat," he said, out of the blue. The First Lady smiled, apparently not taking the suggestion seriously. "Now, Charlie, you know that wouldn't be practical or possible."

I had known Hillary Clinton since my last year at Yale Law School, in the fall of 1969. I was a "senior" in my third year, she was an incoming "frosh," a graduate of Wellesley already famous for a moving valedictorian speech summarizing the historic legacies of the 1960s, the most important of which was a call to public service.

That New York Senate seat had been won by Robert Kennedy in 1964. In 1976, Democrat and then U.S. ambassador to the United Nations Daniel Patrick Moynihan won the seat, and served until the year 2000, when he announced his retirement.

The open seat formerly held by Democratic Party hero RFK was a prize that many well-known New York Democrats and leading members of the House delegation immediately expressed interest in running for. So when Charlie Rangel turned to Hillary and said, "You can win, Hillary, you can win," she laughed, with the characteristic belly laugh that I had known and loved for more than thirty years.

But it suddenly clicked in my head, and I had the feeling, as did all the other Hillary friends in that small group surrounding Charlie Rangel, that he was right. Probably the smartest and most public-service-committed person I had met at Yale Law School (perhaps her only equal was her husband, Bill Clinton, whom I met the year after I graduated) would make an outstanding U.S. senator—we had no doubt. But could she win?

Charlie Rangel had no doubt. "You are a superstar, Hillary. DeLay's partisan, hateful crusade to bring your husband down failed. And there is a huge well of sympathy and support for you in my state. And I guarantee, you'll win my congressional district in any Democratic primary by 90 percent or better." (He turned out to be right.)

Hillary rolled her eyes, and laughed again—that infectious laugh that made everyone laugh with her, sometimes without knowing why. But beyond the laughter, knowing her as well as I did, I could see, knowing her for so many years, that there was a glimmer of interest in her eyes. As she walked away, I pulled Charlie aside and for the next hour or two, while the rest of the White House Friends-of-Bill celebrants were toasting and cheering the end of the partisan impeachment nightmare, Charlie and I talked politics.

I was impressed by how politically and intellectually sharp Charles Rangel was—not just another pretty face from Harlem. He went through all the potential rivals in the Democratic and Republican parties and discussed why the "carpetbagger" issue wasn't serious. ("Remember, the last one they called a carpetbagger—and he was a resident of Massachusetts parachuting into New York to run for the U.S. Senate—was Robert Kennedy. So give me a break! Hillary can overcome that!")

From that night on, through the 2000 Senate campaign when I spent time with Rangel campaigning for Hillary, I came to respect him greatly.

I felt the same way as all the other Hillary loyal friends on that amazing election night when Hillary Rodham Clinton was declared the winner—without Charles Rangel, this could never have happened. I vowed to help him in any way I could in the future.

So some eight years later, when I saw Charlie was in trouble when I read the first *New York Times* article attacking his living in rent-stabilized apartments, I called him to urge him to stop being hostile to the media and answer all their questions—even if they were writing nasty stories. I offered to help him get the facts out and the stories over with.

"Why should I help you embarrass me?" was his response.

On Friday, July 11, 2008, the first of several *New York Times* front-page Rangel articles suggesting wrongdoing by Representative Rangel was published, written by award-winning *Times* investigative reporter David Kocieniewski. The article concerned Rangel and his wife's residence for over twenty years in rent-stabilized (below-market) units in the famous central Harlem Lenox Terrace apartment complex, on 135th Street between Lenox and Fifth Avenues.

There was no way to read this article without believing that Mr. Rangel had done something at least improper, possibly in violation of House ethics rules, and maybe even illegal.

This article was headlined FOR RANGEL, FOUR RENT-STABILIZED APARTMENTS, and the crucial lead paragraph read: "While aggressive evictions are reducing the number of rent-apartments in New York, Representative Charles B. Rangel is enjoying four of them, including three adjacent units on the 16th floor overlooking upper Manhattan in a building owned by one of New York's premier real estate developers."

I read and reread this article to see if I could discern why it deserved front-page treatment in the *Times*—knowing that such placement by the *Times* would likely trigger an avalanche of pile-on reporting conveying at least the appearance of scandal and of favoritism granted to Representative Rangel.

The overall suggestion was that Mr. Rangel had received special treatment by the landlord and had been allowed to maintain four rent-stabilized apartments in the same complex. While the lead paragraph referred to other "aggressive evictions" in general, significantly, it did not report that such "aggressive evictions" had occurred at the Lenox and that Rangel had been oblivious to them in his own apartment, suggesting a double standard. So where's the beef? I wondered.

The only fact that I could find in the entire article that even suggested that there was a possible legal violation was contained in the second paragraph—in a statement that Mr. Rangel had rented a "fourth" apartment six floors below to be used as a "campaign office," "despite state and city regulations that require rent-stabilized apartments to be used as a primary residence." While the article didn't say so, it didn't appear that having more than one rent-stabilized apartment was a violation of any law.

The rest of the article, to me, appeared to have far more innuendo than actual fact showing wrongdoing or violations of law, or at least violations of House ethics rules. For example, anonymous "congressional ethics experts" were quoted as suggesting that acceptance of more than one rent-stabilized unit for residential purposes "may" or "could" violate the House above-one-hundred-dollars gift ban, since the difference between the market rent and rent-stabilized charge was more than a hundred dollars.

"May"? "Could"? Those weren't assertions of legal violations—they were pure speculation.

To make matters worse, then came a quotation from someone named Meredith McGehee, who, while admitting she didn't know the "particulars" about Mr. Rangel, opined that under House ethics rules, a gift is defined as any "discount . . . having monetary value." This McGehee person, I thought, not knowing her at all, struck me as the typical go-to source to support a reporter's thesis, someone willing to speculate even without facts, not minding innuendo that cast a negative light on someone's character. I wondered: Is McGehee suggesting that every member of Congress who purchases a car at more than a hundred-dollar discount off the sticker price "could" be violating House ethics rules? Is that fair, much less correct?

There was some nasty "pay for play" innuendo—without facts to support it—in the article as well.

In one paragraph, the article reported that Sylvia Olnick, an "owner" of the landlord company, had donated the legal limit of two thousand dollars to Mr. Rangel's political campaign in 2004, four years before, and twenty-five hundred dollars to his political action committee in 2004 and 2006. Then the next paragraph stated that in 2005, "a lobbyist for the Olnick Organization met with Mr. Rangel and Mr. [David] Paterson, who was then State Senate minority leader [and future New York governor] as the company set out to win government approvals of a plan to expand Lenox Terrace and build another apartment complex in the Bronx."

Oh, I get it, I thought: So Rangel got the rent-stabilized apartments and campaign donations in return for doing favors for the landlord, that is, for helping the landlord to "win government approvals" of an expansion plan, *after* meeting with the landlord's lobbyist.

But wait. That was the innuendo. Where were the facts to support it? I searched and searched. No facts—just innuendo.

The article also reported that State Senator Paterson also lived in a rent-stabilized apartment.

That word "as" was curious—the connecting word between the meeting with the lobbyist and the landlord seeking "government approvals" for an expansion. It's a temporal word—meaning the meeting took place "at the time of." Since this sentence came immediately after a reference to a campaign donation by Ms. Olnick of seven thousand dollars during the prior four years, there was a strong implication that the political donations to Mr. Rangel were somehow related to the lobbyist's meeting with Mr. Rangel and Mr. Paterson and the effort to obtain government approvals for expansion.

Since a congressman and a state senator have nothing to do

with the issuance of building permits, what could the unnamed lobbyist possibly have been asking? How could there possibly have been a quid pro quo for obtaining the expansion of "government approvals"?

The answer was provided in the next paragraph. A spokeswoman for Olnick "said that Mr. Rangel was not asked to do, nor did he do, anything for the company. A spokesman for the governor said he also did not act on Olnick's behalf."

And then, the next paragraph was a simple sentence:

"Neither project has advanced."

What? This sentence stated that there was, in fact, no quid pro quo. Nothing happened at all as a result of the lobbyist's visit. And no facts showing any connection between the campaign donations, the lobbyist's visit, the plans for expansion, and the fact the Rangels had lived in rent-stabilized apartments for twenty years. So what was the innuendo about?

It beat me.

I did notice, however, that Mr. Rangel had refused to talk to the reporter.

"Mr. Rangel, 78, declined to answer questions during a telephone interview, saying that his housing was a private matter that did not affect his representation of his constituents."

Then Mr. Rangel was quoted as saying, "Why should I help you embarrass me?" after which he abruptly hung up.

Ummmm. Not good, I thought.

The counterintuitive crisis management answer to Rangel's question, of course, is that by answering nasty questions directly and honestly you are maximizing the chances of getting the story over with as well as getting it right.

The next day, Saturday, July 12, came another article, with the lead paragraph denying a nonfact that had only been implied in the first article.

"Representative Charles B. Rangel on Friday angrily defended the unusual housing bargain he had been granted by a major real estate developer, saying he did not believe he was being allowed four rent-stabilized apartments because of his status as a congressman."

Rangel told a group of reporters who had gathered at the entrance to the Lenox Terrace building that he didn't see anything unfair about his living in a rent-stabilized apartment for over twenty years or renting an adjacent studio as an office. As to the twelfth-floor campaign office, Mr. Rangel did seem to concede he might have made an honest mistake. He said that if his staff concluded that it violated the state and city requirement that rent-regulated apartments be used only as primary residences, "that is something I have to look into."

In fact, within weeks, Mr. Rangel confirmed that he had made a mistake in renting the small campaign office on the twelfth floor under the rent-regulated program, and he immediately took steps to move the office to a commercial building nearby.

Moreover, in this second-day story the *Times* clearly reported that Mr. Rangel had acted lawfully when he rented more than one rent-stabilized apartment for his residence (but not necessarily his use of a rent-stabilized unit for his campaign office), which was on the sixteenth floor. "State and city laws allow tenants to lease more than one rent-stabilized apartment." Why wasn't that fact reported in the first-day's story? I wondered.

The article added that landlords are allowed to "evict tenants who have more than one," but omitted another fact that I subsequently verified from top officials of the landlord—namely, that at the time the Rangels first rented these units in the Lenox building and for many years thereafter, the apartment was not fully occupied. Kind of a relevant fact, I thought—since that would explain why the Olnick organization wouldn't "evict" a tenant and would allow a discounted rented unit when it was having a hard time filling the place at market rates. It also might have been the explanation for why the landlord was happy to rent the twelfth-floor campaign office space to Rangel at rent-stabilized rates, even though the landlord could have insisted on higher market rates since Olnick knew the unit was not being used for residential purposes.

Well, I thought, that should have been the end of that story. I called Charlie to congratulate him for getting through the story. Although he had admitted that he might have made a mistake in using the twelfth-floor rent-stabilized apartment as a campaign office, the story reported that he had violated no laws regarding his multiple rent-stabilized units.

ANOTHER SHOE DROPS

That was when Charlie uttered a sentence that crises managers dread: "There's another story coming." But, he added, this one isn't going to be too serious.

On July 15, four days after the first *Times* story, Christopher Lee, a *Washington Post* reporter, wrote a story about Representative Rangel's using his official congressional stationery to write some letters seeking to raise money for the Charles B. Rangel Center of Public Service of City College of New York (CCNY), to be built in Harlem and aimed at encouraging underprivileged minorities to seek higher education and train for public service.

But, I asked, was using official congressional letterhead for fundraising a violation of House rules if it is only for a charity or public purpose?

He said he wasn't sure and wanted to seek advice from the House Ethics Committee. He had already prepared a letter seeking advice on whether living in rent-stabilized apartments constituted a "gift" above one hundred dollars.

The reaction to the *Washington Post* story seemed to be relatively benign. The fact that Representative Rangel had asked for the Ethics

Committee to rule, and that the letterhead was used for a charitable purpose, without any apparent personal financial benefit for Rangel, seemed to take the steam out of the story. In fact, most of the media seemed to ignore it, and it seemed as if the worst for Rangel was over. But then . . .

Still another shoe dropped.

I blamed myself for not asking.

I blamed myself for not seeing around the next corner.

In Kocieniewski's first story about the rent-stabilized apartments, the last few paragraphs reported on various assets that Charlie owned, as disclosed on his congressional financial disclosure forms, which required listing all assets owned or co-owned with family and all outside income earned.

Among the assets listed on his disclosure form was a villa in the Dominican Republic that was listed as worth "$250,000 to $500,000."

A villa in the Dominican Republic? Why didn't I ask him about that—and the rest of his disclosures on his financial statements filed with the clerk of the House? Why didn't I ask to review the statements just in case they raised questions that hadn't been asked by an inquiring reporter, or by a partisan Republican organization looking to bring Mr. Rangel down?

I should have thought: Charlie Rangel wasn't just any representative. He was chairman of the House Ways and Means Committee, the most powerful committee in the Congress, because it writes all the tax laws—and dispenses all the tax loopholes.

I knew that Mr. Rangel had to be cleaner than Caesar's wife when it came to his congressional disclosure filings and certainly paying all his taxes. I should have known the next stories, if any, would be about "follow the money."

On August 24, 2008, the day before the Democratic National Convention, I received a phone call from David Kocieniewski of the *New York Times*, who by then knew I was assisting Representative Rangel in responding to press inquiries and advising him on addressing whatever concerns had already been raised about financial and other disclosure issues.

He told me that he had evidence that Mr. Rangel had received distributions of proceeds from the Dominican Republic villa that he had owned for some twenty years, which tax laws required treating as taxable income. He said it appeared that the distribution reduced his mortgage to zero, but that he could find no income reported on his financial disclosure forms reflecting these distributions of condo proceeds.

My heart skipped a beat. Let me get back to you, I said. I am here at the Democratic convention in Denver, so it may be hard to get in touch with Mr. Rangel and to get you all the answers.

For the next three days, in between appearances on the Fox News network and various radio talk shows talking up the Democratic Party's chances for recapturing the White House in 2008, I spent all my time on the phone with Mr. Rangel, his accountant, and the Puerto Rican attorneys who represented the condominium property owners and who could gather the information about by how much income exceeded expenses among all the units, and thus, how much would be distributed as credits, reducing the amount owed on the mortgages.

To my great relief, I learned from Charlie's accountant and the Puerto Rican lawyers for the property owners that there was an understandable reason why Charlie didn't realize he owed taxes: He had not received the kind of regular tax notice forms that are customary in the United States to inform an individual of "imputed"—that is, noncash—income. Those forms were sent intermittently to his accountant or to his wife, Alma. That offered one possible explanation for why Mr. Rangel had made this error. Charlie vaguely remembered being notified on one or two occasions about a distribution of proceeds, but he told me it never dawned on him that the expenses didn't outweigh the distributions and that there would be any tax liability.

I was even more relieved to learn that over a twenty-year period, Charlie's total tax liability was relatively small. The original purchase price, I learned, had been $125,000 in 1988 or so when he purchased the condominium unit. He had put down a deposit of $50,000, leaving a mortgage of $75,000. Over that twenty-year period, the excess proceeds had paid the mortgage down to zero, which had just recently occurred and which Charlie told me he didn't even realize had happened.

Charlie's accountant finally gave me the (relatively) good news on the Big Question: How much in unpaid taxes did Mr. Rangel owe? The answer: Over the twenty-year period, even including interest and penalties, Mr. Rangel probably owed less than ten thousand dollars, or *less than five hundred dollars per year over ten years*. When depreciation and other tax credits awarded under Dominican Republic law that could apply against taxes owed to the IRS were considered, the accountant told me, it could well be that Charlie owed no taxes at all.

TIME FOR THE PREDICATE STORY

Once I had all these relatively good facts surrounding a very bad one —that the chairman of the House Ways and Means Committee had failed to pay federal taxes over a twenty-year period, however small the amount—I knew it was time to make the tough recommendation to Charlie, which I knew he would regard as bad-tasting medicine: to offer Kocieniewski the exclusive story and to help him write it.

"You are asking me to help this reporter who screwed me once to screw me again? How could you ask me to do such a thing?"

It was a question I had heard before, in fact many times, in the Clinton White House and since from other clients.

But I knew it was the right crisis management strategy. As I explained to Charlie, in a well-rehearsed response, "Because this story is coming out soon, and probably by Kocieniewski, we need to be sure he gets it right and get out in front with our comment, which is true, that this is a modest amount of money owed and that there were understandable reasons why you made this error and didn't pay the taxes—and it certainly wasn't intentional."

After heated discussion, Charlie understood my strategy and that it was best to give this story to Kocieniewski, who I kept stressing to Charlie was a good reporter, though I believed he had written too much innuendo in the initial stories. So Mr. Rangel reluctantly allowed me to give the exclusive story to Kocieniewski.

I called Kocieniewski, and when I told him what I had and was prepared to help him write, he seemed flabbergasted as well as delighted.

This was correct crisis management strategy: Get out a bad story that can be written all at once, giving all the facts, good and bad, and providing the predicate story for other reporters to write, with the best chance that the story would be ended as quickly as possible. And we had the best and most influential newspaper of all in which to publish the predicate story—the *New York Times*—and the reporter who seemed most invested in the Rangel story.

My only "deal" was to ask Kocieniewski to take his time and wait for me to get all the facts about exactly how much Mr. Rangel owed in back taxes and the full circumstances and explanations for why and how he didn't pay taxes. I would provide, as best as I could, access to all those who had documents and information to answer his questions about what happened and why. I would encourage others to talk to him "on background"—without attribution—including Mr. Rangel's accountant and the attorney for the condominium property. I promised I wouldn't "shop" the story if he delayed. He said okay.

My core message, boiled down to two words: innocent mistake.

I told him that these two words were the ultimate oxymoron in cynical Washington, but they were the truth.

So I went through the usual back-and-forth process, in the middle of the historic 2008 Democratic National Convention that nominated Barack Obama as its presidential candidate, sometimes off-camera while I was on the Fox News Channel set, to answer Kocieniewski's questions—calling Mr. Rangel's accountant, the Puerto Rican lawyers, Mr. Rangel's congressional staff, Mr. Rangel, even Mrs. Rangel.

Altogether, I probably had a dozen telephone conversations with

Kocieniewski in two or three days, answering his questions, pushing back at his interpretations, and pushing him to seek more information to round out the story.

It wasn't until a few days after the convention, in early September, that Mr. Rangel's accountant confirmed that I could use the number "under ten thousand dollars" as the maximum Charlie owed the IRS over the twenty-year period, including interest and penalties, and he still hadn't calculated the offsets under Dominican Republic law recognized by the IRS, which might reduce that amount virtually to zero.

Finally, with the story ready to be published, I called Charlie and tried to give him the tough-love advice that the best way to prevent the Republicans from exploiting this story was to "get out in front" and offer to step aside, "temporarily," as chairman of the House Ways and Means Committee.

I suggested he could do this only if the House Ethics Committee would promise an expedited investigation to confirm the modest amount owed and the understandable factual circumstances that led him to make this unintentional error, perhaps negotiating an expedited settlement in which Representative Rangel would accept a modest "admonition" (or something short of a "censure").

"You'll take the wind out of their negative hurricane energy," I said to Charlie, referring to the expected partisan Republican exploitation of Rangel's innocent mistakes. It wasn't surprising to me that these GOP congressional leaders were ready for "payback time" for the House Democratic 2008 campaign mantra (which I considered demagogic at the time) about the Republican "culture of corruption," after the conviction and resignation of several Republican incumbents due to taking bribes and personal corruption.

But Charlie would hear none of any possibility of even a temporary resignation from his leadership of Ways and Means.

"I am not giving up my chairmanship, after all these years of waiting to have this position, over a minor, honest mistake where these guys didn't even send me the forms regularly to remind me of my mortgage being paid."

I knew I couldn't persuade him. I thought (wishful thinking): We might be able to survive this, if this is all there is. The facts speak for themselves. It was a small amount of money owed in past income taxes. The circumstances seemed understandable, although embarrassing for a chairman of Ways and Means.

The *Times* published the taxes story on Friday, September 5, headlined: RANGEL FAILED TO REPORT $75,000 IN INCOME.

The story was almost everything we could have hoped for, using the technique of the predicate story: It contained all the facts, good and bad—especially the mitigating facts, such as the noncash distributions credited against his mortgage over twenty years that made it understandable that Rangel hadn't realized that unpaid taxes were accruing; the fact that he hadn't received the normal IRS forms notifying him of these noncash distributions; and most important, the modest amount of taxes owed over twenty years (amounting to an average of less than five hundred dollars a year).

My quotations in the story were limited to the focused message— honest mistake, with the concession that it might have been the result of carelessness, not intentional tax evasion.

Two weeks later, on September 16, 2008, Charlie agreed—to my surprise—to hold a press conference in the House press galleries to get out in front of the story and announce his intention to hire a forensic (investigative) auditor to review all twenty years of his tax returns and his financial disclosure reports, to correct any inadvertent errors, especially in the congressional financial disclosure reports, and to promise to release all twenty years' worth of tax returns after the audit was completed.

Regarding the congressional financial disclosure reports, during the prior couple of weeks I had received several press calls, not only from Kocieniewski but from several others, indicating that the next "shoes" to drop involved errors or omissions from the annual financial disclosure reports required to be filed with the clerk of the House of Representatives.

I knew that any such errors in these congressional reports, no matter how minuscule, would constitute another dot to be connected to the pattern of, at the very least, carelessness by Mr. Rangel in the conduct of his financial affairs. In fact, I had learned, it was Mr. Rangel's chief of staff for many years who was supposed to be responsible for checking on the accuracy and completing these reports. But for a variety of reasons not his fault (such as failure to have access to all the personal records of Congressman Rangel and Mrs. Rangel) these reports did not reveal all the transactions by Mr. and Mrs. Rangel over these years.

So, I realized, these reports needed to be scrubbed 100 percent and fixed ahead of time before the press caught up and reported on these deficiencies one drop at a time.

So we planned the press conference to be a preemptive strike to clear the air on all these financial issues—and to reinforce the central, simple message of an honest mistake.

Mr. Rangel and I walked into the small room in the House Office Building reserved for press conferences, with easy access to print, Internet, and broadcast reporters who cover the House. The room was filled. Our script was for the congressman to announce that he was seeking an independent audit of all his finances—his tax returns and his congressional financial reports—seeking to correct "inadvertent" errors, in the spirit of full "transparency," errors for which he took full "responsibility" as a result of his "carelessness taking care of my own finances."

The quoted words were the four core message points I had written on a three-by-five card for Mr. Rangel. He stuck to them as agreed: "inadvertent," "transparency," "taking responsibility," and admitting to "carelessness." I hoped the headline would be that Mr. Rangel not only was initiating an independent investigation of himself but would also publish the results, as well as all twenty years of his tax returns—

a man-bites-dog story in Washington, D.C., accustomed to bunker-style "no comments" and even cover-ups in the middle of a scandal.

My only surprise was Mr. Rangel's ad-lib at the podium, in which he described his carelessness as "gross" and used the word "apology"—a word I didn't think he ever would use in public, given his private anger and outrage at the media and the partisan attacks on him from Republicans.

I was delighted and even optimistic that Mr. Rangel's willingness to do this offered the best hope of escaping from a downward spiral of "scandal" stories that could doom his political career.

In a CNN-posted story that day, headlined (as I had hoped) RANGEL PROMISES INDEPENDENT INVESTIGATION, I was quoted as stating that Mr. Rangel "wanted to show in as many ways as he possibly could that he did not do anything intentionally wrong," and he planned to hire an independent investigator to prove that he "never meant to conceal his finances." Perfect! I thought. The story also quoted me disclosing what I had learned from Charlie just as we were walking into the press conference room—that Democratic minority leader (and soon to be Speaker) Nancy Pelosi had said "she was pleased that Mr. Rangel had initiated an investigation of himself" in the spirit of "full transparency."

"Full transparency." Yessss! I thought. Success! Message delivered and received! We had done it.

Now whatever the results of the House Ethics Committee investigation—and I was sure they would show multiple errors in financial filings over the years—I was convinced they would be less damaging since Mr. Rangel himself had initiated the process and had proven that, if he had made mistakes, they were not deliberate and in no way showed dishonesty or even the slightest hint of self-enrichment or corrupt motives.

I actually thought this was the end of the crisis—and the only unknown was the "rap on the wrist" sanction that would come after the House Ethics Committee completed its investigation.

The Ethics Committee was a bipartisan committee, divided 8–8, and while its members were committed to applying the facts and the rules of the House neutrally, without regard to politics, its members were all members of Congress, and of course they might be sensitive to media and political messages and pressures.

My job was essentially over. I had no experience in litigating before the House Ethics Committee, and a major Washington, D.C., law firm with expertise in congressional ethics investigations took over the Rangel representation. I knew the attorneys, and they were outstanding specialists at ethics rules and committee litigation but not necessarily inclined to answer all media questions. The problem, I believed, is that media coverage can be especially influential during a congressional investigation. Members of Congress are, after all, politicians who keep up with news coverage more than most people.

THE SAD OUTCOME

In late September 2008 Charlie went to the floor of the House to make a spirited defense of himself after the House minority leader, Republican Representative John Boehner, introduced a censure resolution.

The statement was angry and expressed his genuine outrage that he should be compared to truly corrupt Republican ex-members who had been convicted of bribery. But all it did was fan the flames, further inflaming a Democratic House leadership increasingly worried about the outcome of the congressional elections.

After Charlie's angry speech on the floor, on a Saturday afternoon, the phone rang at our house at Deep Creek Lake, in western Maryland.

It was a familiar voice from my White House days, the voice of someone who was at times a tough critic and later became a friend and ally at the White House but someone whose temperament was, let us say, somewhat volatile.

"What the ?%!# are you and Rangel doing? You had it right with the press conference. It was 'tell it all, tell it early' classic Davis preemption strategy. Now Rangel has launched missiles again just as we have our guys back on message in the congressional races. Why don't you tell him to shut the ?%!# up?"

Yes, it was my quiet, shy, bashful, soft-spoken buddy from the White House, then Congressman Rahm Emanuel and now Chicago mayor. Rahm was then the chair of the House Democratic Congressional Campaign, and he had a right to be concerned about headlines about Charlie Rangel rather than headlines about the congressional Republicans on the run and Democrats fighting for the middle class—which I knew was Rahm's very focused message.

I explained to Rahm that I no longer represented Charlie and was sorry I couldn't be of more assistance, but he needed to consult Charlie's lawyers, who were Ethics Committee experts and would be the best ones to call.

Rahm uttered a long string of expletives, remarkably diverse, many both alliterative and almost poetic, all of them preceding the single word "lawyers." It was not the first time I had heard Rahm describe lawyers that way. After that colorful sentence, Rahm did his gracious good-bye on the phone when he is angry—he hung up—without even saying "good-bye" or "I love you."

One night in late November 2008, *Times* reporter David Kocieniewski called me at home. He had grown accustomed to being able to talk off the record with me, to test out whether the story he was working on had factual validity. He complained that the attorneys for Mr. Rangel wouldn't return his phone calls or, when they did, wouldn't answer his factual questions directly. And he said the latest story he was working on could prove damaging to Mr. Rangel and he wanted to give Mr. Rangel a fair opportunity to respond, as he had done when I was working with him on Rangel stories, but that the current set of attorneys were not answering his questions, at least in a timely way.

He told me he was about to report a story that I had feared the first time I heard that Charlie had solicited donors to help build the Charles B. Rangel Center for Public Service. Ever since he had done the "nonpayment of taxes" story he had been researching whether anyone who had contributed to the Charles B. Rangel Center fund had ever lobbied Mr. Rangel on a tax matter before the House Ways and Means Committee—the one story I feared the most, since it touched on the "pay for play" theme that was always an explosive political scandal story.

Sure enough, which didn't surprise me, Kocieniewski found an individual who had given a contribution and then sent a lobbyist seeking support for a tax position over which the Ways and Means Committee had jurisdiction. Eugene Isenberg, CEO for Nabors Industries, had given $1 million to the Rangel Center fund. I researched Mr. Isenberg's business and charitable-giving background and talked to a few people who knew him. He had an outstanding reputation for philanthropy and business integrity. He also, it appeared, seemed to be unaware of the negative aspects of sponsoring a lobbying visit to Mr. Rangel on an issue that might benefit his business while also contributing money to the Rangel Center. The issue involved modifying a provision of tax law that might retroactively require Mr. Isenberg to pay additional taxes.

But Mr. Rangel had long stood for the principle that it was unfair to apply a tax change retroactively except in the rarest of circumstances. His staff pointed out to me that he had opposed retroactivity in this particular tax measure even before Mr. Isenberg had sent his lobbyist to him. "It's just not fair," Charlie told me, speaking of his long-standing opposition in general to retroactive application of a tax change.

I knew that I could work this story well, the way I had worked the back-taxes story, to get the good facts into it, such as Rangel's long-standing principle opposing retroactivity. And thus, what appeared to be cause-and-effect was, in fact, correlation—Mr. Eisenberg's views and Mr. Rangel's views were the same, regardless of the contribution to the Rangel Center.

But in Washington optics count more than in most places on earth. I knew that without someone working with Kocieniewski on this story, it would at least strongly suggest "pay for play" or some such or would raise ethical issues at exactly the wrong time for Mr. Rangel.

When I read Kocieniewski's story in the *Times* on November 24, 2008, I knew it could have been much worse. It looked as if the reporter had gone out of his way to be fair and to reflect some of our prior conversations without quoting me. Because it was after the elections, in which Barack Obama had won the presidency and the Democrats had taken over the House, there was little of the political or media furor that usually follows a hot *New York Times* scandal story. (This was also partly because, I felt, Kocieniewski had gone out of his way to be fair.)

During the next year, 2009, the ethics investigation puttered along and, aside from a shot here and there in the tabloids, there was not much adverse press activity about Mr. Rangel. Indeed, on the several occasions I saw Charlie, he seemed cheerful and optimistic that the Ethics Committee would recognize that he had made "honest mistakes" and perhaps give him a rap on the wrist but that would be that.

I was of course concerned that he had given in to his lawyers, so he told me, and had reneged on his commitment during the September 2008 press conference to publish his last twenty years' tax returns and to hire an outside accounting firm to conduct an audit of his financial statements and make all the corrections needed to make them error-free. I feared that if he didn't follow this proactive course, after the 2010 elections, which seemed to be heading for a Democratic loss of seats or even worse, the Ethics Committee would be pressured to move against Charlie. And without "getting out in front" and fixing the problem and offering voluntarily to accept some type of admonition before the Ethics Committee had a chance to vote sanctions, it would be difficult for many of the Democrats on the committee to resist voting for the most severe penalties for his multiple mistakes, unintentional though they were.

On September 14, 2010, Charlie won a resounding victory in the

Democratic primary against four or five serious opponents, winning more than 50 percent of the votes and a nearly two-to-one margin over—of all people—the son of Adam Clayton Powell, whom Mr. Rangel had defeated in 1970 in a Democratic primary.

On November 2, 2010, not surprisingly, Charlie's overwhelmingly Democratic district in Harlem reelected him by a landslide. Rangel had proven that, at least according to the voters in his district, all the *New York Times* articles and charges and innuendo in the tabloid press meant little. They loved . . . and trusted . . . their man Charlie, as I had witnessed during my brief stroll with Charlie in the summer of 2008 to the famous Harlem restaurant Sylvia's.

But there needed to be an ending to the Ethics Committee process that involved some sanction for Charlie; we all knew that, even Charlie. In retrospect, it appears that he showed contrition and a willingness to take responsibility too late. Now he was ready to accept a reprimand but resisted the harsher penalty—harsher in the small world of congressional culture and those who knew congressional history—of censure.

What surprised and disappointed me was how few Democrats stood up to defend Charlie. Indeed, it seemed that many started to treat him as a pariah, especially as the trend seemed to move heavily toward congressional Republicans in the 2010 House races. Few Democrats pointed out the clear difference between instances of high-profile Republican ethics problems in recent years, in which there were bribes accepted and personal enrichment, and Congressman Rangel's situation, in which no one had even suggested that he had personally enriched himself.

Even President Obama couldn't resist piling on a bit. At a press conference on July 30, 2010, Mr. Obama called the ethics charges against Charlie "very troubling." He added that Mr. Rangel "should end his career with dignity"—a not too subtle suggestion that Charlie should resign, even before trial. Since Mr. Rangel just faced "charges" and thus there was no verdict on the facts yet, the president's comment seemed untimely from our perspective.

Charlie Rangel, however, wasted no time in telling his own Democratic president what he thought of the remark. A few weeks later, Mr. Rangel responded to President Obama's comment: "Frankly, he has not been around long enough to determine what my dignity is."

As expected, on November 2, the Republicans shocked the nation (and themselves) and won back the House of Representatives with a net gain of more than sixty seats.

With partisan lines hardening and Democrats on the defensive after what President Obama frankly described as a "shellacking" in the elections, the chances of Charlie Rangel's negotiating a sanction other than censure had diminished to about zero.

However, two weeks later, after the November elections, the House Ethics Committee completed its investigation. Despite last-minute negotiations and pleas by Mr. Rangel to be allowed a hearing with new attorneys and a willingness to accept a reprimand rather than censure, the bipartisan committee voted to recommend censure of Mr. Rangel, based on four core violations:

- Errors and omission in his personal financial disclosure statements;
- The use of the twelfth-floor rent-stabilized apartment as a campaign office that violated lease provisions and might have violated state and city laws;
- Failure to pay taxes related to the Dominican Republic villa;
- The use of official House letterhead to solicit donations to the Rangel Center.

But the four violations cited did not allege any intentional violations—which had been my point of view in the development of the first core message, "innocent mistake," and the "get out in front" strategy of going transparent. And none of them involved personal enrichment or monetary gain—the only real definition of "corruption" (despite the loose and irresponsible use of that word by Republicans to describe Mr. Rangel's errors)—nor that living in rent-reduced apartment units was an unethical "gift" or that needed to be reported on House disclosure forms (which was an important part of the first *Times* story that began the whole controversy).

And I was especially happy to see that there was no finding of an ethical violation regarding the solicitation from Mr. Eisenberg, despite all the huffing and puffing in the media by Republicans about a "pay for play" or quid pro quo having taken place.

The next day, on November 17, 2010, just weeks before the scheduled vote by the Ethics Committee on what was likely to be a censure recommendation, I wrote a column for *The Hill* newspaper, my weekly column, called Purple Nation, which focuses on the theme that bipartisanship is needed to seek solutions for America's problems.

I identified myself as a former attorney for Mr. Rangel and reminded readers that whatever mistakes Charlie Rangel had made, none of them involved findings by the Ethics Committee—or anyone—of personal enrichment or corruption. I stated that the staff director of the committee, Blake Chisam, who played the role of the "prosecutor" of the case in making recommendations to the full committee, had expressly stated that there were no instances of corruption at all supported by the evidence.

I concluded: "So please, everyone, whatever sanctions the ethics committee decides are appropriate—and I won't comment on that subject—let's stick to the facts about Rangel. He made honest mistakes. Yes, he was careless. No, he shouldn't have been if he were perfect. But: He did not personally enrich himself. Those are the facts. . . .

"I, for one, forgive his honest mistakes and am proud to consider him a friend."

On December 2, the day of the scheduled House vote on Charlie

Rangel's censure, he went to the well of the House and finally, after so many months of anger, took responsibility and asked to be forgiven by his colleagues on both sides of the aisle.

I sat in the House gallery, in tears, as I listened.

"I brought it on myself. I do believe that senior members should act in a way as a model for new and less experienced members. I do believe there should be enforcement of the laws, and there should be sanctions. But if you are breaking new ground"—he was referring to voting for censure where there were not findings by the Ethics Committee of personal enrichment or corruption—"I ask for fairness."

He concluded: "I want to continue to serve this Congress and this country. And do what I can to make life better for other people, and I think we all agree that in forty years I have tried to do my best to do that."

ANGER AS THE ENEMY

On December 2, 2010, Charlie Rangel was censured by a vote of 333–79, the twenty-third member in the history of the House of Representatives to be censured.

Months later, I had lunch with the staff director of the Ethics Committee, Blake Chisam, who told me that there might have been a time, earlier in the process, when Charlie could have obtained a lesser penalty—such as a reprimand—if he had expressed contrition and volunteered to accept that lesser sanction.

I said to Mr. Chisam: "Charles Rangel is a good man. And he'll continue to be a good man and a good congressman."

Mr. Chisam nodded. I felt good about his doing that, despite everything.

But then Chisam said, in frustration: "Why didn't Mr. Rangel continue to be transparent with the media and the committee? Why didn't he just step up to the line earlier . . . without his lawyers . . . and just take responsibility?"

I shrugged. "He was angry—outraged—at the injustice of the charges against him, which suggested intentional and willful misconduct, when he and I never believed that was the case."

I also believed it had been a mistake to shut down talking to the media. And while it was understandable, the anger felt and shown by Mr. Rangel wasn't the best way to achieve results in the middle of a crisis and to find a reasonable face-saving settlement for all sides.

In fact, anger is the worst way.

It clouds judgment. It diverts attention from the true goal— defeating the smears and the innuendo with facts and truth and fairness.

The best crisis management strategy, I knew, was to replace anger (and adjectives and adverbs that tend to be used when there is anger) with the facts—and get them out early and often, good and bad, take responsibility, and move on.

I don't know if the ending for my friend Charlie would have been different had he followed the original strategy of transparency and accountability, perhaps by stepping down as chair of the House Ways and Means Committee as a self-penalty and asking the Ethics Committee early on for a reprimand.

But it certainly represents a good "what if" speculation as one strategy versus the hunkered-down, virtually media-silent, defiance-almost-to-the-end strategy before the Ethics Committee that led to the sad (and I believe unjust) outcome of censure.

7.

GENE UPSHAW AND THE
NFL PLAYERS ASSOCIATION

Time to Draw the Line

"I'm going to break his damn neck."

That was the gentle, understated comment made to the *Philadelphia Daily News* by Gene Upshaw, then executive director of the National Football League Players Association (or NFLPA, as the players union was called) in early June 2007, in response to a comment made by Buffalo Bills' NFL Hall of Famer Joe DeLamielleure, one of Upshaw's most vocal critics from a retired NFL players group. DeLamielleure had said it was his "daily goal" to get Upshaw fired as the head of the players union.

For months, Upshaw had been the object of these kinds of personal, public attacks by retired players associated with a group headed by Chicago Bears legendary coach and superstar defensive player Mike Ditka. Ditka was quoted most often with attacks on Upshaw as being stingy and hard-hearted in what he described as inadequate disability, pension, and health-care benefits paid to retired NFL players. The NFL players union shared responsibility with NFL owners in deciding on pensions and disability eligibility and benefit decisions.

And it wasn't just Ditka. Sports journalism is dominated by sports columnists, who use their editorial opinion perch to engage in any kind of subjective critical comments about coaches, players, and especially Gene Upshaw. If you just read the stories or columns about Upshaw, you'd think he was a horrible, cruel man who didn't care about retired players. And there was no serious counterpoint from Upshaw or even any of his friends.

But how could that make sense to sportswriters? After all, Upshaw was retired himself. He had played with and against most of his critics in Ditka's group and had been friends with many of them. Now he headed a union in which he was elected each year by current players.

When I read Upshaw's "break your neck" statement and saw how it had gone viral on the Internet as proof that Upshaw was temperamentally unsuited to lead the players union, I knew that Upshaw was in a deep hole in the media and his leadership and effectiveness as head of the NFLPA were at risk.

This was, at first blush, an obvious case of the need to follow Crisis Management Rule 101 about getting the facts out—"Tell it all, tell it early, tell it yourself."

So why didn't he, I wondered?

About four weeks later, in early July 2007, I got a call from a friend who worked for Upshaw in the NFLPA's Washington, D.C., headquarters office. This person told me that after much pleading, Upshaw had finally agreed to call me to ask for my advice; and maybe even to come to meet me.

The next day, the phone rang. I picked it up and heard a gruff, deep-sounding voice, and I knew instantly who it was:

"Okay, I'm here—you're the famous 'tell it all' Master Spinmeister—but I ain't responding to these jackasses who are attacking me and their media lackeys publishing any junk they are told, no matter how false, except by giving them a dose of the BS [Note to reader: He used the full expression for BS] they are throwing at me. That's all I have to say."

"Nice to talk to you, Mr. Upshaw," I said. "I am glad you called. At the very least I'd love to meet you and get my ten-year-old son your autograph. Actually, I'd like it for myself—I've been a fan of yours for a long time."

"Don't BS me, Lanny, I'll come over to meet you. But I am not following your 'be nice to the press' advice that your friend told me you were going to advise me. I don't talk to the media, because they hate me and I hate them. And I am not going to be nice to the liars in the retired players group who are engaged in a character-assassination campaign against me."

Boy, this is going to be tough, I thought. I invited him to come and see me and we would discuss what he wanted me to do.

When the six-foot-five, 255-pound Upshaw walked into my office several days later, I was struck not only by his physical size—he was BIG—but by the physical presence of the man, the tough-looking expression on his face as we shook hands. He was intimidating.

I recalled reading about how he opened paths for runners lucky enough to be running behind him—by hurling his body as virtually a lethal weapon at linemen, defensive ends, linebackers, safeties, whoever he could find standing between the runner behind him and the goal line. And I knew that in his wake would often be human wreckage, no matter how big they were, as they tried to stand in his way.

I quickly decided I didn't want to be one of those bodies standing in Upshaw's way.

THE UPSHAW-TAGLIABUE PARTNERSHIP

Upshaw has been described as the greatest NFL "pulling" offensive guard of all time—meaning, he pulled off his position as left guard on the line, circled behind the line, and then led the runner behind him, clearing a hole—highway is more apt—for the runner to run through by throwing his body at 250- and 300-pound men, sometimes breaking their bones and some of his own with abandon and either courage or recklessness, depending on your point of view. Upshaw was an NFL Hall of Famer and went to the Pro Bowl in almost every year he played. He was one of only two NFL players who played in Super Bowls in three decades (Jerry Rice of the San Francisco 49ers is the other).

For many players and labor-management relations experts, Upshaw's greatest achievement, as I learned from extensive reading overnight before I first met him that day, was not only how he fought and won recognition for an NFL players union, but more historically, the unique business partnership he developed with then NFL commissioner Paul Tagliabue.

In 1987, Upshaw, with no money and a union that appeared to be busted by tough tactics by NFL team owners, decided his only chance was to call a players' strike, which led to an NFL season in which replacement football players were used, unsuccessfully as it turns out, to play the season.

Then Upshaw turned to the legal system to get recognition by the NFL owners and genuine collective bargaining. He "decertified" the union, meaning that since they were no longer a union recognized by the National Labor Relations Board, they had standing to sue the NFL for violating antitrust laws, on the grounds that the clubs, as competitors, did not have the right, under the federal antitrust laws, to collude and cooperate on business matters, player salaries, and other issues affecting players.

This led to a series of cases in which the players, led by Upshaw (who was basically broke, living on loans and gifts from friends), were successful in the courts, ending up with a successful outcome in the U.S. Supreme Court.

Finally, in 1993, after the then commissioner Paul Tagliabue and Gene Upshaw met secretly many times and got to know and respect each other, they reached a deal—which Tagliabue and Upshaw were able to sell to the owners and the players, successfully, but not easily.

On the players' side, they won union recognition and, most important, Upshaw and Tagliabue reached a historic collective bargaining agreement with a brand-new management-union structure virtually unprecedented in U.S. management-labor relations.

The new system seemed to be a genuine business partnership or joint venture between owners and players. Players would get a fixed percentage of the gross revenues of the entire league (reaching a peak of 60 percent of gross revenues to the NFLPA in 2006). Under this partnership system, all payments and benefits to players—salaries, disability benefits, and retirement benefits—were paid by the NFLPA.

Upshaw wasn't a socialist—but he did believe that as the tide rose and NFL players helped NFL owners receive substantially increased revenues from TV rights, franchise and player brand licenses, games, endorsements, and various other revenue generators, the players should share in that revenue growth.

In addition, players could bargain with other clubs as "free agents" once their contracts expired—but in return, they had to accept a "salary cap" on all players' salaries, per club, according to a proportional formula based on population-based geographical markets.

So there were some gains for owners, too, under this new agreement—since the salary cap acted as a limit on players' salaries and allowed clubs with less money and in smaller TV markets to have a chance to compete against teams with a lot more money and TV revenues. Among the league owners, there was also a form of revenue sharing to try to level things out a bit more.

When Upshaw explained the history of this precedent-shattering NFL-NFLPA "revenue-sharing" collective bargaining agreement, I finally understood why Upshaw was being blamed for allegedly inadequate disability payments, pensions, and other benefits. It was because all salaries and benefits were paid out of the NFLPA's 60 percent share of revenues (that percentage had gradually increased over time since the first NFLPA-NFL contract was negotiated in 1993).

Yet, I found, the attacks were all personalized around Gene Upshaw—as if he made the personal decisions on paying benefits (when, for example, disability decisions were made by experts and a board comprising three player representatives and three owner representatives). My crisis management strategy quickly evolved: Depersonalize and get back to the facts—the process of decisions and the facts of what benefits actually were paid by current NFL players to retired players through the collective bargaining agreement.

The harshest critics came from a retired-players group, led by the famous NFL player and coach Mike Ditka. Unfortunately, the sports press covering the NFL seemed all too willing to report uncritically on Ditka's and his colleagues' criticisms of Upshaw without checking on the actual facts of the process and the amounts current players were paying retired players in benefits.

Maybe, just maybe, I suggested to Upshaw, at least some of the press corps (not all of whom, I tried to convince him, were biased and hated him) had been influenced to write one-sided anti-Upshaw stories by Gene's refusal to return their phone calls or, on the rare occasions when he did, by his cursing them out and hanging up on them.

I worried a bit about his "I'll break your neck" threat to retired player Joe DeLamielleure when I listened to Upshaw. I still gave him the advice: "Gene, I think it's time for you to open up and tell your story to the media, even the ones you think hate you."

Because of the way he looked at me I thought he actually might break my neck.

As he walked out of my office, he turned and glared at me and said, "Okay, I'll take your advice . . . for now."

I was shocked.

"But you better be right."

As he left, I felt a slight anticipatory pain in my neck.

THE WHITE PAPER ON THE TRUTH SQUAD WEBSITE

Regardless of how difficult a media situation Upshaw faced, or per-haps precisely because of it, we went right back to the fundamentals—and followed the first three basic crisis management rules sequentially.

First, we spent a great deal of time assembling the hard, indisput-able facts that, to our amazement, very few sports reporters knew. Sec-ond, we came up with a simple core message. And third, we got out in front of the bad stories and personal attacks and went into war room/rapid-response/let-no-distortion-go-unchallenged mode.

The complicated facts with which to address all the criticisms were difficult to assemble into a simple presentation. But we worked hard with Gene and NFLPA senior staff, especially the staff and out-side attorney who worked with the disability board; studied compara-ble figures in other professional sports; and interviewed key members of the NFLPA Executive Committee—and of course, all along the way, Gene Upshaw showed amazing knowledge about details, numbers, and histories.

The more we dug, the more amazed we were that the actual truth was as far removed from the perception as could be—in fact, the NFLPA under Upshaw's leadership had been on the high end of payments to retired players compared to other professional sports, and aside from the generosity of current players paying out of their own paychecks, we found that Upshaw had personally and privately written checks to retired players and helped them more than anyone knew.

But Upshaw hadn't told anyone about that, and when I told him we wanted to include his own personal generosity in the White Paper on the Truth Squad website, he told me that I was not to do so, and if I did, he might "break your neck, too."

We also explained in bullet points the revenue-sharing system—the core (and surprising) fact that every then current NFL player con-tributed eighty-nine thousand dollars a year out of his 2007 salary to pay retired players for their disability, retirement, and health-care benefits. It was amazing to me that virtually no reporter knew that fact—and they doubted it when we first posted it on the Truth Squad website, until we proved it over and over.

This was my favorite fact—never challenged by retired-player critics—that we listed in the White Paper: "Each NFL player currently playing in the NFL writes a check for eighty-nine thousand dollars per year out of his paycheck to help retired players."

It was a core fact, because it is a game-changer in terms of perceptions. Once people got their heads around this fact, meaning they understood the revenue-sharing system, then they would stop blaming Upshaw personally and go on to understand the other facts, especially the quasijudicial system for determining disability eligibility and the payment levels for disability based on the degree of seriousness of football-related injuries as compared to other professional sports leagues.

We also presented facts, facts, facts about the disability board decisions, case by case, which had often been misstated and distorted by the Ditka group, and showed how favorably the NFLPA contributions compared to other professional sports and other industries.

Then I needed to extract the "garden hose" message from the "waterfall of facts," and that came more easily than usual. We found it almost without trying. We wrote the White Paper on all the facts concerning NFLPA's support for retired players, and we called the website that we created to post the White Paper, with a link from the official NFLPA website, the NFLPA Truth Squad website.

When we saw the title of the website, we knew we had our simple message: This is just about truth—facts, facts, facts and nothing but the facts.

And third and finally, we had to get the facts out to get ahead of the bad stories and misinformation about Upshaw—both proactively, calling journalists and getting stories written about the White Paper and the facts, and reactively, establishing a war room/rapid-response capability. And we vowed—no false or misleading statements from then on would go unchallenged.

"REACH OUT TO REPORTERS WHO HATE ME?"

Shortly after Upshaw returned from his annual August vacation at Lake Tahoe, I asked him to allow me to sit down in person with a leading sportswriter for the *Washington Post*, Les Carpenter, who covered the Washington Redskins. At times Carpenter had written about the retired-players benefits/disability issue and quoted critical comments about Upshaw. I had called Carpenter and talked to him and decided he would give Upshaw a fair chance to tell his story. And the *Post* remained an influential paper not only in Washington, D.C., but in the United States. When I asked Upshaw to sit down with Carpenter, he looked at me menacingly—I swear I felt my neck twitching again.

"You expect me to reach out to reporters who hate me? What do you think I am, a masochist?"

I was instantly reminded of similar sentences from prior crisis clients—from a former president of the United States to Representative Charles Rangel.

"Yes, I do. But they don't hate you. It's just that you don't answer their calls or give them the facts. And Les Carpenter does, after all, work for a pretty powerful hometown paper where you work."

Upshaw cursed a few times when I mentioned Carpenter but finally said okay—as long as I would allow him to throw the reporter out of his office if he had too much of an attitude.

"No, I won't allow you to do that," I said. "But you will anyway even if I tell you not to."

I called Carpenter and he agreed to the interview, expressing amazement that Upshaw was willing to do this. I decided not to tell him that he might be bodily thrown out of the office.

On September 5, 2007, Carpenter published a balanced article in the *Post* that pleased Upshaw, although he didn't really want to admit it. For me, there was a passage that people in my trade would call the "pivotal message quote": "Upshaw said he has fought to squeeze benefits from the owners and has gotten them to move, albeit begrudgingly.

'I'm not going to be unsympathetic,'" he said. For Gene Upshaw to be quoted talking about his softer side—even in the double negative— was a good thing.

I knew that Carpenter's piece would be a signal to other reporters that it was time to do a pivot and start reporting the facts that we had posted in the White Paper, with Gene Upshaw available to fill in the gaps with his own personal comments about his concern for retired players. And it started to work.

We also called other leading sports reporters and columnists covering the NFLPA/Upshaw issue, most of them very critical of Upshaw, and invited them to sit down with Upshaw to interview him and get his side of the story, or to call Upshaw, who would talk to them on the phone if they had any questions. Many reacted in disbelief that Upshaw was willing to do this. Most doubted that he would say very much that would show generosity and respect to at least some of his critics. But he surprised them by doing exactly that.

I had one condition, and only one condition, before I permitted them to sit down with Upshaw. And that was they had to read the White Paper on the Truth Squad website. I kidded them that there was one other condition—I would administer a hundred-question true-false exam on the facts contained in the website and they had to pass with a B or better to get the interview. I might have been joking—but my message, I hoped, was clear. We need to get your journalism out of the realm of accusation and get back to the facts. I also challenged every reporter to call Ditka and his cohorts and ask them to cite one statement in the White Paper on the website that was not entirely accurate. I was told that most reporters did make those calls, and not once did they ever hear of an instance in which there was something factually inaccurate on the Truth Squad website.

More and more reporters were calling themselves to talk to Gene, and he accepted more and more calls, and more and more stories were appearing that seemed more and more balanced.

It was working.

We also established war room/rapid-response capability to fight back immediately if and when the Ditka group or other retired players made inaccurate or distorted public attacks on Upshaw and the NFLPA.

As soon as I read about a statement or a press conference held by Ditka, we were ready to pounce—posting corrections of all misstatements on the Truth Squad website, and sending out a press release and calling key sportswriters about the posted corrections. And I named names. I called on the specific individuals who had made (or repeated) the misstatements and asked them for corrections.

It got to the point that the retired players who had previously been attacking Gene Upshaw started attacking me for the challenges to their statements that we posted on the Truth Squad website—but what they didn't do was dispute the facts.

Gene called me to express satisfaction one night that I was being attacked rather than him, saying, while chuckling: "You may not have my body, Davis, to take the hits, but you have the facts on your side."

I knew that his mood was changing in a positive direction, now that we were fighting back and getting his story out.

And overall, there seemed to be a shift in media reporting in Upshaw's direction, subtle but real.

I was tempted to tell the media about Gene's quiet financial gifts and assistance to injured and hurting retired players. But he was determined to keep that private. I had to honor that. I knew that if I outed him for being a softhearted good guy, contrary to the take-no-prisoners exterior he wanted the world to believe, I might end up as one of those non-prisoners.

Coincidentally, on the same day as the *Post*'s Carpenter article on Upshaw, September 5, Bob Costas broadcast a pre-taped interview of Upshaw that evening on his well-watched and influential sports interview program on HBO.

A month before, in early August 2007, I received a phone call from Costas's producer. He said that Costas was doing a special piece on the retired-players/benefits/Upshaw controversy and wanted to interview Gene on camera. I inwardly winced. I knew the unbreakable rule that Gene could not be disturbed on his summer Lake Tahoe vacation, certainly not for press reasons.

Moreover, as it was a TV piece, even though Costas had a great reputation and was at the top of his craft, editing could distort the truth even when the journalist didn't intend it.

When I reached Gene at Tahoe, he resisted, as I expected.

"They are just trying to set me up," he said. "They'll edit out the good stuff and leave me looking like a fool."

I told him I respected Costas and urged him to take advantage of this TV platform with a wide viewing audience to leave a positive personal impression.

I kidded Upshaw that if he did his "growl" and "grunt" shtick on TV he would fail, since TV was more about demeanor than about content.

"Okay," he said. "You win again. I'll do it."

The Costas interview was taped while Gene was at Tahoe in August and then telecast on that Wednesday evening, September 5.

I thought Costas was fair, as his producer promised me he would be, and Upshaw lived up to his promise to smile, be relaxed, and avoid any anger displays. He came across as a compassionate man, concerned about the retired players, well informed, able, and ready to restate the facts and figures taken directly from the White Paper.

My only complaint about the interview, which I expressed in a brief phone call to Mr. Costas after the broadcast, was that we had not been informed that spliced into the interview would be critical on-camera comments by Ditka and his group, who apparently had been assembled while they were all together at what seemed to be a golf tournament. In other words, there would be negative attacks on

Upshaw on the issue of his failure to support retired players, and then there would be a clip of Gene responding to a similar question asked by Costas.

The effect was that Upshaw was constantly on the defensive, as if he were directly responding to the players. In fact, of course, the material was edited—the players were commenting at a different time and place and then Upshaw's response followed.

I was not told this would happen, nor was Gene. Had we been told, I would have objected—or at least insisted that Gene not be put in the position of always responding to an attack. To his credit, when I talked to Mr. Costas after the broadcast, he heard out my argument that Gene should have been informed about what comments he would appear to be responding to in the editing process. Mr. Costas acknowledged that we should have been told about the setup and that that was a mistake.

After I watched the HBO broadcast, I hesitated to call Upshaw and disturb his vacation again, and I anticipated that he would be angry with parts of it. Then the phone rang and I heard the familiar deep voice. He said hello with something that sounded like a grunt. Then—surprise—the tone was friendly. "That you, Lanny-boy?"

I started to apologize for the editing and the critical comments preceding his in the interview, when he interrupted: "Hey, man, that wasn't so bad," Upshaw replied. "I didn't let Mr. Costas get under my skin like you thought I would. He was actually a nice guy and gave me a chance to speak. I got my points in. You told me to smile, and I did—and my wife thought I was great!"

I thought of Macy's CEO and chairman Jim Zimmerman liking the graphic descriptions of the holding cell and was reminded that a crisis manager isn't usually a good predictor of the reactions of a client in the middle of the controversy—either good or bad.

CONGRESSIONAL HEARINGS—PUSHING BACK

Two weeks later, on September 18, 2007, congressional hearings focused on the retired-players benefits controversy were held by the Senate Commerce Committee. The hearings were presided over by then North Dakota senator Byron Dorgan. Illinois senator Dick Durbin was also concerned about the issue. Upshaw critic Mike Ditka, who headed the anti-Upshaw retired-players committee, was also called to testify, as well as other Upshaw critics and NFL commissioner Roger Goodell.

From the call that I received from the committee staffer inviting Upshaw to testify, it sounded as if there would be a stacked deck of panelists, with Upshaw alone, surrounded by Ditka and other Upshaw critics and severely injured players whose sympathetic stories would inevitably criticize Upshaw and the NFLPA. The issue of disability payments would be central at the hearings, which would be broadcast live on C-SPAN, perhaps also on TV cable, and would be massively covered by the sports media and some political reporters as well.

The first panel on which Upshaw would appear was the one everyone wanted to be there to witness: On the far end of the panel table were Mike Ditka; the legendary Chicago Bears back Gale Sayers, an Upshaw critic but only in the sense that he wanted more money for injured players, not attacking Upshaw or his character and motives personally; and Roger Goodell. And at the other end of the table, as far as possible away from Mike Ditka, was Gene Upshaw.

"Let others engage in this food fight," Upshaw said when we had a meeting at the NFLPA headquarters to debate whether to participate in the hearings. "I am not going to the hearings. I won't dignify it."

There was that expression again, which Gene frequently used to justify not responding to calls from critical reporters.

Upshaw had been widely criticized, I knew, for refusing to show up for the June 2007 hearings held by a House Judiciary Committee subcommittee on the same subject. That had been before he retained me.

I knew that ducking the Senate hearings would be even more damaging to him, given the attendance of both Ditka and Commissioner Goodell (who was both fair and sympathetic to Gene Upshaw on this issue)—and to the cause of getting the facts out about how much he and the NFLPA had actually done for retired players—the mission for which he had retained me.

"So you would rather let them dignify it alone—attacking you and the NFLPA unfairly, without Senators Dorgan and Durbin hearing the other side of the argument?"

I had known both Senators Dorgan and Durbin for many years and I knew both of them to be fair and accurate. And, of course, our strategy was to trump the emotional and sensational charges we expected from Ditka with irrefutable facts from Gene, calmly presented.

I knew that the NFL's new commissioner, Roger Goodell, would also be testifying. I knew that Mr. Goodell, the son of the former New York Republican U.S. senator, was an honest man who was not comfortable with the attacks being made on Upshaw.

"I think Roger Goodell will be fair," I said. And I was right.

The actual testimony and outcome of the September 18 hearings were anticlimactic—and, thus, disappointing to the members of the media who had gathered to watch a food fight. There were few direct attacks on Upshaw. Even Ditka showed restraint. I'd like to think it was because we had the facts ready to challenge anything inaccurate, rather than the more likely reality that Upshaw's physical presence so close by was a disincentive to attacking him personally.

Upshaw's testimony, which we collectively drafted keeping KISS ("Keep It Simple, Stupid") in mind, laid out the simple core facts—especially the eighty-nine-thousand-dollar-per-player contribution and the comparable disability payments among other professional sports. Senator Durbin's questions were fair and Upshaw's answers were crisp and factual.

At one point, Upshaw followed his script and asked rhetorically, looking to the right and left to some of the panelists who had been critical of him in the past: "Is there anyone here who wants to challenge the facts as I have stated them?"

The silence was obvious to everyone—and provided the perfect exclamation point for our crisis management message.

We used one crisis management technique that proved to be successful. Rather than being on defense, Gene and I came up with three positive legislative proposals for Congress to enact that would improve the position of injured retired players seeking disability payments and medical care: expediting the disability process; giving the NFLPA the power to decide on disability payments, rather than a shared board with NFL owners; and prohibiting the option of players' taking lump-sum payments and thus waiving their rights in the future to receive disability payments and medical care.

The next day's *New York Times* contained the following paragraph:

> Lanny Davis, a crisis management specialist and former advisor to the Clinton administration who works with Upshaw, said Upshaw would immediately begin approaching members of Congress to see if they would be interested in introducing these three pieces of legislation.

We did begin working with members of Congress on these three initiatives. The feedback was that Upshaw had "gotten out in front" and demonstrated that far from being hostile to retired players, he was taking the initiative to facilitate and expedite the disability process for players. That proactive stance in and of itself defused the anti-Upshaw slant of the hearings that had been expected and, indeed, left a positive impression about Upshaw.

Even more positive for Upshaw, in a way, was the photograph that I had envisioned but doubted would be possible—Upshaw being gracious to his worst critic, Ditka. We had discussed this, and of course Gene looked at me menacingly, but he refused to respond, except with the usual grunt. But the moment came—and I wasn't surprised that the soft and gracious Upshaw, bottled up inside the tough exterior, inevitably came through.

It came after the hearing was over, when Upshaw walked down the row and shook every panelist's hand. When he got to Ditka, with all eyes (and cameras) watching, Upshaw stuck out his hand and said, "Hi, Coach." Ditka, somewhat surprised, stood up and shook Gene's hand. Gene had a big grin on his face.

That photograph appeared in virtually every newspaper in the country the next day, including the *New York Times*. Mission accomplished!

Later, Upshaw walked over to me, leaned over, and whispered: "We certainly kept them quiet, didn't we?"

I couldn't resist.

"And all their necks remain unbroken," I said. "And you didn't dignify anything—you kept your dignity and carried the day."

He nodded. "Okay," he said. "You win this round. Your neck is safe!"

LEARNING TO FIGHT BACK—WITH FACTS, NOT BLOCKS

The most important lesson I learned in representing a difficult client like Gene Upshaw was that when you have the facts on your side, combined with an inner goodness and decency in the man being attacked, you will come out ahead if you follow the basic rules.

The painstaking assembling of all the facts and responses to the charges against Upshaw was, of course, key. But the ability to get those facts out with a simple message and to push and push and push them out proactively and in rapid response is the tough part.

And the toughest part of all is convincing the client, beaten up by members of the media, to reach out to them and turn them around by cooperating with them and answering their questions.

By using a Truth Squad website concept, with a White Paper to explain the system and all the basic facts and figures about how much the NFLPA/Upshaw paid retired players each year, we were able to refer everyone, whenever there was an attack, to the website. "Go look at the facts—and tell me whether any of them are untrue"—that was our mantra for every reporter.

This also put the critics dealing in misstatements on notice—either do you homework and stick to the facts or you will be called out publicly for not doing so. Eventually, we discovered, their attacks quieted down, because they were aware that they would be challenged.

And ultimately reporters don't want to be embarrassed by getting the facts wrong. It's one thing if they have subjects who won't answer their calls or their questions—then they have an excuse for getting it wrong. But once the transparency regime is in place—and the Truth Squad or White Paper of facts has been posted, without anyone disputing their validity—reporters lose that excuse.

In short, winning the credibility war with the media, even media that has been negative for a long time, is possible—but only by persistent pushing with facts, facts, facts, combined with a more media-friendly and transparent attitude.

The final outcome—vindicating Upshaw and the NFLPA as having been fair to retired players on disability, retirement, and other benefits under their unique 60 percent revenue-sharing deal with the NFL owners—proved that if you are stubborn about pushing the facts out and don't give up even when the press remains hostile, sooner or later the fog can be lifted. Not always, but following the fundamental rules offers the best chance.

UPSHAW THE PROPHET

Criticism of Upshaw died down after these September congressional hearings.

The Ditka group kept beating the drums in the winter of 2007 and spring of 2008, but most reporters had tired of their public attacks on Upshaw and, having read the White Paper, were aware that these criticisms were simply not based on facts.

I called Gene in May 2008 to tell him that my then eleven-year-old son, Joshua, had been invited by my Yale College fraternity brother and friend President George W. Bush to visit him in the early afternoon at the White House. Josh had read about Upshaw when he learned I was working for him and had expressed an interest in meeting him and getting his autograph. I asked Gene if he could see Josh in the afternoon after we had seen President Bush. But Gene said he was free in the morning and Josh had to be in school then, so we would try for another day.

"Do you mean you consider the president of the United States more important for your son to meet than me?" he asked me.

I laughed.

"Josh is going to be disappointed if he doesn't meet the Great Upshaw," I said. "We'll stop by to see you another time."

Upshaw told me he'd be busy until he left for his annual August retreat at Lake Tahoe, but we'd catch up in September when he returned and I should bring Josh by then.

I wished him well on his vacation and congratulated him again that his critics seemed to have lost their energy and the press their interest.

"It's not over, Lanny . . . just you wait."

"What's not over?" I asked.

"Just remember my prediction: When I am gone, the new head of the players union will not have my history or position of bargaining strength. Things will change. You'll see. For example, good-bye to the players' right to receive sixty percent of all revenues, for starters. The owners force a reduction in that percentage and a lot more, and there will be a lockout if the players don't cave."

"What do you mean, when you are gone? You will be around forever."

"Mark my words, my good friend," he said. "When I am gone, things will change."

I wished him well and told him to please try to relax and have a good vacation.

That was the last time I ever talked to Gene Upshaw.

On Saturday night, August 16, Gene had complained to his wife of having a stomachache that was pretty bad. By Sunday, August 17, Gene's pain had grown worse. After much resistance, Upshaw was forced to go to a hospital to be examined.

Three days later, on the evening of August 20, 2008, Gene Upshaw died of pancreatic cancer.

I cried when I heard the news.

And when my son, Josh, heard the news, he too was tearful. We had the same thought—wishing we had gone to see Gene that May morning just three months before, then President Bush in the afternoon.

I remembered wondering about his last words to me—about what would happen to the NFLPA after he was gone.

THE MEMORIAL SERVICE—BITTERSWEET MEMORIES

A few weeks later, I attended Gene's memorial service at the Kennedy Center. Attending the funeral were many of the men who had made Gene Upshaw so miserable in life, attacking his character and his heart, ignoring the facts. I was angry when I saw them. The hypocrisy of it was stunning. I wanted to say to them "Take it all back! Go read the Truth Squad page."

But I didn't.

And then I remembered Gene's words—"When I am gone, good-bye to sixty percent revenue share, for starters."

In 2010, two years after his death, the NFL owners announced that they would not extend the collective-bargaining agreement. When the players balked at changing the terms, a player lockout occurred—that is, the owners shut down their playing operations, barred players from using the facilities, and the war of waiting and attrition began.

As Gene had done in the late 1980s, the union decertified itself as a bargaining unit, which is what provided the NFL with an exemption under the antitrust laws. The players then brought an antitrust suit against the owners. After a lot of litigation and a lot of negotiation, a new collective bargaining agreement was finally arrived at—and just as Gene predicted, the 60 percent level of revenue sharing was now down significantly (reported to be 47 percent), and the players made other concessions, such as caps on rookie salaries.

Upshaw was a truly great football player, a great leader, a great man, and a great friend to retired and current players and to me.

As it turned out, he was also a prophet.

8.

DAN SNYDER AND THE WASHINGTON REDSKINS

Fighting Back and Taking the Heat

I called Dan Snyder, whom I had met shortly after I left the Clinton White House, after I read a lot of negative press about his decision to file a defamation suit against a small Washington, D.C., free-distribution weekly newspaper called *City Paper*. The suit had been filed by Snyder against the paper first in New York City on February 2, 2011, because that was the location of its hedge fund owners. The suit pertained to an article the newspaper had published by a columnist, David McKenna.

The front-page article, "The Cranky Redskins Fan's Guide to Dan Snyder," had been published on November 19, 2010. It was written alphabet-style, from A to Z, presenting a list of criticisms of Snyder's role as owner of the Washington Redskins and other activities in his life, implying that he was much to blame for the Redskins' poor performance since he had acquired the team. One specific assertion by McKenna stated—on the front page of the paper in the introduction:

"That's the Dan Snyder who got caught forging names as a telemarketer with Snyder Communications. . . ."

To anyone who understands plain English, the reporter said "Snyder" himself had been "caught" committing forgery while he was "with" his company. On the inside page, buried toward the end next to the letter "S," was the word "Slamming"—defined by McKenna as the "illegal practice of switching a customer's telephone service without authorization." Then McKenna wrote: "Florida authorities fined Snyder's pre-Redskin outfit, Snyder Communications, $3.1 million in 2001 after investigators uncovered more slamming in its offices than you'd find stagefront at a Limp Bizkit show."

I did some quick Internet research and it took me about five minutes to learn all the facts and see what McKenna had gotten wrong. First, on April 25, 2001, the Florida attorney general, Pam Bondi, in a press release, announced a settlement of "allegations" against GTE Communications Corp (later renamed Verizon), its local Florida company, Verizon Florida, Inc., and Snyder Communications, Inc., that the two companies had engaged in "slamming." The release stated that the companies agreed to "payments without admitting any wrongdoing." The total payments were $2.5 million, jointly paid by GTE/Verizon and Snyder Communications, Inc.—with GTE/Verizon paying an additional $600,000.

So it didn't take long to confirm that McKenna had not only gotten wrong the charge that Snyder personally had been "caught" for forgery—he hadn't, ever; but also that his company had paid a "fine" of $3.1 million, when the amount he shared with GTE/Verizon was less than $2.5 million, with the latter paying an additional $600,000. Moreover, McKenna implied that the companies had pled guilty—he omitted that both companies had denied wrongdoing, an omission that was clearly material and misleading. Moreover, McKenna used the word "fine"—which is imposed by a government after a finding of guilt—when, in fact, the payment made was to settle the charges, without admitting to guilt. That's a difference—and surely the publisher and editor of *City Paper* (and their lawyers) knew the difference.

As I read the almost unanimous condemnation of Snyder's decision to sue *City Paper* (beginning the "Goliath vs. David" anti-Snyder narrative), I was struck by the fact that few commentators expressed concern about whether McKenna's assertions were true or not; or whether McKenna was careless in his reporting; or whether Snyder had tried to get a correction, had failed, and filed the case only because he saw no other alternative to clear his name (which turned out to be the case). There was also early reporting that Snyder had tried to get McKenna fired. That turned out to be false—and the reporter who originally reported that told me months later he was wrong. Yet the original false story was picked up and reported without challenge and was repeated over and over again so that it was generally accepted as true.

I was curious as to why Snyder had taken the trouble to file a case. He must have known, I figured, that the reaction would be negative among the public and media, regardless of the merits. From a crisis management/public relations perspective, Snyder was clearly in a hole.

SNYDER—EASY SCAPEGOAT

Over the years since Snyder had acquired the Redskins, I had watched and listened as the Washington, D.C., media, blogosphere, and sportswriters—and Washington Redskins fans—almost unanimously dumped on Dan Snyder. This was a D.C.-area habit that almost everyone seemed to enjoy. So long as the Redskins continued to experience losing seasons, fail to win the Super Bowl, or even get into the playoffs, I had no doubt this habit would continue.

Sure, Snyder had a lot of personality traits that rubbed people the wrong way, coming across sometimes as disdainful of others or overconfident. The Dan Snyder I knew and admired was an incredibly loving son of his dad (now deceased) and a young man who made every nickel the hard way, by working hard, harder than his friends, harder than almost anyone, and became successful the hard way, through that kind of hard work.

People who resented his wealth seemed not to know, or to intentionally disregard, that he had earned his wealth by hard work. Period.

And many resented that he had the wherewithal to come to own the beloved Washington Redskins. Miraculously, it seemed, this young local guy had somehow managed to edge out a lot of other very wealthy bidders to leverage his own money, bringing in other investors, to purchase the Washington Redskins in May 1999 at the age of forty-two, and to schmooze NFL owners into approving him over a rival bidder.

He was raw, at times; showed his youth, sometimes to a fault; definitely showed signs of having a healthy ego. But above all, I liked his authenticity—he was all there, like it or not; and within that authenticity was a love for family, his wife and children, and that moved me. When he talked first about his love for his dad, I was very moved.

While I saw a lot in Dan to like and admire, I also winced at times when he made public or business decisions that seemed to play to an unfair caricature that I believed wasn't Dan Snyder as I knew him. But I saw some of his excesses as those of the ultimate Redskins fan. And I forgave him for that and other reasons. I wondered why other people didn't.

But as I would often say to others when I responded to critical comments about Dan Snyder at dinner parties or cocktail parties or among friends, "Whatever you say bad about Dan Snyder—I'll bet you would suddenly start to like him if the Redskins started winning and went to some Super Bowls—am I right?"

Some people would protest that that was not correct, but then I would always bring up George Steinbrenner. I pointed out that Steinbrenner wasn't exactly a beloved person or personality in New York, and he was especially detested by New York sportswriters and fans when the Yankees were mediocre in the eighties and early nineties. But between 1996 and 2001, the Yankees won five out of six pennants, and four of five World Series—including, remarkably, three straight in 1998, 1999, and 2000. Guess who suddenly became popular with the New York sportswriters and Yankee fans? Steinbrenner was now praised for being a character, a real Yankees fan who cared maybe too much but was an outstanding owner! I saw a lot of similarities in the rough treatment Snyder received from the D.C. media and Redskins fans. As I said, just let the Skins win a Super Bowl or two and suddenly people would recognize his finer qualities.

So I knew that Snyder's most important problem was that the Washington Redskins were losing and he was the new owner. Still, his conduct and image could use some moderating, and he certainly lacked a media strategy to emphasize his positive attributes—especially, as I would tell him from time to time, that he grew up in the Washington area and was a Redskins fan through and through. Indeed, many of his perceived personality flaws came from the fact that he loved the Redskins so much, and wanted them to win so much. "You are the best Redskins fan—and you need to remind fans of that," I often reminded him.

Since his purchase of the Redskins, the team had had multiple (seven) coaches, general managers, quarterbacks, and players and had experienced seven out of ten losing seasons. Snyder was personally blamed, more than most NFL owners, because he also had an image (most of it exaggerated) as too much of a hands-on owner, getting too involved in decisions on hiring coaches, signing players, maybe even calling plays. Although the last was clearly untrue, critics of Snyder were never bothered by the truth when they wanted to personally attack him.

DRAWING THE LINE

In March 2011, after getting fed up with the frenzied vitriolic attacks on Snyder, with so many media and Washington citizens apparently indifferent to whether the accusations against Snyder were true or not,

I called Snyder and offered to help him. He invited me for dinner at his home in Potomac, Maryland, just a mile or so from mine, to meet with his senior media and legal advisors.

Most of the discussion was about whether Snyder should or should not withdraw the lawsuit against *City Paper*. The charge that he "got caught forging names," Snyder felt strongly, crossed an important legal and business line. He believed that charge went to the heart of his integrity and reputation as a businessman. First he asked for a retraction and apology to be published by *City Paper* but then, if that was not forthcoming, he would file a defamation lawsuit.

He filed his lawsuit in New York City because that was the location of the hedge fund that his attorneys believed owned *City Paper*. In his press statement about the case, Snyder explained that he would contribute all damages won in the suit to charity and would withdraw the case immediately if *City Paper* would retract the charge and apologize.

The publisher of *City Paper* refused to do so (as did the owner, a wealthy New York hedge fund that had purchased the tabloid out of bankruptcy at a fire sale price). She wrote that she and the newspaper had no reason to believe that "Dan Snyder got caught forging names." She wrote: "In fact, we have no reason to believe he personally did any such thing—and our story never says he did."

"Our story never says he did"?

But those were exactly the words used by McKenna—Dan Snyder was "caught forging names."

The publisher seemed to be suggesting McKenna didn't really mean what he wrote—or that no reader would believe the plain words that were written.

Snyder told me that night in his basement den that he could take a lot of attacks, personal and professional, but when a paper accused him of being a criminal and refused to take it back when they admitted they didn't believe it to be true, he had no choice but to take them to court.

Of course that decision was criticized even by Snyder's friends and senior management, because—the standard criticism of the decision by any celebrity to file a libel case against a tabloid newspaper—Snyder's lawsuit would have the counterproductive effect of publicizing and amplifying the charges.

Had I been asked ahead of time, I probably would have advised Snyder to let it go and not bother to sue. But I also would have been torn. I knew from my professional work as well as personal experience that nowadays even good journalists feel some freedom to stretch beyond the facts in writing "opinion" pieces that readers enjoy. And in the blogosphere, especially, the notion that assertions that are not true and could be harmful to someone's reputation should be corrected seems, to many, antiquated, "so retro," as one blogger once told me after I complained about false or misleading statements she had written.

After the suit was filed in February 2011, Dan's explanation of why he sued was not effectively communicated. Even if it had been, the explanation would have been drowned out by the counternarrative that *City Paper* and the media in general quickly generated a furious pounding in all venues—sports sections, cable TV, Internet sites, bloggers: David (*City Paper*) versus Goliath (Snyder), with Goliath trying to crush a little community paper without money or resources to defend itself.

The "David versus Goliath" theme (effectively put out, it seemed to me, by *City Paper* representatives or sympathizers) was further fed by an unfortunate sentence in the Redskins' attorney's letter to *City Paper* asking for a retraction. The attorney made the sensible point that instead of spending a lot of money on legal costs, an apology and retraction would be a better way to end the dispute. But this statement was twisted, repeatedly, into proof that wealthy giant Dan Snyder and the Redskins were attempting to intimidate and kill financially the little *City Paper*.

That narrative ignored the basic fact that the lawsuit was about *City Paper* printing a defamatory falsehood—with no dispute that it was a falsehood (as the publisher herself admitted)—and refusing to retract it. It also conveniently ignored that the "little" *City Paper*, supposedly without financial resources to defend itself against the "Goliath" Snyder, was actually, at least reportedly, owned by a multibillion-dollar hedge fund.

Respected journalists and attorneys defended *City Paper* and McKenna on First Amendment grounds, with Snyder portrayed as trying to thwart freedom of the press. But under long-standing Supreme Court precedent, libel of public officials and public figures could be found if the facts showed that the publication or the reporter had "actual malice"—either publishing with "actual knowledge of the falsity" of the assertion or with "reckless disregard for the truth." The latter might be found in McKenna's ignoring published facts, mixed with his obvious personal dislike of Snyder in this and other articles.

In any event, I certainly understood why Snyder had reached a point to draw the line and say enough. His attorney had written *City Paper* and asked for a retraction and apology. (As stated above, he never asked for McKenna to be fired, as was widely reported.) He also said that he would contribute any damages he won from the lawsuit to charity.

GETTING HIS STORY OUT

By the end of the evening, I came down against withdrawing the lawsuit. I argued that he had filed it for a strong reason—to protect his reputation against an indisputable false charge that he personally had committed forgery. To withdraw the case for now would be counter to that "drawing line" stand. But when the attorney said that night that the case needed to be refilled in Washington, D.C., for legal and jurisdictional reasons, I had an idea.

When Snyder filed his original complaint in November 2010, he had cited several other separate instances or "counts" of false and defamatory statements contained in the McKenna article other than the false assertion that he was "caught forging names," such as false and misleading accusations about other business activities outside of the Redskins. When I talked to Snyder in January 2011 and he told me his attorneys had advised him to refile the case in Washington, D.C., for jurisdictional and legal reasons, I saw an opportunity for him to hit the reset button, explain himself better (not only why he filed the suit but himself personally), and change the negative perceptions of him, even a little. I advised him to focus on the clearest instance of defamation— the false assertion that he had gotten caught forging signatures—and ignore the other counts. I also was ready with a simple suggestion as to how to "frame" (explain simply) why he was doing what he was doing when he filed his new case in Washington, D.C.: It's time to tell your story, yourself, I said, in your own words.

Dan was uncertain he wanted to speak in his own voice and dignify the slimy and false charges and personal attacks of the tabloid paper. "Why should I dignify these people, who don't care about sliming others, with my response?" he asked me.

This was not the first time that Dan Snyder and his response to this media crisis reminded me of Gene Upshaw. The irony hit me immediately: I had represented the head of the players union, Gene Upshaw, the labor-negotiating adversary of a football team owner, Dan Snyder, and they had in common the anger at being falsely accused in the media and the dilemma of not wanting to dignify or give media attention to the false assertions.

"This is your time, Dan, to reframe the narrative about what this is really about—the truth and the facts," I responded. "You may not get another time that your message will get through."

The night we met at Snyder's home I met Snyder's new communications director, Tony Wyllie. Tony was a savvy press guy who knew the sports media and clearly understood the pile-on that Dan's filing of the lawsuit against *City Paper* had created.

But he took the responsibility for the decision to file. "I said to

Dan, 'You've got to do it—you've got to draw the line,' " Wyllie told me as we sat downstairs in Snyder's den.

"What's our proposal?" Snyder asked.

"You write your own op-ed piece in the *Washington Post*," I said. "I know the headline—WHY I SUED *CITY PAPER*—but you have to write the piece in your own voice, expressing your true feelings."

Snyder's lawyers, based in Los Angeles, were preparing a revised complaint to file in Washington, D.C. As it turned out, the hedge fund that owned *City Paper* had established a subsidiary company in the District that was the legal owner of the paper, so the suit should have been filed in a Washington, D.C., court.

We developed a timetable for the suit to be revised and refiled in the District, with Dan's op-ed piece explaining why he filed the suit published on the same morning as the suit was refiled. That way, he would "get out in front" of the news cycle, getting his message out first into the media—"This is about the truth and drawing the line on a journalist who doesn't care about the truth"—rather than allowing *City Paper* to resume and dominate with its "David versus Goliath" message.

I called an editorial-page editor of the *Washington Post*, whom I had known for many years, and asked him if he would review the Snyder-written piece on an off-the-record basis. Then if he thought he could commit to publication, we would need to agree to keep it off the record until we made the final decision to file the lawsuit. After all, if Dan changed his mind and decided to withdraw the case as opposed to refiling it, then the op-ed explaining why he filed the case would become moot.

I knew this was a lot to ask, since it was news that Snyder was refiling the case in Washington and was writing an op-ed piece—for the first time speaking in his own voice, explaining his reasons. But those were the ground rules we asked for, and if they were unacceptable, the *Post* could decline and we could try to place the Snyder op-ed piece elsewhere.

The editor suggested I send over the final draft of the op-ed off the record and he would decide whether it was worth publishing. Dan had just completed the final version. I sent it over to the *Post* editor for review.

The next morning, I got a call from the editor. He said the piece was well written and he would agree to publish it online the evening before the morning paper, when it could be posted on the *Post* website by a *Post* reporter, and then published the next morning in the paper.

The crisis management strategy, which I had used before, was to break news in a predicate story on the morning of the announcement or press event—so that other reporters would have a foundational story to go to for their own reporting, and thus, would be likely to depend on that narrative as the basis of their reporting.

Now came implementing the plan—calling a *Post* reporter to see if he or she would agree to the ground rules—getting an advance copy of the Snyder op-ed piece and the amended complaint, and refraining from calling the *City Paper* to inform it about Snyder's decision to re-file the new complaint in Washington, D.C., until the suit had actually been filed in the court.

This was not difficult. The reporter I talked to, Paul Fahri, had reported on the Snyder story before, and he saw this as a good story for the *Post* to break. He asked me if he could share the story with a sports reporter who covered the Redskins, and I said of course, so long as the ground rules on timing and breaking the story were agreed to.

WHY I SUED *CITY PAPER*

The op-ed piece was published on April 26, 2011, in the *Post*'s morning paper—and was posted online, as we previously agreed, late on the evening of April 25. It was titled, simply: "Why I'm Suing Washington *City Paper*."

Dan began by explaining that this "writer" (he didn't name

McKenna) had written more than fifty-five negative pieces about him, calling his media representative only three times to check his facts. And on the occasion when the "tabloid writer" had falsely accused him of committing forgery, he never called his communications advisor to check out the facts.

Then he got personal, mentioning his dad. "I am the son of a University of Missouri School of Journalism graduate whose professional pedigree included working at United Press International and *National Geographic*. I am proud of that legacy from my dad and understand the journalist's perspective and challenges."

And in the two paragraphs that meant most to me and his communications team, because—perhaps for the first time—they revealed that Dan Snyder was a feeling human being who admitted to weaknesses, his biggest being that he loved, loved, loved the Washington Redskins, perhaps too much, he wrote:

> I am not thin-skinned about personal criticism. I consider myself very fortunate to own the Redskins. Criticism comes with the territory and I respect it. I have never sued people who publish critical opinions of me, nor have I previously sued any news organizations.
>
> I understand the anger people feel toward me when the Redskins have a losing season or when we sign a veteran player who does not meet expectations. I have been a Redskins fan all my life, and I get angry, too, including at myself. I am the first to admit that I've made mistakes as an owner. I hope I've learned from them. All I want is for the Redskins to win!

Snyder got to the ultimate message we wanted to deliver—and the main point of his writing the op-ed piece. To answer the Big Question on everyone's mind: Why on earth did he file this lawsuit, knowing he would get killed in the media and the Internet and blogosphere from legions of Snyder-haters for doing so?

I also hope that people understand why sometimes, especially in the age of the Internet, when an uncorrected lie can live forever, you have to draw the line.

You have to draw the line.

That was the sentence Snyder had said over and over again the March night I sat in his basement talking to him about why he filed the case.

Then Snyder, with the help of those of us who had legal experience in First Amendment law, wrote the key sentence about why the case was not about an attempt to suppress protected First Amendment speech.

I honor vigorous free expression in the media. But even a public figure can sue for defamation when a tabloid paper publishes a harmful assertion of fact, not an opinion, that it knows to be false or recklessly disregards the truth.

As to the "David versus Goliath" theme that had been hurting Snyder in the public portrayal of his suit, Snyder went right at it:

Let's be clear what this lawsuit is not about. It is not about money. I have already publicly committed to donate any financial damages I win to help the homeless. . . . The large for-profit corporation [the hedge fund] that owns the Washington *City Paper* could have checked the public facts and done the right thing: required its paper to retract the false charges and apologize. Had they done so when I filed the lawsuit, I would have immediately withdrawn the case. If *City Paper* in the next several days retracts the false statements cited in my lawsuit and apologizes, I am still willing to withdraw the case.

In other words, all the paper had to do was correct the false statement and apologize and there would be no financial expense at all. Snyder also directly corrected the false report that had asked that McKenna be fired.

> Nor did I or any of my representatives ask for the tabloid writer
> to be fired, despite published reports to the contrary.

Finally, Snyder got to the heart of his motivation—in human terms:

> Simply put, this lawsuit is about the truth—and the need to cor-
> rect the record, even when you are a public figure, when your
> character and integrity are falsely and recklessly attacked. This
> is the case whether you are a public figure or a private citizen.
> Nothing more and nothing less.
>   Enough is enough.

The rest of the day—April 26—was spent following the plan to brief the press by conference calls and then for Snyder's top litigator, who would be leading the attorney team in the case, Patricia Glaser, a brilliant and charismatic trial lawyer from Los Angeles, to call in to the various morning sports talk shows with a significant audience in Washington.

The *Washington Post* op-ed piece was Dan Snyder's true voice—finally. And it was a voice that ultimately didn't ask to be liked or loved but, simply, understood. A lot better than remaining silent. But certainly not enough to win over his most vitriolic critics.

I discovered, in the days and weeks that followed, that at least some who still remained critics of Snyder found the op-ed piece surprising and positive evidence of Snyder's humility.

I was surprised to hear from so many people whom I talked to and who did not know I was involved in helping Snyder in this matter "get it"—that at some point, everyone has a right to draw a line in demanding a correction of a false and damaging published statement and suing if necessary to vindicate one's reputation.

But no matter what, almost everyone agreed with me: The only real answer to Dan Snyder's public relations problems was a Washington Redskins Super Bowl win.

"WHY I WITHDREW MY SUIT"

As it turned out, it was a lot easier to explain why Snyder sued *City Paper* than it was to explain why he had decided to drop the case.

In early September 2011, I received a phone call from the Redskins general manager, Bruce Allen (son of the legendary Redskins coach George Allen, and brother of the former Virginia governor and U.S. senator George Jr.), who had called to tell me that Dan had decided to withdraw his case.

The owners-union dispute that led to a lockout of NFL players was heading to a final resolution and the new football season was about to get started.

Snyder understandably wanted to focus all his attention on the Redskins and the coming season. The lawsuit was heading for a period of heavy "discovery"—meaning, under U.S. procedures, that *City Paper* would have the right to take Snyder's deposition, dig into a broad range of topics beyond the specifics of the case, and cause substantial distraction at the very time Snyder and his organization wanted to concentrate on the new football season.

Bruce Allen called to ask me what I would advise about explaining the decision to withdraw the defamation case. He and others around Snyder feared that *City Paper* and McKenna might try to spin the story as vindication of McKenna's original story and proof that Snyder's lawsuit was baseless.

I agreed that if there was no strategy and message surrounding the withdrawal of the case, that was exactly how *City Paper* and the media would play the story—it would be impossible to resist another chance to poke Snyder in the eyes and to do an "I told you so" crowing that Snyder's original case was about nothing more than Goliath attempting to squash David.

My first reaction to Bruce Allen was to follow the model set by former Vermont senator George Aiken in the late 1960s in advising President Lyndon Johnson how to get out of the disastrous Vietnam War: declare victory and get out.

So, I reasoned, Dan has, in fact, been vindicated. Even *City Paper*'s lawyers won't defend McKenna's accuracy or reporting. Their only defense (under some First Amendment precedents) was that McKenna's false statement was acceptable hyperbole and wasn't meant to be taken literally. But that defense was *an admission that McKenna's statement was false*. Thus, it was time to declare victory and get out.

So based on that concept, we constructed the message to explain Dan's decision to drop the case—in addition to his desire to focus on the Redskins.

Now we had to get to the *Washington Post* reporter who had previously covered the story, Paul Farhi, and give him the story of the withdrawal first—again, using the same strategy of getting our story out first before *City Paper* had a chance to declare victory.

Farhi agreed to embargo the story about the withdrawal of the case until we had received signed agreements from *City Paper* and McKenna to agree to the withdrawal, and that each side would "bear its own costs"—meaning Snyder would not be required to pay *City Paper*'s legal fees, or vice versa.

The "without costs" part of the deal wasn't a question of money. It was about not allowing *City Paper* and McKenna to claim they had won because Snyder was willing to pay their costs, thus compromising the principle that the case was always just about the truth, and nothing but the truth.

I also urged Farhi to call *City Paper* attorneys immediately, since they already knew that Snyder intended to withdraw the case and were waiting for *City Paper* and McKenna to sign the "dismissal without costs" agreement, so his story could reflect both sides at the same time, and that would be the end of the story.

Usually we prefer to get a preemptive-strike message out first before the other side has a chance to respond and leak the story. But in this instance, the objective was to get out in front with our message declaring vindication of the principle of truth—and by including *City Paper*'s counterargument, the *Washington Post*/Farhi story should be closer, or at least leave other journalists only to follow up on the message in the *Post* story.

Nothing in crisis management strategy works perfectly, but this was as close to fulfilling the objectives as we could have wanted—get in, get out, over quickly.

So, consistent with our timing strategy, just about at the moment that we received the signatures of the *City Paper* representative and Mr. McKenna agreeing to the dismissal without costs, Farhi posted his story. At the same time, Snyder and the Redskins issued an official press statement that was sent to the *Post* sports desk first and then simultaneously to the news and sports wires. The statement carefully set out our basic preemptive messages, based on the facts. I will insert my own comments about the message point after each one is made:

"The [defamation] lawsuit was pursued as means to correct the public record following several critical factual misstatements in the Washington *City Paper* article," said team spokesman Tony Wyllie.

Message: The case was about correcting the record, not about Goliath squashing David.

In the course of the defendants' recently filed pleadings and statements in the matter the Washington *City Paper* and its writer have admitted that certain assertions contained in the article, which are the subject of the lawsuit, were in fact unintended by the defendants.

Message: The decision to withdraw was largely triggered by recent statements by *City Paper* attorneys that the accusation against Snyder was not true, that is, that it couldn't be read literally.

> Therefore, we see nothing further to be gained at this time through continuing the lawsuit. We prefer to focus on the coming football season and the business at hand. We remain committed to assisting with responsible reportage of the Team and the many people involved in our organization, including Dan Snyder, and the principle that the truth and the facts matter in responsible journalism has been vindicated.

Core message: Dan Snyder was first and foremost a Washington Redskins fan—and that was his priority, now that he had been vindicated in correcting the record.

The end. The crisis management objective was accomplished—the story was over—no more stories on the Snyder–*City Paper* controversy. And even better, now the focus was back to Dan Snyder and the Washington Redskins.

Unfortunately, the Redskins suffered a disappointing 5-11 record, getting walloped 34–10 by their archrival Philadelphia Eagles at home on January 1, 2012, in their final game.

I still believed that despite all the personal vilification of Snyder, one Super Bowl victory would cause a miraculous DNA transformation and suddenly Snyder's obsessive Redskin-mania would be seen by the fans as proof that he really was a great Redskin, and all his excesses could be forgiven once the Skins won the Super Bowl.

DEFEATING THE INTERNET-FED MEDIA FRENZY ISN'T EASY

Media crises are usually caused by a huge gap between the truth and way the facts are being distorted in the media, and especially on the Internet.

Following the fundamental rules of crisis management—getting the facts, developing a simple message, and getting out in front of the story—may not be entirely effective. Making a bad story better is often the best you can hope for. And most important, you must overcome the reluctance to give more media attention to the smear or false statement and fight back with the facts, over and over again, until the offender knows he or she won't get away with future misinformation without challenge. This was the situation Dan Snyder faced, and the outcome, with he himself explaining why he filed the case and why he withdrew, early and clearly, was probably the best he could have hoped for.

And even when it was over, the ultimate public relations problem Dan Snyder faced hadn't changed at all as Redskins fans looked grimly ahead to the 2012 season: the Redskins needed a first-rate quarterback, something beyond my expertise of crisis management.

Little did I know not only that Snyder would find one in the April 2012 NFL draft—the Baylor University Heisman Trophy superstar quarterback Robert Griffin III (known as "RGIII")—but, for the first time, I would hear many people praising Dan Snyder for his skill in getting RGIII. I wasn't surprised when, the very next day, a friend of mine who had been one of Snyder's harshest critics and who knew I liked him and had helped present his point of view regarding his decision to sue City Paper, called me. "Well, I have to say I am growing to like Dan Snyder. He really got it done."

On December 30, 2012, the Washington Redskins, led by RGIII and a remarkable 200-yard, three-TD performance by rookie running back Alfred Morris, ended their season with their seventh straight win.

This meant they went from a 3-6 opening record to a final record of 10-6, winning their first National Football Conference East Division title since 1999. Adding to the pleasure of Redskins fans was the fact that this final do-or-die victory at home at DC's FedEx Field was over their ultrarival, the Dallas Cowboys, by the decisive score of 28–18.

As the year ended on New Year's Eve the next night, there was even "Super Bowl" talk in the air—in the neighborhoods, on Capitol Hill, and, so the buzz went, all the way to the top of 1600 Pennsylvania Avenue. And even Dan Snyder won some credit, albeit begrudging, from some Redskins fans and in the media. He had notably refrained throughout the season from interfering with Redskins head coach Mike Shanahan. This was remarkably noted in a headline in the *Washington Post*, on January 4, 2013: DANIEL SNYDER REDSKINS OWNER ADOPTS HANDS-OFF ROLE. No one doubted that Griffin was a great quarterback and was likely to become the franchise quarterback the Skins have lacked since Sonny Jurgensen more than thirty years ago, and Snyder was given some credit for signing him, as well as Morris and backup quarterback Kirk Cousins, the former Michigan State star. Cousins had replaced the injured RGIII to help win two crucial games at the end of the season.

Despite the disappointment when the Skins lost the first game of the playoffs to the Seattle Seahawks, 24–14, on Sunday, January 6, after RGIII reinjured his knee, there was still great hope for next season. And who knows? Miracles can still happen! A healthy RGIII could lead the Skins to a Super Bowl title in January 2014 and Dan Snyder could then be the most popular person in Washington next to Barack Obama!

9.

SENATOR TRENT LOTT

When Nothing Else Works, Pray

"Lanny, this is your old Republican friend. I have a Republican friend who very much needs your help. It may be too late, but if anyone can help him, you can. I'd appreciate your taking his call."

It was the morning of December 18, 2002. I recognized the foggy, famous voice right away. It was Jack Kemp, former congressman, presidential candidate, cabinet secretary, and superstar quarterback for the San Diego Chargers and Buffalo Bills. Jack and I had become close friends over the years, despite our strong political differences. He was then in private life, with his own company, in partnership with his son, and we had done some work together and had become even closer friends.

Jack passed away on May 2, 2009—a truly great man, mourned by Democrats and Republicans alike.

My friendship with Jack really began during the Clinton impeachment crisis.

Kemp had reached out to President Clinton in the early days of the

House GOP effort to impeach Clinton in late 1998. He was then in private life, but still a major respected figure not only in the Republican Party as a whole but among its conservative base.

So when he publicly opposed impeachment, not because he approved of President Clinton's conduct but because he believed it did not justify impeachment, that was seen as significant by the Clinton White House and by some in the media.

Jack worked with us in the Clinton camp, getting briefed before doing TV appearances, which we greatly appreciated. While Jack and I differed on politics—I am a liberal, Jack was one of the most famous "supply side" economic conservatives—we had come to be close personal friends. He and his wife, Joanne, attended one of our ecumenical (and bipartisan) Seders on Passover night two years before he passed away.

My response to Jack's request to do a favor for a friend of his was immediate. "If it's a friend of yours, Jack, of course I'll help. Who are you talking about?"

"Trent Lott."

"Trent Lott?" I was thunderstruck. "He's too far gone, Jack—you know I know and like Trent, but there's nothing I can do at this point."

"He knows that. But he still wants your help. Please take his call—for me," Kemp said. "He's got a particular problem with a particular individual—and you may be the best person to help him out."

"Okay, Jack—of course I'll take his call, even though I honestly don't think I can help him at all. But, as you know, I admire Senator Lott, although I disagree with his political views."

One of the main reasons I felt this way was that Senator Lott had quietly worked with Democrats in the Senate in 1999 before the Clinton impeachment trial to try to avoid the necessity of a trial—which he knew would result in the acquittal of President Clinton because he knew there weren't sixty-seven votes for conviction—in return for President Clinton's agreeing to sign a harsh self-censure resolution for his conduct. The approach failed after the GOP House managers strongly objected. But those of us in the trenches arguing that the impeachment process was partisan and illegitimate were appreciative of Senator Lott's private, pragmatic efforts to achieve a compromise.

Of course, that and other efforts by Lott to work with Democrats on center-right compromise solutions for the benefit of the country didn't sit well with partisan Republicans. And he hadn't made a lot of friends in the Bush White House when he didn't always toe the political and policy line they believed was best.

So when I prepared myself for the phone call from Senator Lott, I knew that one problem was that he had not only alienated the left by his long-standing conservative views, but he couldn't look to the Republican base on the right to protect him in a time of difficulty.

And I knew, from the national headlines, that Senator Lott faced, to say the least, a time of difficulty.

PILING ON, WASHINGTON-STYLE

By December 18, virtually everyone in America knew about Mississippi senator Trent Lott's pending demise as Senate Republican majority leader. But you had to be a Washington insider or student of the media-political complex scandal-pile-on machine to appreciate the pain and humiliation that Trent Lott and his family were going through.

The triggering incident occurred only two weeks before Kemp's call, on the evening of December 5, 2002. And it was almost entirely missed by the media—a classic example of the tree falling in the forest with no one there to hear the noise. Then after it was missed, once it was found out, it produced—in my view—an entirely disproportionate and excessive adverse reaction, which led to Senator Lott's forced resignation as GOP Senate majority leader.

On that night of December 5, Senator Lott stood up to toast South Carolina senator Strom Thurmond at his one-hundredth birthday party. What he said—he later described his mood and the room's mood as "lighthearted"—was the beginning of his nightmare that wasn't just a bad dream:

"I want to say this 'bout my state [of Mississippi]: When Strom Thurmond ran for president, we voted for him. We are proud of it. And if the rest of the country had followed our lead, we wouldn't have had to deal with all these problems over the years, either."

C-SPAN cameras were rolling and picked up the toast live. There were reportedly twelve or more political reporters at the event as well. But apparently the reporters and the C-SPAN audience didn't see the significance of what Senator Lott had just said.

But one young broadcast media representative, ABC TV news reporter Ed O'Keefe, a "non-on-air" reporter covering the event just in case, did take notice. He later said he immediately thought: This is news. He looked around and, it seemed, no one else in the media or among the guests had any reaction at all to what Lott had just said. Years later when I read about O'Keefe's singular reaction to Lott's Thurmond toast, I was reminded of my favorite scene in the Watergate-journalism Academy-Award-winning movie, *All the President's Men*.

The young *Washington Post* reporter Bob Woodward (played by Robert Redford) is sitting in the D.C. local criminal courtroom when the Watergate burglars are being arraigned. One of them, James McCord, is asked by the judge, "Who is your current employer?" He answered, "The Committee to Re-elect the President" (that is, President Nixon). Then the judge asks McCord, "And who was your previous employer?" McCord responds, so quietly Woodward can barely hear him, "CIA." The judge asks him to repeat his answer, louder. And he does—this time allowing Woodward to clearly hear the three letters: "CIA."

The close-up of Redford in the movie shows a look of shock—and then Redford/Woodward whispers to himself: "Holy shit."

I can imagine something like those two words going through O'Keefe's mind.

When O'Keefe got back to ABC's studios and reported the toast to his producer and said it was broadcast live on C-SPAN, the producer is said to have responded: "No, I don't think this is anything." The reporter did manage to get ABC to report on the Lott toast the next morning, on December 6—at 4:30 a.m. Again, a tree falling in the forest . . . no one else in the mainstream media picked up O'Keefe's report that day.

But this was 2002, and the Internet and the blogosphere were alive and well—unlike the archaic age of newsprint and deadlines of hours, not seconds, during the early-1970s Watergate era. This, I knew, was crucial to understand and appreciate if you were going to be an effective crisis manager in the era of the Internet. The rapidity of the virus of negative information, which, whether accurate or not, circles the globe or spreads throughout the mainstream media in seconds or even less, cannot be underestimated.

So while almost everyone missed the O'Keefe/ABC/4:30 a.m. report, a few bloggers had heard about it through the grapevine of the blogosphere—Josh Marshall and Glenn Reynolds, to name two. They started doing research on Lott's prior position on race issues and also on the 1948 campaign of Strom Thurmond, when he ran as an independent "States Rights Party Democrat," or Dixiecrat. For example, they found the following ugly quotation from Thurmond during that campaign:

> I wanna tell you, ladies and gentlemen, that there's not enough troops in the army to force the Southern people to break down segregation and admit the nigger race into our theaters, our swimming pools, into our homes, and into our churches.

The result was that others started to connect the dots and put Lott's toast into a much more negative context. As a media analyst, Jay Rosen, wrote years later about the slow burn of media interest in the Lott toast, which was energized by the early blogger research and postings in the few days after the December 5 toast:

What news was heard that night when Lott rose to speak depended entirely on prior knowledge that a journalist either did or did not have about race, Southern politics, and the re-alignment of the political parties during the civil rights era. The blogs provided, almost overnight, that short course on Dixiecrat politics.

Then the news moved from the blogosphere into the mainstream media, as it sometimes does—and then, look out! A highly respected *Washington Post* political reporter named Tom Edsall heard about the toast and started doing his own research about Lott.

He found a report of a comment made by Senator Lott twenty-two years before, on November 3, 1980, published in the Jackson, Mississippi, *Clarion-Ledger*, at a Ronald Reagan rally in downtown Jackson, when he was introducing the keynote speaker, then South Carolina senator Strom Thurmond. "You know, if we had elected this man thirty years ago, we wouldn't be in this mess today."

Also by then, the racist history of Strom Thurmond, as expressed in his 1948 presidential campaign speeches, had produced across-the-board shock, regardless of party, among many who had forgotten, or were too young to remember, the raw and ugly racism of America, segregation, and Jim Crow in the Deep South in that era.

So by the time Jack Kemp called me on December 18, I already knew—who didn't?—that Senator Lott was in serious political trouble due to a toast he had made on the evening of December 5, 2002, to South Carolina senator Strom Thurmond at his one-hundredth birthday party.

His Thurmond toast had already alienated the Democratic Party partisan left, which regarded it as evidence of his suppressed, if not continuing, racism. And the Republican right, as noted above, had already been alienated by Lott's outreach to the Clinton White House before and during impeachment, including his tendency to reach across the aisle to achieve bipartisan solutions.

Leading GOP figures—such as Governors Jeb Bush of Florida and

196 | LANNY J. DAVIS

Rick Perry of Texas—had already criticized Lott for his remark. So had conservative columnists and editorial writers. And rumors were strong that Tennessee Republican Bill Frist was the White House (and GOP conservative establishment) selection to oppose Senator Lott for majority leader at the January 6, 2003, Senate Republican caucus. On the other hand, South Dakota Democratic minority leader Tom Daschle had gracious words to say about Senator Lott—comments that mirrored my own feelings perfectly.

"There are a lot of times when he and I go to the microphone [and] would like to say things differently and I'm sure this is one of those cases for him as well," Senator Daschle said. Liberal senator Patrick Leahy also had sympathetic words for Senator Lott—probably not helping Senator Lott's cause with right-wing Republicans.

Thus, as I heard from many friends who were GOP conservatives, the base—and many in the Bush White House, including reportedly the "Architect," Karl Rove—were happy to watch Lott—to use the phrase made famous during the Watergate scandal—"left twisting in the wind."

"SHOULD I TAKE THE CALL"

So that was the context the day I heard from my friend, former representative Jack Kemp.

Then Kemp told me the reason Senator Lott wanted to call me.

"It's about a call he just got from Reverend Jesse Jackson—who has asked him to call him back. I told him you were a good friend of Reverend Jackson, and Senator Lott wants to know whether he should call the reverend back."

"Well, of course he should," I responded. "Why wouldn't he?"

Jack took a moment to respond.

"He is concerned that Reverend Jackson might be tempted to use his taking the call politically—to make it public and embarrass him," he said. "He knows he's probably too far gone for his majority leader position to be saved—but he just doesn't want any more pain or humiliation for himself and his family."

I said I would be happy to advise Senator Lott that Reverend Jackson would never do such a thing—and I would guarantee that.

I had known Reverend Jackson since the 1960s and had met him shortly after the assassination of Dr. Martin Luther King. He was by Reverend King's side when the assassin's bullet struck him and I knew him as an inspiring religious and political leader and eloquent spokesman for the civil rights movement.

I also knew him to be a highly empathetic and spiritual person who was at his best when counseling a person in trouble, regardless of party or political philosophy. I knew that he would never attempt to exploit another person's personal pain and anguish.

An hour or so later, the phone rang.

"Hello, Lanny, this is Trent. Trent Lott. I appreciate your taking my call. Jack told me it was okay to call you to ask your advice."

"Of course, Senator. I've heard a little about the issue you are concerned about."

"I want to do right here," Senator Lott said. "I know I've made a mistake and offended my friends in the black community and many others, and my toast was a terrible mistake. I didn't mean it in my heart, but few people believe that now."

He continued: "This isn't about politics—this is about repairing who I am and what I am. I don't know if I will have the votes to continue to be majority leader but I am guessing I won't."

He mentioned that Reverend Jackson had called him and wondered why, and whether he should return the call.

"I know it's probably too late for me to save my position as majority leader. But my question is: Will Reverend Jackson try to hurt me even further if I return his call?"

I was impressed, even amazed, that I didn't hear more bitterness and self-pity from Senator Lott. After all, while he had made a mistake in his toast, and perhaps it reflected long-ingested insensitivities from being raised in segregated southern Mississippi, he could have been angry at the Bush White House and his fellow Republican senators for throwing him over the side so quickly and putting up Tennessee Republican senator Bill Frist as his replacement. It was obvious to everyone that Bush White House political leaders (rumors were that Karl Rove was behind it) were pushing for Frist to replace Lott.

My crisis management advice to Senator Lott—the same advice I would have given Representative Anthony Weiner when he got caught in his misconduct on the Internet—was to forget about politics, or political consequences, and to deal with this issue on the most personal level through soul-searching and seeking counseling.

In other words, here the third rule of crisis management—to get out in front of the facts and the crisis—was applicable, but with a twist: The objective was not to "solve" the crisis (that is, to keep Senator Lott's position as majority leader)—since, realistically, that objective was not very likely to be achievable. So the new objective, I suggested to him, or at least his highest priority for the moment, should be a far more personal one for him and his family—to find closure, and rehabilitate himself with dignity, to at least leave open the option of being able to continue in the U.S. Senate with some inner peace and ability to be effective. In effect, this would be "getting out in front" of his own pain and his family's pain—personal crisis management.

In this case, I knew Jesse Jackson well enough—because I had seen the friendship, counseling, and empathy he provided to Bill Clinton at critical moments during his personal crisis—to know that no matter what, Reverend Jackson would give Senator Lott wise advice.

I knew Reverend Jackson would personally extend the hand of forgiveness if he decided that Senator Lott was sincere—which I knew he was. Whether that helped or hurt Senator Lott politically, in my view, had to be irrelevant at this point.

That was the advice I gave Senator Lott—to call Reverend Jackson back.

He accepted it. But then I hesitated. Before he made the call, I made a quick decision.

"Let me call Reverend Jackson and ask if I can be present when you call him—that way, there may be further ideas we can discuss about ways for you to repair your political relationships on the left and the right and perhaps save your position as Republican Senate leader."

"Well, Lanny," I recall Senator Lott saying, "I'd rather not consider the politics of this—your advice was right on that. I need Reverend Jackson's personal counsel. But if you would like to be there for the call, that is fine."

I called Reverend Jackson. "Jesse—I know you have called Trent Lott. I'd like to facilitate that call—he needs your counsel."

The reverend didn't disappoint.

"Why am I not surprised that even Trent Lott calls you for help?" he said, as we both laughed. "But all I wanted to do is reach out to offer him a chance for spiritual peace—it wasn't about politics."

I didn't want to insult him by asking whether he would exploit the phone call. I knew that it was impossible for him to do so.

I also didn't want to insult him by asking the following question, but I did so anyway: "Would you mind if I came over to your office and sat with you when Senator Lott calls you?"

Reverend Jackson laughed. "So you want to monitor me, Mr. Davis—no problem. Come on over."

"Not 'monitor,' Reverend," I responded. "Just bear witness."

It was then 2:00 p.m. on December 18, 2002. So we set the call for Senator Lott to make to Reverend Jackson about four that afternoon. I went over to the reverend's office town house, went down to the basement office, and he sat at his desk waiting for the call. We talked quietly and I simply told him that Senator Lott was a good man with a good heart who had made a bad mistake and wanted to be forgiven.

The phone rang, and the reverend answered and said, "Hello, Senator Lott . . . nice to talk to you."

Then I sat for about twenty minutes. Reverend Jackson didn't say too much. He nodded once in a while, said "I understand" several times, and looked at me with a look that seemed to be both sympathetic and in pain, as if he was sharing Senator Lott's pain.

I was engrossed by this scene. And then the moment came that I shall never forget.

"Okay, Senator Lott. I believe you are sincere. I believe you should be forgiven. And now what I have to say is this: Let us pray."

Then it hit me: Who could possibly believe that the famous liberal civil rights leader, friend of Dr. Martin Luther King, Jr., and spiritual advisor to President Clinton—Reverend Jesse Jackson—would be talking to Senator Trent Lott, conservative senator from the Deep South state of Mississippi and the Republican Senate majority leader, and would be conducting a private prayer for him in the midst of a national controversy in which his own conservative base was after his scalp?

Only in America, I thought. No one could believe this scene actually occurred, I guessed.

My amazement was interrupted when I heard Reverend Jackson begin his prayer, extemporaneously, which moved me greatly. It lasted about ten minutes—and its theme was human frailty, sin, pain, the process of acceptance of responsibility, forgiveness, and spiritual peace.

I was drawn to tears. And, I was told much later by Senator Lott, so was he.

So as the reverend began his prayer, I sat, not knowing what to do, feeling both awkward and almost surreal in what I was witnessing. Instinctively, I could do only one thing: Bow my head.

Years later, Senator Lott told me that he had a staff member with him to witness the conversation. And when Reverend Jackson said, "Let us pray," loud enough for his aide to hear, he had a look of amazement on his face that must have been the same as mine. And, Senator Lott told me, both also bowed their heads as Reverend Jackson delivered his prayer, loud enough on the phone for his aide to hear. And both, he said, had tears in their eyes when he was done.

As I strongly suspected that day and as Senator Lott did as well, it was too late for him to survive politically. Two days later, on December 20, 2002, Senator Lott announced he would not seek reelection as GOP Senate majority leader, although he would remain in the Senate. Senator Frist announced he already had fifty-one committed votes from Republican senators to replace Senator Lott.

While Senator Lott had lost his role as GOP Senate leader, it was not too late for him to repair himself—teaching me another important rule of crisis management when the crisis is about personal embarrassment and humiliation due to a personal misstatement or serious misconduct.

He was hurting a lot—personally—and was in great pain when I talked to him after his announcement. But he set a standard for how to conduct himself during this embarrassing, self-inflicted crisis. He was gracious, took responsibility, and gave in only after taking the high road.

After his resignation as GOP majority leader, I became close friends with Senator Lott. He truly seemed to have emerged a far better person as a result of his personal and political crisis.

Senator Lott was reelected in 2006 for his fourth term, but a year later, on December 20, 2007—almost exactly five years after he had announced he would not seek to be reelected majority leader—Senator Lott announced he was resigning from the Senate to pursue a career in private life in Washington. His comments on his announcement were typically gracious. The words sounded very much like the words of spiritual advice and wisdom that Reverend Jackson had offered to him in his prayer five years almost to the day before:

"I have no anger or complaints. I have nothing but heart for my future."

SOLVING A CRISIS EVEN WHEN LOSING POLITICALLY

What the crisis management tale involving Senator Trent Lott taught me was not too different from the lesson that President Clinton learned when he suffered through his personal crisis involving his private life and his family: When the crisis is so personal, and so painful, that the only way out is no way out; that the only political solution is no political solution; then the only way to manage the crisis is to look inward and seek answers from within . . . and to repair relationships with people who have been hurt by the mistakes.

I also discovered, in the experience with Senator Lott, that when political crisis and personal crisis mix, the degree of hurt and humiliation suffered by the politician or celebrity who is in the crosshairs of the media frenzy (or the other metaphor I tend to use, in the pool bleeding with the media piranhas circling), the level of pain and public humiliation is beyond the pale.

The biggest challenge for a crisis manager is how to get the client through the intensity of the frenzy and to the point that the client is able to make rational decisions that in the long term are the best pathway to rehabilitation and repair. The most important rule: Deal with the personal—spouse, family, yourself—first. Heal and repair and get time to settle things down.

It may seem corny to say it, but I learned here again that crisis management in this situation is about finding peace in the soul—and from that inner peace can come a new day and "turning the page," the ultimate "solution" in this situation for the crisis manager's client.

FIGHT FOR THE TRUTH USING LAW, MEDIA, AND POLITICS

10.

RENT-WAY

The Risk of Telling the Truth

In late November 2000, on a cold and wintry night in Erie, Pennsylvania, with winds blowing strongly off the mostly frozen nearby Lake Erie, I sat over dinner with a very nice man, a gentle man, in his mid-forties.

It wasn't a happy dinner or a social dinner. I was there to console a man who was CEO of a company he had founded and who was in the middle of what seemed to be a massive accounting fraud in his own company.

He was a man in obvious great pain, a man who spoke to me with intense sincerity mixed with doubt—doubt that I would believe anything he had to say.

I felt like a priest hearing a confession, someone pouring his heart out. But what exactly what was he confessing to?

"I screwed up, badly," admitted Bill Morgenstern, the CEO of a rent-to-own publicly owned company, called Rent-Way, headquartered in Erie.

We were eating dinner alone in a small Erie private eating club, more like a dining room in a small home than a restaurant.

"I should have known. I don't know why I didn't. I can't sleep. I am ashamed. I am ready to give up."

Each of these sentences moved me, uttered as they were with staccato fierceness, one after the other, each one hitting me like a quick electric shock. The last one especially.

But there was something off here, something paradoxical, I thought.

"But you say you are innocent," I interrupted. "How can you be ready to give up if you are innocent? Why would you? If you are innocent, why are you talking and walking and acting like you are guilty?"

I realized I sounded—indeed was—angry.

He responded, a hurt look in his eyes.

"Look at the press, look at what everyone in the company thinks, look at what my closest friends think who are reading the press—even the lady at the cash register at the supermarket who I know invested in Rent-Way and has lost most of her life's savings looks at me like I am a criminal," he said, his eyes tearing up.

What Morgenstern and I were talking about was a massive accounting fraud that had been uncovered a few weeks before in his company. Tens of millions of dollars, perhaps more, of inflated profits had been invented and reported to the stock market and investors. This was a crime and people would probably go to jail for criminal securities fraud—including Morgenstern, if there was any evidence that he had known about it.

Headlines blared in the *Wall Street Journal* and all the major national business newspapers, especially in his local newspaper, the *Erie Times-News*.

"I didn't know—didn't know a thing," Morgenstern said. "That's what I am guilty of . . . stupidity. But I didn't know," he kept repeating, trying to convince me, but also seeming to be trying to convince himself.

His eyes teared up. "I just don't know how to explain this," Morgenstern went on, defensively. "No one will believe me that I didn't know, that I couldn't have known—the fraud was so clever, unless you are looking for fraud, you couldn't have found it. Even the outside accountants didn't find it."

"But I thought you just told me you should have known. If it was impossible to detect unless you are a forensic accountant digging and looking for fraud, and even then it would have been hard to find, how can you blame yourself so much?"

"Because I let everyone down. And maybe I pushed too hard, hard to cut expenses, hard to increase sales, hard to increase profits," he said. "I told them to go out and find additional profits by reducing expenses so we could make our numbers for the next quarter—but I didn't think they would find it by making up numbers in the accounting department."

So now I understood.

This wasn't about law or fraud.

It wasn't even about negligence or indifference.

It was about a man who felt responsible—an internal moral code, a feeling that he, Bill Morgenstern, was responsible for pain he had caused his employees, his company's shareholders, his friends, his family.

I was an attorney, a crisis manager who knew something about getting the facts out to close the gap between what the media reported and what the reality was.

But I wasn't a grief counselor or a psychiatrist.

"Bill," I remember saying clearly as if it were yesterday rather than more than ten years ago, "you've got to tell the truth and let others decide your moral guilt. And don't worry whether people believe you. Just tell the truth and let the proven facts speak for themselves."

Long pause.

"Help me get my story out," Morgenstern said.

I looked at him for a while, not wanting to say anything that would make matters worse for him. We hadn't touched the food we had ordered.

"Tell me the story," I said, knowing that was exactly what he wanted to do.

UNCOVERING FRAUD WHEN YOU ARE NOT
LOOKING FOR IT

Rent-Way was his baby, his pride and joy, he said.

He began in the rent-to-own business in 1979, when he worked as a store manager and then a district manager for Rent-A-Center in Fort Worth, Texas. When he returned to his home town of Erie, Pennsylvania, he opened his first store with his friend Gerald A. Ryan. They formed a company and called it Rent-Way. Morgenstern and his wife, Shelley, ran the first store themselves, getting to know each customer and their families personally, one at a time.

The rent-to-own or "rental purchase" business is often criticized for charging "rent" to poor people who can't afford to purchase simple appliances, TVs, furnishings, and other home-related merchandise but can afford to pay a small weekly rental payment. The criticism was always about adding up the full rent total to the term of the lease, which was usually two or three times the retail purchase price. Some consumer activists saw this as a ripoff—"legal usury," as some would call it, since if you calculated the interest rate leading to the total payments made at the end of the lease, it would be extraordinarily high.

But Bill Morgenstern saw it differently.

His business was giving poor people a chance to have middle-class appliances and home entertainment—people who couldn't get credit, who were terrible credit risks, people who didn't even have checking accounts and had to use cash, living from paycheck (or welfare check) to paycheck.

He set up his business to make it as easy as possible for his lower-income and heavily minority customers. They could cancel their lease agreements at any time. If they failed to return the appliance, the cost of repossession of a relatively inexpensive TV or couch probably meant it was cheaper to write it off than go through the legal and physical difficulties of seizing it. And of course there was always the risk that even if the merchandise was returned, it would be damaged or even beyond repair.

Even so, he never charged for wear and tear when the merchandise was returned. His store offered free pickup and delivery. His company's motto: "Welcome, Wanted, and Important."

"I trusted my customers," he said, his eyes shining with pride, the previous mood of despondency and grief now gone. "I gave them a chance, took a risk, and they trusted me, and we rarely got burned." He told a trade magazine, "We think it's critical our customers feel satisfied by the products we offer and the treatment they receive."

It was the 1990s, and there was plenty of equity investor money around to finance expansion, with a plan to "go public"—with an "initial public offering," or IPO, to sell public shares to raise money to acquire other rent-to-own chain stores. And so in 1993, Rent-Way went public and raised hundreds of millions of dollars in new equity to be spent on buying other rent-to-own chains. The goal was to acquire more and more chains and to try to capture 6 to 10 percent of the estimated $4.4 billion rent-to-own industry by the year 2000.

And so they did. The rate of growth, which would be a factor in Morgenstern's sudden confrontation with fraud and scandal, was described by stock market analysts as a "breakneck pace." He went from nineteen stores in 1993 at the time of his IPO, with $8 million in revenues, to eleven hundred stores in forty-two states with $600 million in revenues by 2000.

In the summer of 2000, for the third time in the last four years, Rent-Way was profiled in *Fortune* magazine as one of America's hundred fastest-growing companies. Its share price of eight dollars in 1993, when it first went public, had more than tripled to more than twenty-five dollars a share about seven years later, in October 2000.

Investors in Rent-Way stock, many of them local Erie, Pennsylvania, residents, and relatives, friends, and neighbors of the Morgensterns, took pride in this local-company success story and, incidentally, made lots of money and kept buying more and more Rent-Way stock. Morgenstern was a popular man in Erie. He was a local hero. Cash register attendants at the supermarket would shake his hand and thank him for what he had done for Rent-Way and for their investments.

Jeffrey Conway, previously vice president and chief operating officer, who had been promoted to president in January 2000, told business media that by the end of the next year, Rent-Way would approach $1 billion in revenues.

"We had proven we could be successful while still doing right by our customers who needed help the most," Morgenstern said that night, with pride.

Rent-Way's last acquisition, costing more than $300 million, was an eighty-six-store chain, RentaVision. However, that chain in several states had a number of stores that were losing money and had worn-out or nonworking electronic merchandise.

In the summer of 2000, Morgenstern recalled spending much of his time supervising the closing of a number of RentaVision stores and helping management decide how much of run-down or nonworking merchandise in various stores needed to be sold at a loss or completely written off and thrown away, with the reduced market value deducted from income on tax returns as a loss.

"We grew so fast, we took on so much, that maybe that's where we lost track of things," Morgenstern said, trying to second-guess himself again.

Morgenstern was a cheerful, almost cherubic-looking man with a dynamism and charisma that inspired everyone who worked with him, from store managers and floor salespeople to senior management and the board of directors to his secretary, who once described him to me as an "Energizer bunny" who never stopped moving. And no doubt he pushed people who worked for him to the limit—especially when it came to making financial targets and earnings (profits) each quarter.

He prided himself on being hands-on, walking the hallways, asking questions, talking to store managers, tracking the details of how the company was doing. For example, virtually every morning Morgenstern would review the previous day's computerized financial results from Rent-Way's stores across the nation, dissecting the numbers to see where profit margins were dropping or costs rising above targets, and then trying to find out why and how he could fix the situation.

These were the days in the late 1990s when stock market prices moved up and down depending on whether the "earnings targets" or "guidance" per quarter were met. Company executives then (and mostly now, too) would "predict"—or offer "guidance"on—what the next quarter's earnings or after-tax profits per share would likely be.

As insane as it may appear to rational people, if the earnings target was below "guidance" by even a few pennies per share, then the quarterly earnings announcement would likely result in a drop in the stock price, sometimes a significant one (if there were rumors that this was just the beginning of steeper drops to come).

I asked Morgenstern that night whether he had ever pushed his management to be sure they met the predicted earnings targets.

"Absolutely," Morgenstern said. "But I meant they needed to increase their efforts to increase revenues by greater selling efforts, or by reducing expenses—not by cooking the books in the accounting department computers."

So when did you first find out there was accounting fraud going on? I asked him. "Tell me what happened."

He told me that his then chief financial officer, Bill McDonnell, was going through a final draft of the quarterly financial statements on October 24, 2000, in preparation for a forthcoming board of directors meeting, when a junior staffer in the controller's office had given him a last-minute change in the list of company merchandise assets—an increase of $16.6 million.

Normally in a company with revenues in the hundreds of millions, such a change would be insignificant. But there was something about the manner in which it had been communicated—sort of a "last-minute urgency," as Morgenstern described it—that raised McDonnell's suspicions.

McDonnell went to the new company president, Jeff Conway, to ask him whether he knew about it, and Conway waved him off, saying it was a minor issue and he would check it out.

That further raised McDonnell's suspicion.

The next day, Wednesday, October 25, McDonnell went to see Matthew Marini, the company's controller or chief accounting officer, who was responsible for supervising the computer entries of all consolidated financial information from all Rent-Way stores. Why the last-minute addition in merchandise inventory? he asked.

What Marini told McDonnell "made me dizzy," McDonnell later reportedly said.

Marini said that the change was made "for the purpose of making earnings."

McDonnell was reported to have said: "Did I just hear right?"

He went back to Conway and told him they had to go to Morgenstern.

But Conway didn't wait to see Morgenstern with McDonnell. He told McDonnell not to worry and went in to see Morgenstern himself. He told Morgenstern there was a minor $1 million to $3 million amount of missing merchandise when comparing the "general ledger," where all inventory was recorded, and the computer records, and not to worry.

"I didn't like his eye contact," Morgenstern told me. He called in Conway and they compared notes. They were now very suspicious.

Over the next two days, Morgenstern and McDonnell quietly questioned individuals in the accounting department about what they knew and whether there was anything going on that wasn't on the up-and-up. He couldn't get a straight answer, but he and McDonnell were more and more certain that the accounting records had been manipulated—they just didn't know how and by how much.

Morgenstern was frightened, panicked. This couldn't be happening. No one would believe that he had no idea, he thought. Even if he convinced them, they would ask: Then why didn't you know? How could you not know?

I interrupted Morgenstern, as I saw over the dinner table he was stuck, having a hard time continuing.

I asked him whether he had ever considered trying to fix the problem himself by changing the computer entries back to reflect the real numbers and reduced earnings?

He stared at me, knowing I was asking him whether he had ever considered compounding the crime with a cover-up?

I felt guilty—but I had to ask the question.

He looked shocked—then understanding.

"Of course not," he said, his eyes filled with tears. "Not for a second."

He called Gerald Ryan, cofounder of Rent-Way and member of the board; his close friend and attorney, John Zak, at a leading Buffalo law firm of Hodgson Russ, one of the oldest law firms in the nation; and William Lerner, the chairman of the board's audit committee, a distinguished lawyer with a reputation for integrity and the highest standards of corporate governance.

Morgenstern told each the same thing: that he thought there was serious accounting fraud in the company, that he needed them to begin planning for an independent investigation, and that the company needed to delay making its quarterly earnings report the following week.

Then he called Matthew Marini, the company controller, the man who supervised the entries into the company's computerized financial system and who had told McDonnell about the need to meet earnings targets. He asked Marini to come to his office the next morning, Saturday.

Marini said okay, sounding nervous, not asking why.

Near midnight on that Friday night, October 27, Morgenstern was home preparing for bed. He re-called a woman in the accounting department, someone who appeared very nervous when she had been questioned by Morgenstern and McDonnell that afternoon, and asked her once again whether she knew anything about phony numbers being entered into the computer accounting system to bolster earnings artificially. She denied it again, forcefully, and hung up on Morgenstern before he could say more.

An hour or so later, just before midnight, she called back.

In tears, she admitted that she had been lying, and told him that for a long time she had been entering phony numbers into the computer accounting records. They were in as many as a dozen or more separate categories of "expenses"—and in each case, she had changed the numbers from higher to lower, meaning by reducing "expenses," she had increased "profits" dollar-for-dollar.

Morgenstern was thunderstruck. He knew right away that this was a crime, in his company, in his baby, now grown up, sophisticated enough to be a criminal enterprise.

How could he have missed it? He had followed the numbers in his stores, in his company, every day. The RentaVision acquisition had cluttered the computer screen, with all the bad merchandise, losing stores, and write-offs occurring all at once. But that was no excuse.

How could he have missed this?

Later, he took little solace from the fact that—as was frequently pointed out to him by leaders of the outside auditors at PricewaterhouseCoopers—this type of fraud, cleverly executed in twelve or fourteen line items of reduced expenses spread across many weeks and months over at least a year—was virtually impossible to detect unless you were looking for it.

"Seeing fraud by hindsight is easy," one of the top PwC forensic accountants later told Morgenstern.

But that was Bill Morgenstern. It happened on his watch. He was CEO. He was responsible. Maybe he should have worked harder, been more careful. Maybe . . .

He felt dizzy. He felt nauseated. He thought he was going to throw up.

"Who told you to do this?" he asked the young woman.

She hesitated. Her boss, Matthew Marini, the company controller, she said.

Who else knew? he asked.

She said she thought that Marini was working with the company president, Jeffrey Conway. But, she said, she never received instructions from Conway, and he could probably deny knowing about it.

How far back does that go? Morgenstern asked, holding his breath, afraid to hear the answer.

At least the last year. Maybe more, she said.

"Oh, my God," Morgenstern thought. "Oh, my God."

Shortly after dawn on Saturday morning, October 28, after a virtually sleepless night, Morgenstern got to the office early and placed a bat under his desk. He was about to accuse a man—a big man, heavier than himself—of being a crook. He was prepared for the worst.

Morgenstern sat alone behind his desk as Marini walked in, looking nervous. The headquarters office was empty on a Saturday morning. They were alone. Morgenstern recalled hearing his heart thumping. The baseball bat under his desk was just by his feet, ready for action.

Morgenstern asked Marini point-blank, "Have you been cooking the books?"

Marini evaded. Asked him why he was asking.

"Because I happen to know that the books have been tampered with and we have fraud going on in this company and I am going to get to the bottom of it," he answered.

Morgenstern at first couldn't get a direct answer from Marini. Finally, he admitted that he had presided over an operation that had reduced expenses artificially in a variety of expense categories. And after further being pushed, he said company president Jeffrey Conway was aware and had directed him to do this, although he didn't want to know any details, to preserve his "plausible deniability," as he expressed it.

"But why?" Morgenstern asked. "Why?"

"You pushed us to make earnings, to make our quarterly numbers—you know you did, all the time," Marini said, referring to the quarterly earnings-per-share predictions that Morgenstern was always concerned be met or exceeded to avoid adverse reaction from the stock market and drops in the share value.

"But I meant to do it in our stores, in our business, the kosher way—to sell more or cut expenses," Morgenstern recalled shouting back at him in exasperation. "I didn't mean to do it by cooking the books!"

Marini got up and left.

Once Marini had left, Morgenstern knew what he had to do.

DOING THE RIGHT THING—"TAKING THE HIT"

Working through the weekend, Morgenstern and a team of lawyers led by his friend and attorney, John Zak—whose constant advice to Morgenstern to "do the right thing" was one of the key reasons that Morgenstern was able to survive this crisis with his reputation intact—worked with their outside auditor, PricewaterhouseCoopers, to get at least a preliminary estimate of how bad the accounting fraud was.

They discovered numerous fictitious entries of reduced costs and expenses in the general ledger of the company, where all the direct entries were recorded—reduced operating costs in various stores and categories, delayed or reduced write-offs, credits against amounts owed to suppliers, omitted or reduced depreciation expenses, and so on—hidden across twelve or fourteen different accounting categories. And then they found, with the help of PwC forensic investigators, that these general ledger fictitious entries had been reconciled by similar adjustments in the central computer accounting system records at headquarters.

It was a brilliant if evil scheme. Spreading the relatively minor artificially reduced expenses month after month over so many arcane expense categories, such as accelerated depreciation, vendor discounts, and bad-debt write-offs, without ever affecting the top-line monthly revenues that Morgenstern carefully tracked virtually every morning, allowed the fraud to continue undetected, even by Rent-Way's outside auditors.

"You shouldn't blame yourself," I and others told Morgenstern many times as the extent of the fraud became known.

"Well, I do. I shouldn't have believed that earnings remained the same even after the acquisition of RentaVision when I knew that there were a lot of losing stores and beat-up merchandise when we bought them out," he responded.

The investigators knew they didn't have the full picture, and some on the team counseled delay before making any public announcement.

It is possible, several reportedly argued, that the amount of fictitious reduced expenses entered was so small as to be below the level of "materiality"—which, under securities laws, is the level above which there must be a public announcement to warn the stock market traders before they make additional buy-sell decisions.

"If the number we announce in inflated earnings due to the fraud is too big, we will be sued for emphasizing bad news and allowing the short-sellers [those who make money when the stock goes down] to make extra money they don't deserve" was one individual's perspective, according to a source working over that weekend.

"But if the total of inflated earnings we announce turns out to be too small at the end of the day, then we will be accused of fraud by those who lost money when the stock goes down once the larger number is ultimately announced," said another.

"We can't win either way—so let's wait till we are close to being sure what the real number is" was a growing consensus.

But the "final decider," Bill Morgenstern, was not ambiguous and was not going to vote for that consensus.

He knew that his books had been cooked.

He knew something the market didn't know.

He believed it was his fault—not because he knew about the fraud, but because as CEO he had to step up to the line and take the responsibility.

He prayed on Sunday—he is a religious man with a strong faith. He conferred with his best friend, his wife, and family.

"My decision, actually, was easy," he told me that night in the restaurant.

"How so?" I asked. "Seemed to me you were damned if you did and damned if you didn't. Whatever you did, you would be second-guessed by investors and whatever you did you were about to shoot, maybe shoot to kill, your baby . . . the company you began . . . all you had worked so hard for. Sounds like a tough decision to me."

Now he was clear-eyed and spoke with humility.

"No . . . it was the easiest decision of all," he said, with conviction. "I just did the right thing."

On Monday morning, Morgenstern and his team informed a senior official of the New York Stock Exchange of the fraud investigation and asked that trading in Rent-Way stock be immediately suspended. At the time of the call, the stock was trading at about twenty-five dollars per share.

By early afternoon, the team had reached a "rough estimate" of the impact of the fraudulent reduced-expense entries located in the 2000 financial statements to date—and thought it was safe to describe the range as "$25 million to $35 million" in inflated earnings. They were relatively confident that it could not be any better than that—meaning the fraudulent inflation of profits couldn't be any lower. And there was a chance it might be higher, especially if the fraud extended back before 2000. But Morgenstern insisted on disclosing what they knew at that time even if it had to be adjusted in the future.

"We have to tell the public markets what we know now, and if it is worse, we'll revise the numbers and have more egg on our face. We have no choice."

As soon as the NYSE closed, the company issued the press release on Monday afternoon, October 30, 2000, announcing that accounting fraud had been uncovered, the earnings needed to be "restated" and reduced at least $25 million to $35 million, and an independent investigation had been launched.

The press release stated that Jeffrey Conway, the company's president and chief operating officer, had been forced out at the request of the board of directors, with an independent investigation commissioned by the audit committee of the board. CEO William Morgenstern was quoted as saying that this was "the most heartbreaking day" of his career. "I'm going to hold my head high and the company is going to hold its head high. We're going to take the hit and move on."

And then, a mistake: "Company executives believe the errors are limited to fiscal year 2000, according to the release."

Oops.

THE ROAD BACK—CRISIS MANAGEMENT 101

And so the pile-on began—not unusual in any breaking apparently "big" scandal, whether in politics, business, or life.

The next morning, when trading of Rent-Way shares resumed, the price had plunged from $23.44 at the closing on Monday afternoon to about $5.00 on Tuesday morning, October 31.

Peter Panepento of the *Erie Times-News*, who consistently did the best and most comprehensive reporting on the matter and who was followed by all the national business journalists and news organizations, found local Erie investors who were, well, very pissed off. He found a thirty-eight-year-old Erie resident who had purchased about six hundred shares of Rent-Way the previous year because she said it had shown "strong growth and because it was local." But after watching her shares plummet by about fourteen thousand dollars on Tuesday, the day after the company's report of the accounting fraud, she said she was angry and wanted someone to pay.

"I feel that someone needs to be responsible for this," she said on Wednesday, November 1. "I just think it's an unprofessional and unethical way to do business."

A *New York Times* account years later reported the widespread anger in the small Erie community toward Morgenstern.

"Walking through a local supermarket, a shopper confronted Mr. Morgenstern and shouted that he could not afford groceries because his portfolio had disappeared," wrote *Times* business feature reporter Charles Duhigg in an extensive "look back" narrative published at the end of December 2006, more than six years after the scandal first broke.

"Anonymous callers made threatening phone calls to Mr. Morgenstern's home. His children asked to stay home from school because teachers told them that their father was a crook, [Morgenstern] said. Mr. Morgenstern and his wife, meanwhile, spent most of their time locked in their home, afraid to venture outside."

But Morgenstern refused to quit, refused to file for bankruptcy and avoid the class-action plaintiffs' lawsuits, refused to sell Rent-Way at a distress-sale price to competitors. He refused to concede defeat.

"Our employees had invested their entire life savings and would have been wiped out," he told Duhigg. "If I ran away, I would have regretted it for the rest of my life."

In his report, Panepento said that eight law firms had already raced to the Erie federal courthouse, within two days of Rent-Way's announcement, and filed class-action suits against Rent-Way. (I had seen this lawyers' phenomenon before. Class-action plaintiffs' lawyers often race to file first, to enhance their chances of being chosen by the court as "lead" counsel, which gives them the best chance to recover the lion's share of legal fees out of any damages awarded to the "class" of plaintiffs, whom they have yet to meet—they usually find one or a few shareholders of the company to serve as their "plaintiffs" in the suit.)

Apart from the rush to file, plaintiffs' lawyers also engage in charges that might sex up their complaint but that are based not on fact but on pure speculation. One of the class-action complaints charged Morgenstern with being involved in the fraud and also a cover-up, claiming that an accountant with PwC had told Morgenstern of the accounting fraud a year before. The complaint accused Morgenstern of being told that there were approximately $60 million, not $25 million to $35 million, in overstated earnings, but he intentionally announced the lower numbers to further defraud the market.

I was quoted some time later in an *Erie Times-News* report as saying these fact-free charges by the filing attorneys were mere "guilt-by-association and innuendo. They have made accusations of fraud first, but then provided no facts. This is unacceptable as a matter of fundamental fairness—and as a matter of law."

In addition to the unsurprising slew of class-action lawsuits, within the next day or so after the October 30 announcement of the $25 million to $35 million overstated earnings, the New York City regional office of the Securities and Exchange Commission (SEC) notified Rent-Way of an investigation of the company and Morgenstern and company officials, and the local Erie U.S. attorney/federal prosecutors began a criminal investigation.

A few weeks later I arrived at corporate headquarters in Erie for a look-over by Mr. Morgenstern and met with the legal team from the Buffalo, New York, firm of Hodgson Russ, including Morgenstern's friend John Zak, whom he had called first on the Friday night when he confirmed the accounting fraud, as well as Zak's partners, Robert Lane, experienced at SEC investigations and civil litigation, and a white-collar criminal defense lawyer and former prosecutor, Daniel C. Oliverio.

The chair of the audit committee, William Lerner, a former SEC enforcement attorney and corporate governance expert, believed an "independent" investigation had to be conducted by another law firm that reported to the audit committee, not to the company. He was right—for the same reason I recommended to the HealthSouth board that Fulbright & Jaworski be retained to conduct an investigation "independent" from the one I had conducted while representing the company. Lerner retained the New York City firm of Ross & Hardies, led by senior attorney Menachem Rosensaft.

My role was to try to formulate an overall crisis plan to get the Rent-Way story out and over with, thus allowing the company to move on, as Morgenstern had said in his press release.

I expected resistance from the attorneys to following my transparency and proactive strategy with the media and, if possible, with the SEC and prosecutors. But I knew I was not going to make the mistake again that I had made in the Martha Stewart case. I wasn't going to take this matter on unless I was a member of the legal team, with access to all the facts and documents under the protection of the attorney-client privilege. And, additionally, the legal strategy and concerns had to be integrated with whatever legal or transparency crisis management strategy we adopted—meaning we had to work together.

Fortunately, in this case, I was surrounded by a group of attorneys who understood that saving the company and its reputation would require taking litigation risks and trusted me to stay within the approved "fact box" and messages to the media that they knew to be verifiable facts.

Once again, the value of my being an attorney with attorney-client privilege was self-evident. I could never have done this job and been part of the discussions and review of documents with the attorneys representing Rent-Way and Morgenstern had I not shared attorney-client privilege.

Most persuasive to me that we had a chance to make this crisis plan work was the reaction of Bill Morgenstern.

From the outset, he favored the "tell it all" approach. He said he was ready to "open the doors" to SEC investigators and give them everything they wanted, without the necessity of a subpoena requiring documents to be turned over and testimony to be given. He also told his criminal defense attorney, Dan Oliverio, that he wanted to be interviewed by the prosecutors as well. That told me a lot.

My long private dinner with him on a subsequent visit shortly thereafter, described in the opening of this chapter, sealed it for me. Now we were ready to proceed with the plan.

I felt like pinching myself—this was textbook.

A HAPPY . . . AND SAD . . . ENDING

Step by step, the team of lawyers, businessmen, and outside auditors and board members worked closely together on implementing the crisis management plan.

First we needed a "turnaround" predicate in a major newspaper, crediting Morgenstern and Rent-Way for the forthright way they had handled the breaking scandal, buying some time to complete the longer-term, more definitive investigation of how far back the accounting fraud went.

I contacted the *Wall Street Journal* reporter who had been covering the Rent-Way story and she agreed to a sit-down with Morgenstern, getting to know him personally, and then writing the outlines of the narrative of how he discovered the fraud and what he was doing to get to the bottom of it to move the company forward. I was confident that if she got to know Morgenstern personally, as I had, she would believe him and write the story without any presumption against him—and she did.

The story she wrote established the fundamental theme—

Morgenstern was innocent, had acted honorably, and the company had a long slog to get to the end of the road, but it still had a strong business model and had a good chance to survive.

One positive fact we kept stressing—despite the tens of millions of dollars of reduced earnings, the fraud had occurred through reduced expenses. There was no evidence that any revenues had been artificially increased: That is, the eleven-hundred-plus Rent-Way stores were still producing the same more than $600 million per year stream of revenues.

Next, the team of lawyers and Mr. Lerner had to make the most difficult and legally risky decision—going to the SEC and "opening the kimono"— volunteering full and transparent cooperation.

I remember vividly the experience of calling the New York City SEC enforcement officials, together with John Zak and Bob Lane from Hodgson Russ, to tell them of our plan to cooperate with their investigation fully. Their voices over the phone speaker-box sounded shocked, disbelieving, when we told them they could set up an office at Rent-Way and get access to everyone and everything, including the raw interview files by Rent-Way's investigating attorneys, and thus, waiver of all attorney-client privilege. (It reminded me of the sound of disbelief in the voices of the Atlanta office of the SEC investigators when I called to inform them that HealthSouth would waive attorney-client privilege and turn over the results of its own outside investigation by Fulbright & Jaworski.)

During the Rent-Way investigation, I had one SEC investigator tell me that this was the most unusual investigation he had ever experienced—it felt more like a common effort with Rent-Way's team of outside attorneys and attorneys for the board audit committee than an adversarial effort. That was more than a feeling—Rent-Way provided an office in its headquarters for SEC investigators to work out of and access to secretarial and computer IT support if they wanted or needed it.

Particularly unusual, according to SEC investigators I talked to, were the interviews of Morgenstern. They were open-ended—anything and everything could be asked and answered, without the usual interference from an adversarial defense counsel. And the SEC had complete and unfettered access to all Morgenstern's papers, notes, emails, and correspondence—again, no attorney-client privilege was asserted.

During the years of the SEC and U.S. attorney investigation, it wasn't always a straight line to getting Morgenstern and Rent-Way cleared. It didn't help matters when the initial estimate of overstated earnings had to be revised upward twice more. First, in December 2000, just two months after the first announcement, the estimated overstatement of earnings had to be adjusted up to $65 million to $75 million from the original $25 million to $35 million.

Then the outside forensic accounting experts brought in looked back into the 1999 and 1998 books and found more instances of fictitious entries reducing various "expense" items, bringing the total inflated earnings number to $127 million in 1998, 1999, and 2000—meaning those financial statements had to be redone or "restated" to reduce earnings over the three years by that total amount.

That could have damaged the credibility of Morgenstern and the rest of the internal and external investigatory teams, but, because of the credibility built up with the regulators and prosecutors directly resulting from the "tell it all" transparency that Morgenstern insisted on, he and the company were able to escape prosecution or regulatory penalties.

The final result, in July 2003—about two years and nine months after Morgenstern first announced finding financial fraud in his company at the end of October 2000—was judgments by the SEC in a settlement agreement by Conway, Marini, and an operations vice president; and guilty pleas and prison terms for Conway and Marini announced by the U.S. attorney, Mary Beth Buchanan.

The SEC's press release of July 22, 2003, announcing the settlement (based on a lower number than had been previously publicized of the size of the fraud—$60 million in falsely reduced expenses in fiscal years 1999 and 2000)—never mentioned Bill Morgenstern. The SEC imposed fines on Conway, Marini, and another senior Rent-Way official, Jeffrey Underwood, former vice president in charge of operations, who seemed to have been least involved and whose failure appeared to be not second-guessing Conway's instructions when he agreed to defer recording expenses at the end of 1999 and 2000. But significantly, it did not impose any fines on the company itself—a remarkable result for the crisis management strategy and, more specifically, for Bill Morgenstern's strategic gamble to go transparent and just tell the truth and let the chips fall where they might. The SEC explained (in words, I must admit, that warmed my heart as a crisis management advisor): "In determining to accept Rent-Way's settlement offer [to be cited only for "books and records" violations, but no fines and nothing about fraud], the Commission considered that Rent-Way *undertook remedial actions and cooperated with Commission staff*."

The United States attorney for the Western District of Pennsylvania, Mary Beth Buchanan, who brought the criminal cases against Conway, Marini, and Underwood and obtained their guilty pleas, put out a press release on the same day about those pleas. Remarkably, she agreed to add the following words—words that all the attorneys involved had never seen before in this type of a corporate criminal fraud investigation:

"Ms. Buchanan recognized the significant cooperation provided by company officials at Rent-Way and stated that 'this case is a good example of how a company can alleviate some of the significant consequences stemming from misconduct of its former employees, *by fully and openly cooperating with the government*.'"

I have italicized the final words of the SEC and the U.S. attorney because they so clearly prove the effectiveness of the "tell it all, tell it early, tell it yourself" strategy. (Much credit for the additional sentence in the U.S. attorney's press release should go to the Hodgson Russ criminal defense attorney Daniel Oliverio, for staking his credibility with the prosecutors and for trusting me to develop a joint media-crisis management strategy.)

THE FINAL ACT . . . AND AFTER

Three months later, in December 2003, the class-action suits for hundreds of millions of dollars filed against Rent-Way, Morgenstern, and various officers and directors were settled—for $25 million. The lead attorneys in the case won 25 percent, or $6.25 million, and the rest of the money was split among Rent-Way's many shareholders who held or sold stock during the pre-fraud-announcement period and were damaged by the drastic drop in share value after the October 30, 2000, announcement.

"This really does bring [this crisis] to a close," Morgenstern told the media. "It puts the final period to a very long book."

For a while, it looked as if Morgenstern could survive in his position as leader of the company he founded and bring Rent-Way back to economic (and mental) good health. In the next two years, the stock price more than doubled to ten dollars or more. Morgenstern avoided bankruptcy by refinancing his $200 million–plus bank debt, albeit at a significantly higher interest rate. And revenues and earnings continued to improve. Rent-Way opened fifty-four new stores in 2005, and income continued to grow.

And they avoided filing for bankruptcy through it all, unlike in other major accounting scandals involving high-profile companies during the same period, such as Enron, Adelphia Communications Corp., and WorldCom Inc. And Rent-Way maintained its New York Stock Exchange listing.

All in all, one could say, Morgenstern and his team had done a remarkable job of survival and turnaround, keeping their honor and protecting the company and its employees.

Yet, despite all that, the ending for Morgenstern was a sad one.

In the final analysis, the amoral forces of Wall Street and the public markets that continued to undervalue Rent-Way's stock prevailed. The share price went down to $7.62. This despite the fact that in early 2005, Rent-Way had opened twenty-five new stores, had plans to open as many as twenty-five more by September, and had increased same-store revenues at its rent-to-own locations throughout the nation during each of the past six quarters.

On March 24, 2005, Bill Morgenstern agreed to resign as CEO and president of Rent-Way, the company he founded and loved. He described his decision as voluntary. "The time is right for me to pursue some other ideas and dreams," he said. He remained as chairman of the board, however, and he still owned more than seven hundred thousand shares of company stock.

The end came on August 8, 2006, when Bill Morgenstern announced that Rent-Way had been sold to its arch competitor, Rent-A-Center, Inc., located in Plano, Texas.

In a lengthy personal statement, Morgenstern promised that all corporate employees in Erie would be offered opportunities for employment at Rent-A-Center's Texas corporate offices.

"The men and women of the Rent-Way office are my friends and many of them have been like family to me," he said. "Our company has worked hard to inspire our coworkers to be good corporate citizens who give back to our community and look for ways to fill unmet needs where we live and work."

On November 18, 2006, it became official. Rent-Way's stock stopped trading and the name Rent-Way disappeared. The final deal with Rent-A-Center was closed. Shareholders were paid $10.65 a share—a premium of about 30 percent above the share price—valuing Rent-Way at a total price of $576 million.

And where was Bill Morgenstern in 2011, more than eleven years after that traumatic weekend when he learned about massive accounting fraud in his company and when he was convinced no one would believe that he was innocent?

Morgenstern lives in North Carolina and continues as the idealistic "Energizer bunny" for himself, his family, and now for the public good. He is CEO of an international nonprofit microfinance company, called Opportunity International, that provides small business loans, savings, insurance, and training to more than twenty countries in the Third World.

"Our vision is a world in which all people have the opportunity to provide for their families and build a fulfilling life. Our mission is to empower people to work their way out of poverty, transforming their lives, their children's future, and their communities."

On its website are the words "Spread the Joy. The Benefit of Opportunity."

Pure Morgenstern.

"I am doing good," he said to me during a phone call in mid-2011. "I mean doing good for people—and doing good for me and my family, good for the soul."

The name Rent-Way may be gone. But Bill Morgenstern the Lion-hearted and Big-hearted remains.

LESSONS LEARNED

One of the best-kept secrets in the legal profession is how many lawyers, especially in potential criminal cases, start out presuming their clients' guilt.

I remember a very highly regarded criminal defense attorney once giving me the advice that I should assume all my clients facing criminal charges are lying, assume they are guilty, and then see if they can prove themselves innocent to me.

That may work for criminal attorneys. And since many criminal attorneys are former prosecutors who are accustomed to having virtually every guilty person they investigate initially lie to them and protest his or her innocence, there may be some validity to such a presumption-of-guilt rule.

But it doesn't work for an effective crisis manager. I am not saying that a crisis manager should naively believe that all clients are telling the truth. But if you start by assuming the client is guilty, you will too often find it difficult to develop an effective crisis management strategy in time to be effective. And the client will sense your doubt of his or her credibility, and that could be fatal to effective crisis management, which depends on the frail fabric of trust that *must* exist between crisis manager and client.

Nevertheless, the true tale of Rent-Way and Bill Morgenstern shows how a broad multidisciplinary approach—involving an integrated team of attorneys, media strategists, and those who could deal with all the "political" constituencies, such as the board, shareholders, and investment analysts—can help a client survive.

But you have to start with the truth—the verifiable truth. And in the case of Bill Morgenstern, the greater challenge was convincing the principal whose rear end was on the line that the truth matters—and that ultimately, the regulators, the prosecutors, and, most important, his friends and neighbors would believe him.

But in Morgenstern's case, the crisis manager could take little credit. Because it was the client, Morgenstern, who never doubted from the beginning that he had only one course—to tell the truth, even if no one believed him, even though the truth appeared, on its face, to be utterly implausible, and to just let the chips fall where they may. "Don't give me too much credit," Morgenstern would say to me over and over again. "It's who I am."

Another lesson from the Rent-Way experience: The strategy Morgenstern chose to follow proves that when headlines are smearing you, and the stock market has your company in decline and not recovering, and the pile-on of plaintiffs' lawyers and quick-buck artists and fair-weather friends are all convicting you before trial—you have to keep fighting to get the facts out *and* take your chances by telling the truth, all, early, and yourself. Keep fighting, no matter how futile it seems. The truth matters, even in the age of the Internet and the presumption-of-guilt culture of today's media, and especially the blogosphere.

This need to mix law, media, and political strategies isn't unique to crises in the United States. As the next chapter illustrates, sometimes it is necessary in the international arena as well, perhaps even more so. There was one occasion in which law, media, and international politics collided—and to handle that crisis, I found myself with a mandate from the client, and created by the facts and the law as I understood them, to stay in the middle of the road.

But as President Clinton once said to me, "The middle of the road is where all the roadkill is."

I I .

THE HONDURAS CRISIS

The Risk of Truth in the Center

"You have to convince people that what happened in Honduras last week when our president was shipped out of the country in the middle of the night by our military wasn't a 'coup,' as that word is generally understood," the leader of the Honduran Business Council, whose acronym is "CEAL" in Spanish, told me on the phone on July 4, 2009, just as I was about to leave to watch the Fourth of July fireworks.

Oh, really, I thought, and how was I supposed to do that?

The caller was referring to the events of the evening of June 28, 2009, when military leaders appeared at the home of then Honduran president Manuel Zelaya and forced him at gunpoint to board a small private plane in his pajamas and shipped him to Costa Rica.

For some reason, the fact that he was forced out of the country in pajamas became a widely reported detail—probably because it conveyed how abruptly and shockingly the elected president of a small democracy was seized and forced out of the country. It also explained why the media and liberal small "d" democratic organizations and think tanks in the United States reacted so negatively when the first word of what happened broke.

As soon as Zelaya was gone, an interim government was announced. The interim president was Roberto Micheletti, the former president of the Honduran Congress, the constitutional successor, since the vice president had resigned to run for president in the election scheduled for November 29, 2009.

I was on a conference call with several of the leaders of the Honduran Business Council, who had called me on this national holiday in great distress—since they saw their country in crisis with their friend and ally, the United States, which was talking about sanctions and had already announced support for Honduras's ouster from the Organization of American States and refused to recognize the interim Micheletti government.

"We need you to speak the truth and convince Americans and the U.S. government that what happened here was not a coup, but actions under our constitution," the leader of the council continued.

"It certainly seemed like a coup to me," I responded. "Certainly everyone in the media is describing it that way, not only in the U.S. but around the world.

"Didn't the military seize your elected president forcibly on an airplane in the middle of the night, in his pajamas [yes—that word stuck with me, too], and send him to Costa Rica against his will—and not let him come back? If that's not a coup, then what is?"

"You need to learn about the facts, and then you'll agree it wasn't a coup, at least not in the classic understanding of what a coup is" was the response of one of the Honduran business leaders on the phone. "Zelaya was removed under the law because he violated the constitution—the Supreme Court and the Congress found that to be the case, both controlled by Mr. Zelaya's own Liberal Party."

I promised I would look into the facts, but if I found that the military was behind the whole thing and was still in control of the government, I could not credibly deny it was a coup, and would not.

If I couldn't speak credibly as the facts dictated, I would be useless to them. I told them that. I also told them that, regardless of what you called it—a "coup" or whatever—I could never justify the illegal, forced deportation of anyone at gunpoint by the military, without due process. Period.

They said they understood what my limits were.

"So my mission is to get the facts out. And let people draw their own conclusions about what to call what happened. Anything else?"

"We hope you can find a way to win back the friendship and support of the U.S. government" was the answer.

"If we find it truly was a military coup or the U.S. government remains persuaded that it was, you won't be able to do that without returning Mr. Zelaya to his office and using the political process to replace him," I predicted. "I can only make an argument from facts— I can't make up facts—and that argument must be credible if your intention is to persuade the U.S. government and the American people of your point of view."

"Maybe behind the scenes, you can help us find a negotiated solution," one of the leaders of the council said to me during an early meeting in Washington.

"I am not a diplomat," I answered. "I don't work for the American government. I can't do that. But if we stick to the facts and are seen as sticking to the middle of the road, then you as business leaders who are prodemocracy might be able to facilitate communications and a compromise solution and I may be able to help you do that.

"What is your ultimate objective?" I asked.

"Help us move on—we have an election of a new president scheduled for November 29," said a leader of the Business Council. "Help our country get the election recognized as fair and free and the new president, regardless of who that is, recognized by the international community, and then we can move and return to normalcy."

I realized why the Honduran Business Council saw this as their ultimate objective. As businessmen, their concern was not politics but first and foremost political stability and the rule of law, which is necessary for the business community to thrive. It was especially necessary to resume normal commercial relations with the U.S. and ensure its economic assistance, which was so vital to the future of Honduras.

I accepted the assignment, emphasizing that first I had to assess what happened and then develop a strategy—no different from the approach used with any other personal, corporate, or political crisis management client I had represented before. The tricky part about this one, I knew, is that ideologues on the left and the right would be throwing accusations at each other—in Honduras as well as in America—and the facts would get lost (and, I sensed, I might be in the middle of that crossfire as I tried to stick to the facts and avoid ideological stands).

Things developed just as I had feared—and hoped. My client, the Honduran Business Council, was blamed by the left for being apologists for the "coupdistas" and by the right for being apologists for Zelaya and his perceived patron and benefactor, the anti-American president of Venezuela, Hugo Chávez. On the other hand, perhaps because we were attacked by both sides, the council came to be seen by senior officials in the U.S. and Honduran governments as facilitators of a reconciliation, one that would avoid bloodshed and ensure a just solution regarding the return of Mr. Zelaya as well as the conduct of fair and free elections in November for a new president.

I also learned that crisis management was hard enough in the context of U.S. politics—but it was even more difficult when you find yourself in the middle of another nation's politics with the international "community" pulling to the left and right politically at the same time.

From the start of the Honduran assignment, I knew I faced an uphill task, especially from the left-liberal human rights and democracy communities from which I came and whose values I shared.

Leaders of these groups and their outlets in the media and on the blogosphere quickly decided that what had happened to President Zelaya was an illegal military coup. They believed the only solution was for the United States and the Organization of American States (OAS) to force Honduras to reverse the "coup" and let Zelaya come home to resume his presidency (and prosecute those responsible for the "coup").

The OAS met shortly thereafter, and there was overwhelming consensus among most Latin American leaders that what had happened was an illegal military coup, and the OAS came down hard on the Honduran interim government. Honduras was suspended from membership in the OAS. The United States announced a suspension of economic aid and threatened to suspend visas until Zelaya was returned to the country and resumed his office. Most of the international community, including the European Union, made similar pronouncements.

So those were the cards we were dealt as I decided to accept the Honduran Business Council assignment. It certainly seemed, at the outset, a "mission impossible" in real life. I vowed to get the facts out, period, and then let the policymakers in both governments find a way to a reconciliation and a peaceful solution.

STATING THE FACTS—AND LETTING OTHERS DEBATE THE "COUP" WORD

Our attorney's crisis management team began our assignment as we always did—we started to research the facts in as neutral a fashion as possible, without preconceived biases or desired outcomes. I talked to dozens of staff and some members in the Congress, in the State Department, in the foreign-policy think tanks, and in Honduras on both sides, including the cardinal of Tegucigalpa, Oscar Rodriguez, who was at one point discussed as a possible successor to Pope John Paul II.

Here was the background narrative we crafted and used as the basis for our public messages and strategies. We did not publish it, but it guided us as we drafted and redrafted it as new facts and evidence pro and con regarding the "coup" to explain what happened on the night of June 28.

- The then incumbent, Liberal Party president Manuel Zelaya, had initiated a public campaign to hold a referendum on whether a Constitutional Assembly should be called. There was at least a possibility that while Zelaya was not running for reelection in the November 29, 2009, elections, the purpose of calling such an assembly would be to amend the Honduran constitutional prohibition preventing any person from serving more than one term as president so that he could run again for president.

- There was some evidence that the referendum called by then president Zelaya was supported, politically and financially, by Venezuelan president Hugo Chávez, whom Zelaya had openly befriended, to the consternation of even his Liberal Party members.

- Honduras had rewritten its constitution in 1982 with an absolute bar, not only against any president's ever running for a second term, but on his *even attempting to influence an amendment to that constitutional bar on a second term.* The language appeared to be self-executing—any president who attempted to amend the constitution to permit a second term for the incumbent president was rendered ineligible per se. That seemed wrong from a due process perspective—without trial or a judicial finding? But that's what the words of the constitution seemed to say. Significantly, the Honduran constitution didn't provide for removal of the president through "impeachment" or any other process.

- According to the historical research we did, the drafters of this particular constitutional provision were trying to prevent misuse of democratic elections by strongmen, who could corruptly ensure their reelection. This is why the active support of the referendum attempt by Venezuela's anti-American president, Hugo Chávez, was of such concern even to members of Zelaya's Liberal Party—as many people believed Hugo Chávez was a classic case of a corrupt permanent "elected" president, resembling the "democratic dictators" in some of the former Soviet states and in some African nations.

- The Supreme Court—*a majority of whom were members of Zelaya's Liberal Party—unanimously* upheld a lower-court ruling that Zelaya's attempt to fire the head of the military and conduct the referendum with the purpose of calling a constitutional convention was barred under the constitution. The case against Zelaya was filed by his own attorney general. The Supreme Court issued an order barring Zelaya from continuing his efforts.

- But Zelaya defied the Supreme Court's order. He led a large group of his supporters to break into military barracks to seize the Chávez-supplied ballots (Mr. Zelaya in a white hat and suit could be seen on YouTube leading his supporters into the barracks to overrun security guards and seize the ballots).

- The elected Honduran congress—a majority of whom were members of Zelaya's Liberal Party, representing all parts of the country—voted by an overwhelming margin to declare that Zelaya had violated the constitution, supporting the holding of the Supreme Court that he should be removed from office.

- But there were also reports, which the U.S government believed were troubling, that the congress was called too quickly to allow all members to attend and that the vote was pushed through too quickly without sufficient debate—it looked all too much as if this was an orchestrated plan to validate post facto the illegal forced deportation of Zelaya by the Honduran military.

- The U.S. ambassador, in a cable subsequently included in a Wikileaks trove of documents published on the Internet, alleged that there had been a plan among military leaders to intervene and get rid of Zelaya—what could be classically defined as a military coup, outside of the constitution and illegal. These views were supported by senior officials at the State Department and many others in the moderate center. But the ambassador's cable, at least the excerpts I read in Wikileaks, omitted the facts that the Supreme Court and congressional actions, dominated by Zelaya's own Liberal Party, had declared Zelaya's conduct to be illegal and unconstitutional and a basis for his constitutional removal, and that his all-civilian successors under the Honduran constitution were all members of Zelaya's own leftist Liberal Party, and that the leaders of the successor government were all civilians, with no apparent military involvement with official positions in the government at all.

- More evidence of this being a "different kind of coup," to say the least—and this was also apparently omitted from the U.S. ambassador's secret cable to Washington—was the position of the Human Rights Commissioner of Honduras, an independent U.S. version of an "ombudsman," who also opposed Zelaya's actions and supported the Supreme Court decision.

- The famous Roman Catholic cardinal of Tegucigalpa, Oscar Rodriguez, also supported the decision by the Supreme Court and the congress that Zelaya had violated the constitution and supported his legal ouster. Cardinal Rodriguez was famous for tending to the poor and the dispossessed—hardly the "coupdista" of the right-wing caricatures being presented by the left in Honduras and the United States.

- The civilian government that succeeded Zelaya was led by the president of the Honduran congress, Roberto Miche-letti, a member of Zelaya's own Liberal Party, who was the constitutional successor (since the vice president was running for president in the election scheduled for November 29, 2009).

These facts suggested neither a traditional military "coup," overthrowing a democratic government by force, with the military imposing martial law; nor a legal or constitutional process requiring the elected president to step down—in the absence of an impeachment provision in the constitution. It was something in between the right and the left; holding an ambiguous, nuanced position, driven by the facts, which were also ambiguous, the center was a difficult place to be, with a "solution" hard to find.

But that was, in essence, my crisis management assignment— helping my client find and hold the center, facilitate communications and reconciliation, in order to be able to move on and return to stability and democracy, which is what the business community needs.

However, I insisted to my client, the Honduran Business Council, that I could not defend what had been done to Zelaya without due process of law. I told them that the military leaders responsible for forcibly seizing and deporting Zelaya had acted unlawfully and should have been held accountable—as even those in the U.S. government who understood that this looked more like a "constitutional coup" than a "military coup" believed. I recommended, and the Business Council agreed, that it should be our public position to the congress and the State Department that the rule of law had to be upheld—including those responsible for illegally deporting Zelaya out of Honduras.

In the early weeks of July, it appeared that the overwhelming consensus in Europe, Latin America, and the United States was that Zelaya had been removed by an illegal coup and had to be restored before the Honduran government could be recognized and readmitted into the OAS.

Then something happened that triggered confusion among the ideologues who condemned the interim Micheletti civilian government as illegal and the result of an illegal "coup": The nonpartisan, professional Congressional Research Service completed a scholarly, neutral, extensively researched report reaching factual determinations and legal conclusions very similar to those we had reached in the White Paper—that is, that Zelaya had been removed from the presidency due to actions his own civilian government found to be illegal and unconstitutional.

So armed with these facts, reinforced by the findings of the Congressional Research Service, and with a mixed message—no, it wasn't a military coup, but yes, Zelaya was illegally forcibly deported—we were ready to go forward trying to get the facts out on behalf of the Honduran Business Council.

And, notably, because of this mixed, pro-and-con message, driven by the facts, we were in the "middle" between pro- and anti-Zelaya factions, and thus, perhaps, in a position to facilitate communication and some type of compromise and accord to resolve the crisis.

IN THE "MIDDLE" OF A CONGRESSIONAL PANEL

The first public opportunity to get the facts out and express our "middle" position occurred in mid-July 2009, when I was invited to testify, on behalf of the Honduran Business Council, before the important House Subcommittee on Western Hemisphere Affairs, chaired by Rep. Eliot Engel (D-NY) and ranking member Rep. Connie Mack (R-FL).

Not only was our position in the ideological "middle"—on the panel, I was in the geographical middle as well.

As we sat facing the members of the subcommittee on the dais, I was in the middle chair, with three panelists to my left—physically as well as ideologically—who were critics of what they called the "coup" and supporters of the return of Zelaya; to my right were conservative leaders of the Reagan and Bush administrations who hated Hugo Chávez, believed Zelaya to be his pawn, and at least implicitly seemed to support his ouster, even if what had occurred was a military coup.

My testimony restated our middle position that Zelaya's removal had been caused by the nation's civilian supreme legal and legislative entities, under the interpretation of the Honduran constitution that they believed to be the correct one, but that Zelaya's forcible expulsion from the country had been illegal and a violation of his due process rights.

It was an unusual sensation for me to be thanked by the liberal chair of the subcommittee, Representative Engel, and by the ranking member, Representative Mack, while at the same time listening to the critical mutterings of the pro-Zelaya and anti-Zelaya witnesses to my right and left on the panel.

Yet, despite this testimony, I was consistently described from this point on, by the left blogosphere especially, in articles that of course went viral, as "Davis . . . pro coup," with search engines yielding innumerable hits on the Internet, despite the fact that this was untrue—as proven by my public testimony before the House subcommittee (which didn't seem to get mentioned by critics or picked up by the Internet search engines).

I discovered once again, this time with me in the crosshairs, how difficult it is to catch up with the Big Lie on the Internet once it goes viral on the ideological websites and among bloggers. By sheer repetition, through search engines and the habit of repeating what is read on the Internet without fact-checking, the perception that I was a "coup" supporter became so established that mainstream media started repeating it without any fact-checking—such as reading my testimony before the House subcommittee.

But I violated my fundamental rule of crisis management and didn't fight back to correct the record. It was just too overwhelming and exhausting.

At one point my office was picketed by Zelaya supporters, with a huge sign on the office building across the street with a photograph of me, with the words "coup supporter" under my photo. I felt as if I was in a swarm of bees of misinformation, unable to defend myself, with swatting the bees doing no good, because they just kept swarming.

It got even scarier when I received threatening postcards at my home and hate emails that were so extreme that at one point I turned some over to the FBI.

Even years later, when my role in the Zelaya controversy is referenced, I continue to be misdescribed as a supporter of the Honduran Zelaya "coup" in the respectable mainstream media. No matter how many times I cited my public opposition to what the military did, including the summer 2009 congressional hearings, which were recorded in the congressional record—the facts about my position didn't seem to matter to the often anonymous Internet bloggers, with repeated viral misstatements of my position on the Internet.

LOOKING FOR A PEACEFUL, RECONCILIATION OUTCOME

Despite the false characterizations of my position (and that of my client, the Honduran Business Council) as being "pro-coup" by the pro-Zelaya blogosphere, we were still seen by many objective policymakers in Congress and the State Department as in the "middle," and thus, available to be an honest, albeit behind-the-scenes, communications facilitator in finding a possible compromise solution to the crisis.

Shortly after my testimony in mid-July 2009, I began working closely with a senior congressional official whom I shall call Robert. He was a harsh critic of the Micheletti government, was convinced the Honduran military was behind the entire scenario resulting in the ouster of Zelaya, and most certainly believed that the appropriate term for what happened was "coup." We both believed that some compromise was necessary to restore Honduras to America's good graces.

Secretary of State Hillary Clinton had asked the Nobel Peace Prize–winning president of Costa Rica, Oscar Arias, to initiate a mediation process that could lead to the return of Mr. Zelaya and the resumption of his presidency.

Robert knew the outlines of the "Arias Plan" in detail. It required Zelaya's return to Honduras as president, but only under severe restrictions. He could not seek reelection; had to abandon any efforts to hold a referendum on the calling of a Constitutional Assembly; had to agree to support, and not to interfere with, a free and fair election of his successor in November; and there would be some type of "truth commission" to ascertain what had really happened on June 28, the night that Zelaya had been illegally deported by the military, and who was responsible. Legal prosecutions of either Zelaya or the members of the military responsible for putting him on the plane would be deferred. As Robert put it, "They need to kick that can down the road."

Negotiators from the Zelaya and Micheletti camps met in San José, Costa Rica's capital, in the latter part of July, with President Arias shuttling back and forth and each delegation in constant consultation with its principals.

Robert called and asked me if I could recommend to my client, the Business Council, the latest version of the Arias proposal—what he called the "bring Zelaya back and keep him in a cage" scenario. "It's the only possible basis for Honduras returning to normal relations with the U.S., in my opinion," Robert said.

I agreed to transmit his views and to explain the rationale. The Business Council leaders agreed to be a conduit to Mr. Micheletti directly. And thus began a series of back-and-forth telephone calls between Robert and myself, with me carrying messages to the Business Council, which carried messages to Micheletti, and carrying messages back to Robert, to the U.S. Embassy in Honduras, and to President Arias in San José.

We did all this secretly—acting only as communications facilitators.

On a memorable weekend in the latter part of July, while I was driving five hours from Washington, D.C., through the northeastern Pennsylvania hills and mountains to visit my twelve-year-old son at summer camp, I talked to Robert dozens of times, going in and out of cell service, about the outlines of the final "San José Accords" proposal. Then I would call the leaders of the Business Council, who would convey these positions to Micheletti.

I can only describe the sensation as surreal when, at 2:00 a.m., I found myself at a fax machine in a Scranton, Pennsylvania, hotel faxing and receiving the latest revised drafts and redrafts of Arias's San José Accords, with Robert's proposed edits and arguments that he wanted the Business Council to convey to Micheletti and directly to the Micheletti negotiator in San José.

No one would ever believe this tale if I wrote about it someday, I thought, as I stood by the fax machine in Scranton, knowing that far away in Costa Rica were senior diplomats who were trying to make peace and avoid bloodshed, without knowing that Robert and I were working into the evening to facilitate communications.

You can't make this stuff up, I thought.

Unfortunately, with almost all the details worked out, at literally the last minute, Mr. Micheletti, the interim president who seemed to truly hate and thoroughly distrust Mr. Zelaya, decided not to take the risk of allowing him to return and refused to sign the accords. Then, Robert informed me that Zelaya had also rejected signing the Arias proposal.

We were back to square one.

"MAY GOD FORGIVE ME"

But the Business Council wanted me to continue to try to convince the Congress and the administration to send international observers to the upcoming November 29 presidential elections and, on validating them as fair and free, to recognize whoever won the election—the ultimate objective that they had declared at the beginning of the engagement. At the very least, if that happened, there was a chance that there could be a "new beginning," putting the events of June 28 and Mr. Zelaya's ouster and the debate on whether it was or was not an illegal military coup behind them.

In another unusual experience, shortly after I began to focus in the short term on recognizing the newly elected president, I coincidentally found myself seated behind Representative Eliot Engel, the chairman of the Western Hemisphere Subcommittee, and a member of my synagogue in Potomac, on the morning of the holiest of all Jewish holidays, Yom Kippur, the Day of Atonement, when all Jews ask God's forgiveness for all possible sins.

At one point during the service, I leaned over to Representative Engel and whispered in his ear: "Eliot, it makes no sense for the U.S. not to recognize the successor president in Honduras if the election can be certified by U.S. and international observers as fair and free."

He looked at me in shock, shook his head disapprovingly, and then totally ignored me. I realized he must be thinking, I can't believe Lanny Davis has just lobbied me in synagogue in the middle of a Yom Kippur service, God forbid. May God forgive him.

I realized he was right. I quickly looked at my rabbi, to see if he had noticed, thinking: My rabbi will know even if he didn't see me. I avoided any eye contact or further effort to talk to Representative Engel from that moment on.

I then returned to my prayers, even more intently asking God's forgiveness for my latest sin.

• • •

Late in September 2009, another unusual twist occurred—this one, too, in the category of "How did I get into this situation?"

I received a phone call from another government official. He, too, must remain anonymous. I shall call him Arthur.

Arthur knew of my behind-the-scenes communications facilitation work on behalf of the Honduran Business Council, and of my working with Robert to try to obtain agreement among the parties to President Arias's San José Accords proposal. He also knew that the Honduran Business Council was still pressing to get the United States to support a fair and free election of a new president and to recognize whoever won the election, and wanted above all to restore normal commercial and diplomatic relations with the United States. And, when he started his conversation with me, he acknowledged that I, on behalf of the Business Council, had tried to stay in the middle position and to be driven by the facts, not ideology.

Arthur and I met several times for early-morning breakfasts at a diner on Connecticut Avenue in Washington, D.C., where we could avoid being seen together. He reviewed with me new modifications to the Arias Accords that might be acceptable to both sides, explaining that without the return of Zelaya or some type of agreement by Micheletti to agree to the return at some point, there was little hope that the United States would recognize any newly elected Honduran president.

Over the next several weeks, Arthur and I talked several times a day by phone—and I transmitted his and the Zelaya forces' positions to the Business Council leaders, who in turn transmitted the positions to the Micheletti government.

Once again, the council served as behind-the-scenes go-betweens among the various Zelaya and Micheletti factions, trying to facilitate a compromise that would allow the U.S. government to recognize the newly elected president, with only weeks to go before the November 29 election.

I was on the phone frequently with Arthur, sometimes in the middle of the night. Then I would be on the phone repeatedly with the Business Council leaders, transmitting the messages from Arthur and asking them to recommend to the Micheletti government that they accept the new proposed agreement.

It was another amazing and surreal experience—all with the intent of trying to find a way for Zelaya to return—but preferably after the November 29 presidential elections, when there was a new president-elect, a coalition government had been announced, and the Honduran Congress had endorsed the return of Zelaya.

At long last, on October 31, a final agreement, called the "Tegucigalpa San José Accords," was signed by Zelaya and Micheletti—just four weeks from the date of the scheduled presidential election.

Shortly thereafter, the secretary of state announced that the United States would recognize the results of the presidential election.

But then Zelaya refused to name his half of the coalition government, and the Honduran congress didn't act to invite Zelaya's return in a way that satisfied Zelaya. Both Zelaya and Micheletti announced the newest accords were dead.

But the die was cast. The administration did not change its position and recognized the newly elected president on November 29, Porfirio "Pepe" Lobo. There was little doubt that the elections were honest and valid. The independent Honduran Electoral Commission, which all political parties in Honduras had pronounced to be completely independent, had declared the elections to be fair and free. And significantly, turnout was at a higher percentage than the turnout four years before that had elected Zelaya, despite efforts by Zelaya and his more extreme supporters to call for a boycott of the 2009 election.

Yet it wasn't until the end of May 2011 that a final agreement was reached between President Lobo and Zelaya, permitting his return to Honduras. The conditions: Zelaya had to promise to stay out of politics, and a general amnesty was granted for all prosecutions of possible crimes associated with the events of June 28, 2009, and thereafter—including crimes by the members of the military responsible for illegally deporting Zelaya and by Zelaya and those of his colleagues accused of corruption and legal violations.

In the final analysis, the basic rules of crisis management were just as applicable to this international crisis, involving a foreign country and all of its complicated politics and legal and constitutional issues, as they are to one occurring in the United States. Most important was the inevitable first step—to get the facts out.

In the Honduran tale, however, something brand-new took place—because of the middle position we found ourselves in, driven by the facts, my client and I found ourselves as interlocutors or facilitators of communications between the factions, trying to help behind the scenes to find a peaceful and satisfactory compromise to end the crisis and restore normalcy.

While we tried to be successful as backdoor communication facilitators between the opposing factions to produce a peaceful solution, and at the very least, a presidential election with the results recognized by the United States and the international community, we also learned the limitations of trying to play the neutral, behind-the-scenes "conveyor belt" role. We found ourselves, inevitably, in the cross fire, with both sides beginning to blame us. And we couldn't control events, since as long as we had to stay "off the record" and out-of-sight, we had difficulty influencing a positive final outcome.

So the new template I had discovered for dealing with international crises—serving as a facilitator of communications but remaining behind the scenes—had its limitations.

I wish I had understood that the biggest was the inability to influence people and politics in faraway places. There is only so much getting the facts out can do in crisis management—especially when you cannot be sure you have all the facts about what happened on the ground in a foreign nation thousands of miles away.

THE WRONG LESSON LEARNED

As I will show in the next chapter, my contribution, however modest, in working behind the scenes to find a peaceful outcome—i.e., to achieve a fair and legal election and international recognition of a new president in Honduras—led me to believe I could pull off finding a peaceful resolution in the Ivory Coast crisis in December 2010.

Boy, was I wrong.

NEVER REPRESENT YOURSELF IN A CRISIS

12.

A FOOL FOR A CLIENT

The headline on the front page of the *New York Times* on December 31, 2010, didn't exactly put me in the mood to wish everyone, much less myself, "Happy New Year" as midnight struck.

KEY LOBBYIST'S CLIENT LIST

PUTS HIM ON THE DEFENSIVE

The not-so-pleasant lead (since I was the "key lobbyist" the *Times* was referring to) read:

"After decades of work for some of the country's most powerful lobbying firms, Lanny J. Davis, the lawyer who once helped defend President Bill Clinton from impeachment, is suddenly scrambling to defend himself."

"Scrambling"?

"Defend" myself?

After listing a number of my clients suggesting there was something wrong with the work I had done for them, the article continued:

Mr. Davis withdrew from his $100,000-a-month contract with Ivory Coast Wednesday night [December 29], saying that the embattled government refused to accept his suggestion to talk to President Obama. Still, his role in West Africa has stoked growing criticism that Mr. Davis has become a kind of a front man for the dark side, willing to take on some of the world's least noble companies and causes.

"Front man for the dark side"? "Willing to take on some of the world's least noble companies and causes"?

Pretty painful to read that sentence about yourself when you know it is untrue and misleading—especially when your entire family is surrounding you and you are supposed to be enjoying your Christmas vacation.

How did this happen?

I was disappointed about what I believed to be an unfair headline and opening paragraphs, omitting important positive facts, especially my true role in the Ivory Coast matter. If I had read this story about someone else, my first reaction would have been: That guy ought to fire his crisis manager.

But wait—I *was* that crisis manager.

So I had only myself to blame. The old adage appeared to be true: "A lawyer who represents himself has a fool for a client."

Even worse, the person who truly triggered this awful story about me was—you guessed it—me. So the following is offered as an object lesson in what not to do—as well as lessons to be learned about the limitations of crisis management when you can't know the facts for sure and can't control the actions of others thousands of miles away.

TRYING TO SET THE RECORD STRAIGHT

It was I who had called the *New York Times* two days before to try to set the record straight. The previous week, the *Times* had published a story about my lobbying "for" the government of the Ivory Coast and its president, Laurent Gbagbo, who had lost an internationally supervised election to Alassane Ouattara, but was refusing to concede because he claimed there had been massive fraud. But I couldn't tell the reporter who called me, Eric Lichtblau, the crucial fact that I believed would ultimately exonerate me: I was privately helping the State Department find a peaceful way out and had been in touch with a senior official there even before I accepted the assignment from the Washington ambassador to the Ivory Coast, who knew of my behind-the-scenes contact at State. But not being able to tell Lichtblau, whom I knew rather well and had worked with on other stories, this crucial fact violated my fundamental rule of crisis management, to "tell it all, tell it early."

But I had no choice—I had promised my contact at the State Department, whom I called to get advice on how I could help facilitate a peaceful solution, that I would tell no one about my role—except for the Ivory Coast ambassador, who had retained me and who was my client (he signed my firm's engagement letter, meaning I represented the Ivory Coast U.S. Embassy, not the strongman and defeated presidential candidate Gbagbo). The ambassador knew that I was working with the State Department to find a peaceful resolution of what could be a violent civil war, including the possibility of finding a peaceful way for Gbagbo to give up his presidency. I explained that I would not be advocating for Gbagbo's position that he had won an election after the UN observers and the international community and the United States government had declared that he had lost. But I would work with the State Department to find a dignified path out of office that would preserve peace and the democratic process in the nation. The contract we wrote and signed, and knew was going to be public, was supposed to limit my role and avoid being an advocate. This would allow me to work behind the scenes to help avoid bloodshed and find a peaceful solution. I saw this role as a "holding" position. How naive, how wrong, how stupid I was in thinking I could pull off this secret role without it being misunderstood.

Thus, I let the *Times* story get published without explaining my role completely or accurately, believing I had no choice. But once the ambassador told me that Gbagbo would neither speak to me nor take a call from President Obama, ten days later, on December 29, I decided I could not continue the representation, especially in light of reports that Gbagbo had allowed his supporters to engage in violence and human rights violations. I was disgusted and sorry I had ever accepted this assignment.

So I called a *Times* reporter I had known from my work with the Honduran Business Council, Ginger Thompson, late on the afternoon of December 29, to ask her if there was time for her to run a story about my letter of resignation to the Ivory Coast ambassador, which I had just emailed. She said yes—she would post it online—but wasn't sure there was time to get it into the next day's paper version of the *Times*.

I asked her whether she would have the time or interest to write the full story of my behind-the-scenes role in helping the State Department find a peaceful solution in the Ivory Coast—activity that I hadn't been able to disclose to Eric Lichtblau in the previous week's *Times* story.

I told her I really hoped the full story could be written—because in the last ten days the blogosphere and many other news organizations had unfairly attacked me for "defending" Gbagbo and even suggested I was defending the violence and human rights violations of his supporters.

Ginger Thompson said, yes, she was interested. "Let's get the story of your resignation posted tonight," she said, "and I will call you tomorrow to write the rest of the story about what you were actually doing."

THE REAL STORY

It all began, as usual, with the ringing of my phone, in the first few days of December 2010.

I had just read in the major newspapers that the president of the Ivory Coast, Laurent Gbagbo, had lost the election to his opponent, Alassane Ouattara, 54 percent to 46 percent, according to the United Nations team that had supervised the election and the "Independent Electoral Commission" recognized by the UN as the supervisor of the election. The UN, the United States, the European Union, and apparently the African Union had all immediately recognized Mr. Ouattara as the winner, according to news reports.

But, also according to news reports, Gbagbo contended there was voter fraud in the northern provinces, controlled by Mr. Ouattara's opposition party. The country's top judicial body for determining election outcomes, the Constitutional Council, had thrown out what it determined to be fraudulent votes in these northern areas and declared Gbagbo the winner, 51 percent to 48 percent. Of course the Ouattara forces, with good reason, claimed the Constitutional Council was controlled by Gbagbo.

There were also credible news reports that there was mob violence and human rights violations by Gbagbo's supporters.

I was asked by a friend to meet an American from the Ivory Coast with close connections to the Ivory Coast embassy in Washington. I was told the Ivory Coast ambassador to the United States wanted me to come to the embassy, on Massachusetts Avenue, to represent the embassy in making the argument to the U.S. government that Gbagbo had really won the election and that he was being victimized by fraud.

"No way," I said immediately. "I can't verify claims of who won a contested election in a faraway country. We couldn't even do that in Florida in the early days after the 2000 election.

"Hasn't the administration already weighed in here and recognized Ouattara's election and asked Gbagbo to step down?" I asked.

"Yes" was the answer.

"No way," I repeated. "I will have no access to the facts, and the entire international community has already made up its mind," I said, all my instincts telling me not to even consider this.

Still, I wondered whether I could facilitate a peaceful outcome (i.e., a face-saving exit by Gbagbo without bloodshed) so I called a senior official at the State Department, Don Yamamoto, deputy assistant secretary for West Africa, whom I had previously met, and told him what I had in mind. He said he wouldn't approve or disapprove, but he assured me if I took the assignment representing the IC ambassador I might be helpful in facilitating a peaceful exit of Gbagbo.

At the Ivory Coast Embassy, I sat for several hours with a few of my colleagues from my crisis management group, listening to the ambassador describe the evidence of voter fraud in the north. We learned that Gbagbo and his wife were stubbornly insisting not just that there was evidence of fraud that should be investigated, but that he had actually won the election. He was relying on the decision of an election "commission" he had appointed that had ruled as invalid more than six hundred thousand votes in the northern areas that heavily favored Ouattara.

I was skeptical that this was the truth, skeptical that this "commission" was independent. We knew that was a politically untenable position and would certainly not change the U.S. administration's (or the world community's) position that Ouattara was the newly elected president.

For the next week or so, we had various discussions with the Ivory Coast embassy officials and the ambassador about the terms of engagement. I made it clear that we would be willing to serve as conduits only to facilitate Gbagbo's peaceful exit, and would not defend Gbagbo's position that he had actually won the election. Rather, I argued to the ambassador, we had to find a way to align with the U.S. government and President Obama to find a peaceful solution—and that I was ready to work with the State Department to do so—meaning, a peaceful exit of Gbagbo and the transfer of power, consistent with the views of the UN and the world community. The ambassador said he understood and retained me on that basis. I had my behind-the-scenes role in the Pakistan and Honduras matters in mind as to what I could accomplish.

I also made it clear that I would have to charge a substantial three-month fee (of three hundred thousand dollars), because I knew I would have to retain several consultants to assist me—in particular, the Ivorian American who had first introduced me to the ambassador, who knew all the key players at the embassy and many in the Ivory Coast, and importantly, was fluent in French, and whom I needed to translate for me and to liaise with the ambassador, embassy officials, and the government in Abidjan, the de facto capital of the Ivory Coast, and perhaps Gbagbo himself to convince him to give up power.

I doubted the ambassador or his colleagues would accept these terms of engagement—that is, that I would not be representing Gbagbo or defending his position that he had won the election. I showed the ambassador the public statement I would have to issue explicitly stating I would not be taking a position on who won the election on behalf of his government.

I was somewhat surprised the next day when the Ivorian American contacted me to tell me that my terms of engagement were accepted, despite the condition that I wouldn't be defending Gbagbo's position.

First mistake: It never dawned on me that people wouldn't believe that I could be hired by a client and paid a lot of money while not defending the client's position. Even though it seemed implausible on its face, it just never occurred to me that if I put out all the facts, documented by my public statement at the time of the engagement, I would not be believed.

I still had my own doubts about whether Gbagbo himself understood my terms of engagement. "Are you sure you have communicated these terms to Gbagbo and he understands?" I asked the ambassador. "Are you sure he understands that the end result will be for him to accede to the judgment of the international community and agree to a peaceful exit from power, and perhaps from Ivory Coast?"

"Yes," he said.

Several days passed. Each day I was given a different excuse why the ambassador had not gotten through to Gbagbo—usually that his cell phone was not working, or that he wasn't available. (I asked his daughter, who lived in Atlanta, to put me through to him or her mother, but while she said she tried, she told me she was unable to do so.)

Second mistake: On December 18, I accepted the assignment, even though the ambassador was not able to get through to Gbagbo. I did so only after once again showing the ambassador the statement I would be reading at a press conference the next day, clearly stating that I would not be defending Gbagbo's position.

Then I made another call to Deputy Assistant Secretary Don Yamamoto. I had previously worked with Don to persuade the president of Equatorial Guinea to publicly commit to a specific program for political, legal, and human rights reforms, with the result that the program publicly presented by the EG president won the endorsement of these efforts by Nobel Prize laureate Archbishop Desmond Tutu of South Africa.

I told Yamamoto about the terms of my limited engagement by Ivory Coast and asked if I could be of assistance.

What he told me stunned me—literally left me breathless.

"You know, President Obama has tried calling Gbagbo twice to look for a peaceful exit strategy, and hasn't been able to get through. Perhaps you could help facilitate that call."

"*What? The president of the United States tried to call another head of state twice and couldn't get through?*" I asked, incredulous. Yamamoto said that President Obama wanted to offer Gbagbo some dignified options, such as conceding defeat and coming to the United States temporarily to teach at a university. His family and property would be protected and he could always return to run again.

I told Yamamoto that I doubted, from what I heard at the embassy, that Gbagbo would agree to yield his office. But, I agreed, if there was anyone in the world who might persuade Gbagbo to leave office peacefully, it was President Barack Obama, seen by Africans as a hero, with a father born in Kenya. I knew to be effective, I would have to keep my actual role a secret from U.S. media.

Third mistake, which I was about to make: If I couldn't be transparent about my role, that would violate the most fundamental crisis management rule about the truth—"Tell it all, tell it early, tell it yourself."

But this seemed like a good reason for an exception—to help the president of the United States get through to Gbagbo and avoid bloodshed. And I had it in my head that when it was all over, whether I was successful or not, I could put the full story out and, of course, be backed up by Assistant Secretary Yamamoto.

Now, in retrospect, just suppose I was advising a client about to do what I was doing. I have no doubt that I would have said: Don't you dare. If you are not transparent, this engagement is too odd to be believed after the fact.

So what did I do as my own crisis manager?

I ignored my basic instincts. I was too confident that I could pull off arranging the Obama call. How could Gbagbo refuse a call from the president of the United States, especially with me involved working with the ambassador to make the call happen?

Arrogant? Yes, I must admit. Naive? Even a bigger yes.

Not being a complete idiot, I called Don Yamamoto back to have him reassure me that, when all was said and done, success or failure, he would be allowed to talk to the press and confirm my role.

"Yes, you can refer reporters to me," he said. "I will back you up."

Fourth mistake: Under the stress and time pressures, I had made an inadvertent error in the words used in the engagement letter with the Ivory Coast—the same letter that I knew would have to be filed as part of my public registration under the Foreign Agents Registration Act (FARA), a requirement whenever one represents a foreign government involving public comments. This error, as it turned out, was the most serious in contributing to the misperception that I was defending Gbagbo's position insisting that he had won the election and was holding on to power.

The wording of the original letter indicated that, for a fee of one hundred thousand dollars per month (for three months, I thought), which would include expenses for several consultants I had already retained, I would "present *the government's version* of the facts and the law" about the election. This was my way of finessing the role I would be playing—buying time until the State Department and the world community could exert diplomatic pressure to ease Gbagbo out in a way that saved his dignity and protected his family. But in the final version, in the rush of things, I hadn't noticed that the words "the government's version" had been left out—leaving an impression that what I would be "presenting" was a defense of Gbagbo's position when my intent was the opposite.

When I saw the error I called a press conference the next day, primarily to clarify my role as *not* defending Gbagbo's position. Here is the key sentence from the public statement I read at the press conference, with only a few reporters attending, including one from CNN: *"I have not been asked by the Ivorian government to try to prove to the world community who won the election in the Ivory Coast, or who is right or who is wrong."* Instead, I explained, my mission was only to try to find a peaceful "solution."

Looking back, I now realize I was continuing my pattern of making all the crisis management mistakes I would have advised a client not to make.

Normally I would have spent several days preparing key media and international news editors and reporters for the announcement, doing personal "backgrounding" of these reporters about the apparent paradox of representing a government but not defending its ostensible president. At the very least, I would have been sure we contacted major news organizations to attend the press conference—or be available for one-on-one interviews to magnify the message, its distribution, and its reporting, especially on the Internet.

We took none of these basic preparatory steps. With little more than a day's notice, I and my team wrote my statement, wrote the press release, and sent out the announcement of the press conference late the evening before. Not surprisingly, few showed up and even fewer picked up the key sentence concerning my limited role. There were only two TV crews—one from Al Jazeera and another from the Associated Press. A CNN reporter attended, with no camera.

"A tree falling in the forest when there is no one there" was the thought I had as I stood at the end of a long conference table with only a few reporters in attendance.

Realizing that we had utterly failed to get our message out—the early media reports were that I was "defending" Gbagbo, despite growing reports of international community condemnation of his behavior, including reports of human rights violations by some of his armed and militant supporters. We decided to try again—this time in a telephonic press conference, which would allow me to reread my statement with the critical sentence explaining that I wasn't defending Gbagbo's position.

Once again, we failed. The attendance at the telephonic press conference was as meager as that in the in-person conference the day before. Again, I violated all our rules by not having machinery in place to do extensive follow-up—a prearranged list of calls to key reporters from the *New York Times*, the *Wall Street Journal*, the *Washington Post*, and key wire services such as the AP, Reuters, Dow Jones, and Bloomberg, and TV appearances on cable news networks, especially CNN, with the most extensive international audience.

The next day, I did get to do some TV appearances. But sleep-deprived, stressed, and anxious to go home for my twenty-sixth wedding anniversary evening with my extremely understanding wife (but not *that* understanding if I missed our anniversary dinner date), I rushed out to do interviews on CNN and BBC radio and BBC TV. Aside from being tired and cranky, I was also ill prepared. Following my usual discipline of focusing on a couple of key message points and staying "on message," I found myself irritated by the CNN questioner's apparent skepticism that there was any fraud in the Ivorian election. To make matters worse, the reporter asked me questions from a remote location, and it was difficult to hear through the earpiece. I was snappish and defensive.

Instead of calmly staying "on message" and stating that I was not taking sides but only trying to find a "peaceful solution," I got ornery and argumentative.

In short, I made the fundamental mistake on TV that I always had taught my clients never to make—I argued with the reporter rather than simply answering the question. This left the impression that I was actually defending Gbagbo on the merits, which I never intended. Later that day, December 21, as if I needed anything more to make my mood worse, I got a call from *New York Times* reporter Eric Lichtblau. He asked me why I was "lobbying" in favor of Gbagbo. "Lobbying?" I snapped back. "I am not lobbying in favor of anyone. I am trying to find a peaceful solution."

But, Lichtblau said, the contract that you filed with the FARA office says you were hired to "present the facts and the law" about why Gbagbo won. "That sounds like you were defending his position on the merits."

Ouch. This was akin to root canal pain.

But . . . but . . . I explained to him the mistake in the letter and my correction in the December 19 and December 20 public statements at the two press conferences. I pointed out that the words "*the government's version*" of the facts had been inadvertently omitted. And I used my "conveyor belt" metaphor—I insisted that was the only role I had agreed to.

Eric tried to understand—but he was stuck on the apparent paradox of Gbagbo's paying me not to defend him, even if the letter did omit the phrase that I was simply passing on Gbagbo's version of why he had won the election.

And I was now stuck with violating the most important part of my mantra about telling the truth—"Tell it *all*."

I knew that if I disclosed my conversations with Mr. Yamamoto about my efforts to persuade Gbagbo to take a call from President Obama to seek a face-saving exit from power, I could blow the whole effort and, possibly, enhance the chances of violence and bloodshed.

The *Times* story the next day, on December 22, shouldn't have surprised me. But I was still disturbed by the inaccurate impression left by the headline: AMERICAN LOBBYISTS WORK FOR IVORIAN LEADER, with the caption under my photo stating that I was "working for Laurent Gbagbo's government." But I was *not* in any way working *for* Gbagbo— quite the contrary.

I realized I had no choice but to remain silent—not exactly one of my personality characteristics. I could do nothing to correct the words "lobbyists" or "work for Ivorian leader." I just had to suffer through this until I could help get a resolution—always assuming that, when it was time and all was done, I could get the full story out and Yamamoto was there to corroborate my role and protect my back.

I rationalized: It's a few days before Christmas; no one is reading the newspapers anyway. But of course I was fooling myself. This wasn't any newspaper: this was the *New York Times*. And journalists, editors, and bloggers all over the world read and were influenced by the *Times*.

Invisibly at first, and then more and more apparent from emails and calls I began receiving from perfect strangers, the misinformation virus was spreading. What started with the false headline in the *Times* that I was a "lobbyist" for Gbagbo morphed into my being a defender of human rights abuses, murder, and worse.

It was a nightmare. And all the while, I was on the phone trying to assist the State Department and to persuade the embassy to influence Gbagbo to talk to President Obama and to find a peaceful solution.

After Christmas, my wife and family went to our western Maryland house for skiing and relaxing. A time to relax and enjoy my family.

Not quite.

For three days—December 26, 27, and 28, virtually all day and into the wee hours, I was on the phone—with the ambassador, with embassy officials, with the daughter of Gbagbo—an intelligent Ivorian woman married to an American and living in Atlanta—trying to convince Gbagbo through intermediaries to take President Obama's call.

And I was also on the phone frequently with Don Yamamoto, who told me that Gbagbo (or the people around him—he couldn't be sure which) was refusing to see the U.S. ambassador to the Ivory Coast.

Finally, I realized my efforts were fruitless. I called Yamamoto and asked him if he thought I should continue—whether there was anything else I could do to be helpful. He said no.

I realized I couldn't continue. I called the ambassador and couldn't get through to him. I called Atlanta and spoke to Gbagbo's daughter and son-in-law and informed them of my decision. They pleaded with me not to resign. I gave them an hour to get through to Gbagbo one more time to ask him if he'd take the call from President Obama. The daughter called me back to say she couldn't get through.

I then wrote my letter of resignation and emailed it to the ambassador. It was almost 6:00 p.m. on December 29 when I hit the "send" button on the resignation letter email. Now, I thought, I can finally "tell it all" and "tell it myself."

Then I made my most significant mistake.

Had I been a good crisis manager advising a client, I would have advised my client: "This is Christmas week. There are few major media reporters working, or, if they are, they are shorthanded. It is 6:00 p.m. on December 29. Wait until after New Year's Day and give a reporter a few days to work on the story. Line up Deputy Assistant Secretary

Yamamoto to be certain he is available to talk to the reporter you choose to write the story. He is the crucial corroborator of what really happened."

Take your time, I would have said again. *Get it right. You may not have a second chance.*

Instead, in the pressure I felt to get out of this nightmare, I decided to do it myself. To hell with taking my time.

I did think of calling Deputy Assistant Secretary Yamamoto, who was my sole witness. I got him on his cell phone—I was lucky.

I told him I had resigned and had informed the *New York Times.* I asked him whether he would still honor his offer to talk to reporters to corroborate my role, and he said, "Yes, have the *Times* reporter call my cell phone."

I should have asked: "Are you sure you will be available? Where will you be tomorrow? Are there alternative numbers besides your cell phone?" His cell phone was the best way to reach him, but I had learned 75 percent of the time he couldn't answer or his voicemail box was full.

Had I been advising a client, I believe I would have asked those questions. But I was too much in a rush to get out and correct the record immediately.

Then I called the *New York Times* Washington office and asked to speak to Eric Lichtblau, the reporter whom had I talked to before the December 22 story that inaccurately described me as a "lobbyist for Gbagbo" (when I specifically had stated I was not advocating for Gbagbo during my press conference and press releases). But Lichtblau wasn't in, I was told—he was on vacation.

But I thought I got lucky: There *was* a reporter on duty whom I knew from my work for the Honduran Business Council, who coincidentally happened to be working on a Wednesday night, two days before New Year's Eve: Ginger Thompson.

She checked with her editor and thought they could get the story of my resignation into the paper. She asked me to email a copy of the letter of resignation, and I did, and waited for her to call back to ask me questions.

The letter I had written disclosed the interesting and, perhaps, newsworthy fact that I was working behind the scenes to help get a call from the president of the United States through to Gbagbo to achieve a peaceful solution to the crisis, and had resigned after making many fruitless efforts to get the call arranged.

The key section in the December 29, 2010, letter stated:

> In the past ten days, I have spoken repeatedly with a senior of-ficial of the State Department toward this end, and specifically to facilitate a call between the President of the United States and Mr. Gbagbo so Mr. Gbagbo could be presented with options for a peaceful resolution, that would avoid further bloodshed and be in the best interests of his country and the people of the Ivory Coast. There is no excuse for a return to violence or civil war.
>
> Unfortunately, as you know, the decision was made in Abi-djan not to allow President Obama's call to be put through to Mr. Gbagbo, despite my repeated pleas . . . [to do so]. Nor have I been able to reach Mr. Gbagbo directly myself to offer him this ad-vice, despite repeated requests, as recently as the last twenty-four hours. Therefore, without going into further details regarding dis-agreements between me and representatives of the government, of which you are aware, I have reached the conclusion that I have not been allowed to effectuate the mission that I was expressly asked to do by your government, despite all my best efforts to do so.

About 7:00 p.m., Thompson called me back. She said that, unfor-tunately, it was too late to get the resignation story into the *Times'* morning paper, on Thursday, December 30; but she could post a story online that evening. I said fine.

She said she would do a brief story and asked whether, the next day, I would be interested in telling her the full story about my actual role. She asked me whether I could name the State Department official I had referenced in my letter. I said I would be happy to cooperate, and the official was Don Yamamoto; I gave her his cell phone number.

Her last words were "I'll call you in the morning and we'll write the full story about how you got involved, what you were doing behind the scenes, and I will call Don Yamamoto to verify."

I hung the phone up and actually had some time with my family, without too much stress. I got the first good night's sleep in more than a week.

A DIFFERENT STORY THAN THE "FULL STORY"

The next morning, December 30, Thompson called, but what she told me stunned me. She told me that her editor was now less interested in the backstory about my role, but more interested in how I seemed to get myself into situations in which I was defending such difficult and often unsavory clients.

"What?" I asked. "Did you say 'situations'? 'Unsavory'? Is this story about what happened to me with Ivory Coast—or about other clients? I thought you said last night you were going to write the full story of what I have been doing to facilitate the Obama call and to try to find a peaceful solution."

"Well," she said, "we want to broaden the focus of the story . . . but we will also be calling Don Yamamoto to get the backstory as well."

What "unsavory" clients are you talking about? I asked her.

She referred to my defense of the "coup" in Honduras in the summer of 2009. "But I did not defend a 'coup' in Honduras," I reminded her. I told her to read my testimony in July 2009 before the House Western Hemisphere Subcommittee, which was available on the Internet. She said she would.

Then she asked me about whether I had "defended" a "dictator" in Equatorial Guinea.

What? I asked.

I told her I was hired by EG President Teodoro Obiang to help him implement what I described explicitly in my contract, to which he agreed, a "comprehensive program of political, legal, and economic reform." I told her I was responsible for a public speech President Obiang had made before a large worldwide audience in June 2010 at the "Global Forum" sponsored by *Time* and *Fortune* magazines and CNN at Cape Town, South Africa, committing to that program, including the International Red Cross monitoring human rights. I sent her a copy of that speech plus a letter to Obiang from South African Nobel Prize winner Archbishop Desmond Tutu praising the speech and offering to help Obiang implement the program.

She asked me about other clients of mine—could she or her co-reporter on the story, Eric Lipton, call them about my work?

I had to defend myself on many fronts, not just one, on December 30? I asked. How could they possibly be available or reachable at this time of year? Do you really think even if I reach them they would be willing to talk to a *Times* reporter and be included in a story that seemed to depict me, and possibly their companies, negatively?

Well, it would help if we could talk to some of your clients, Thompson said.

I asked Thompson, Do you have any specific clients in mind?

Yes. She mentioned one client, Martek Biosciences, a manufacturer of two naturally occurring fatty acid nutrients found in mothers' milk—DHA and ARA—which they supplied to infant formula companies for women who chose not to breast-feed or could not do so.

DHA and ARA had been found by worldwide medical and nutrition scientific bodies, including the World Health Organization, to be valuable for early infant brain and eye development. Indeed, it was one of the reasons why breast milk was seen as advantageous, because it naturally included these two fatty acids.

She asked me whether I had taken a position on behalf of this client against breast-feeding.

I told her absolutely not. My client strongly supported breast-feeding by women, and was on record doing so over and over again. The only issue was that my client wanted poor women who qualified for federal subsidies to have the choice to purchase infant formula—called the "Women, Infants, and Children" or "WIC" program—to receive DHA and ARA just as wealthy women could, and just as women who chose to or could breast-feed did, since these two nutrients naturally occurred in mothers' milk.

I explained that a group of people who strongly supported breast-feeding wanted to impose a ban on the sale of DHA and ARA to poor women under the WIC program. They had used the device of seeking a study by the agriculture secretary of the cost-benefit ratio of DHA and ARA. In one proposal they managed to get inserted into an early version of the 2010 agriculture bill, they had actually succeeded in banning the sale of any infant formula under the WIC program that included these two essential nutrients.

I explained to Thompson that after several senators objected, the substitute version was simply to propose a "study" by the agriculture secretary of the cost-benefit ratio of DHA and ARA. But my client and others who were prochoice and opposed a ban on poor women having access to infant formula with DHA and ARA were concerned that the true agenda of the more extreme breast-feeding movement—sometimes called "Lactivists"—would be to convince the agriculture secretary to oppose a ban administratively, pending a study.

All this was done without hearings and without full public debate, I explained.

"Do you want me to send you the amendment the Lactivists initially succeeded in getting into the agriculture bill," I asked her, "which would have, in effect, banned the sale of DHA and ARA to subsidize infant formula for poor women pending completion of a study, which might have been without time limits?"

Thompson demurred. I knew this was too complicated and she was facing a deadline.

She said I should explain all this when her coreporter, Eric Lipton, who was working on this subject for the story, called me, which she promised he would. But I never heard from Lipton that day. She asked me if I could suggest other clients for her and Lipton to call besides this DHA-ARA manufacturer.

Again I protested—On December 30, you expect me to reach clients to talk to a reporter, in the middle of Christmas week, people on vacation, people who I have to tell may be putting themselves into a negative story about me and their companies?

"Well," she said, "it's up to you, but it would help if we had more of your clients to talk to."

So I sent out several emails and made several phone calls to former clients, and was amazed that I quickly received emails and calls back, from various vacation spots where I found them, saying, yes, they would talk to the *Times* reporters. I called Thompson back and gave her the names and phone numbers.

My heart was now sinking so low I didn't think it could get any lower.

NO ONE CALLS MY BACK-UP SOURCE

My best hope was that Thompson would talk to Deputy Assistant Secretary Yamamoto, who I knew would back up my story about my true role in the Ivory Coast matter—which I thought the story was supposed to be about, as least when I had talked to Thompson the night before.

Late in the afternoon, Thompson called me back to ask me some personal questions about my age, birthplace, and background.

I then asked again, nervously, "Have you called Deputy Assistant Secretary Don Yamamoto yet?"

"Not yet," she said. "We will."

"But isn't the deadline near?" I asked.

"We will call him—promise," she said.

"Not to worry," she added. "We did get a good quote from P. J. Crowley about you." Crowley was then the official spokesperson of the State Department.

What was the quote? I asked.

This could be crucial, I thought—it would at last clear the air on the misreporting and smears about me on the Internet regarding my "defending" Gbagbo's misdeeds and human rights violations.

She said, "P. J. Crowley said that 'Lanny is a relentless and effective interlocutor' . . . he defended you," she said.

I interpreted that comment to be about my role in the Ivory Coast matter. I was relieved. P.J. must have talked to Yamamoto, I thought. Thank goodness.

But Yamamoto was still needed to fill in the details with the *New York Times*—only he knew them.

So all that was left for me to do was wait until about ten-thirty on the evening of December 30, when the *Times* story for the morning paper of December 31 would be posted on the Internet.

At about 10:00 p.m., on the evening of December 30, 2010, I read the *Times* story posted online, with the headline about my being on the "defensive" due to my "client list," which I described at the beginning of this chapter, and then a second and third paragraph listing five specific clients that were examples or evidence that I had crossed over to the "dark side" in my crisis management work. I was horrified—literally in pain as I read:

> Since leaving the White House, Mr. Davis has built a client list that now includes coup supporters in Honduras, a dictator in Equatorial Guinea, for-profit colleges accused of exploiting students, and a company that dominates the manufacture of additives for infant formula. This month he agreed to represent the

Ivory Coast strongman whose claims to that country's presidency have been condemned by the international community and may even set off a civil war.

Mr. Davis withdrew from his $100,000-a-month contract with the Ivory Coast on Wednesday night, saying that the embattled government refused to accept his suggestion to talk to President Obama. Still, his role in West Africa has stoked growing criticism that Mr. Davis has become a kind of a front man for the dark side, willing to take on some of the world's least noble companies and causes.

But in each of the five instances, important facts were omitted that would have cast my representation in a positive light, contradicting the "dark side" premise of the story. In other words, the omission of positive, indisputable facts can be just as misleading as intentional words that distort the facts. On Honduras, my client, the Honduran Business Council and I had not supported the "coup"—in fact, my public testimony to Congress, easily available on the Internet, criticized the illegal forced deportation of Zelaya. But the article omitted reference to my congressional testimony, even though I had told Thompson about it. On Equatorial Guinea, I had advocated only for transparency and reform, as she knew from the speech I had written, and had won the praise of Archbishop Desmond Tutu for my efforts. The *Times* had copies of both the speech and the Tutu letter, but the article omitted reference to both. On the for-profit career colleges I had represented, I had advocated for lower-income and minority kids who depended on career colleges to get ahead, and pointed out the substantial majority of for-profit colleges that provided an important service to lower-income kids. But omitted was my public criticism, on behalf of my clients, to those "bad apples" in the industry who were responsible for abusive and misleading recruiting tactics and sometimes outright fraud.

On "infant formula additives" as another example of going to the "dark side," as noted above, I was on the side of "prochoice" advocates who wanted poor women who couldn't breast-feed to have access to the same essential nutrients naturally found in breast milk—to have the same "choice" as wealthy women or women who could breast-feed. But the story included this work as part of the "dark side" of the issue—i.e., supporting giving poor women the *choice* of purchasing infant formula that contained nutrients that were already present in natural breast milk. To this day, I have never understood how that position, on behalf of my client, could possibly be described as the "dark side"—by the "Lactivists" who wanted all women to breast-feed or by the *New York Times* in choosing this as one of the five examples to support its headline and lead. And, of course, there was the "rest of the story" on the Ivory Coast. But each of those positive facts was omitted as reported by the *Times*.

Of course I credit the *Times* and especially Ginger Thompson for devoting a considerable amount of space in the bottom quarter of the story allowing me to state my perspective and facts on many of these issues. But that isn't the same, and doesn't carry the objective credibility of the *Times* independently verifying and reporting these counterpoint facts in response to the charges.

The key omission in the Ivory Coast part of the story—the core example cited of my going to the "dark side"—was the promised quotation from Deputy Assistant Secretary of State Don Yamamoto, substantiating the true behind-the-scenes role I played trying to facilitate a call from President Obama to Gbagbo in order to ease him out of the country and avoid bloodshed. But instead of seeing the quotation from Yamamoto, I read a quotation from the State Department spokesman, P. J. Crowley. The first sentence contained the precise words that, as Thompson had told me earlier in the day, Crowley had used to a *Times* reporter: "Lanny is a relentless and effective interlocutor." But then came the "pivot" word "but"—indicating disagreement with what I had done:

But [Mr. Davis] cannot change the basic facts and interests that guide our foreign policy. President Gbagbo scheduled an election and he lost fair and square. That's a fact. President Obiang [president of Equatorial Guinea] has an abysmal human rights record. That's a fact.

Ouch. That sounded like I had advocated on behalf of Obiang of Equatorial Guinea and Gbagbo of Ivory Coast—the "but" word implied that—when the exact opposite was the case. Obviously, P. J. Crowley had not been briefed on the facts by Yamamoto or anyone else.

More important, it seemed that no one had briefed Mr. Crowley about my efforts, at the request of Mr. Yamamoto, to facilitate a call from President Obama to Gbagbo to convince him to leave the country and avoid bloodshed. Nor did Crowley appear to know about my mission for Equatorial Guinea to transition to democracy and human rights protections, the program set out in the speech that I wrote and that was praised by Archbishop Tutu.

When I spoke to Don Yamamoto the next day and asked him why he hadn't given the *Times* the supporting quotation he promised me, his answer left me breathless—"No one from the *Times* called me." To say I was stunned was an understatement—although I wasn't sure if it was true, since it is possible calls were made to Yamamoto's cell phone, which he rarely answered.

Of course, in retrospect, I still blamed myself and not the *New York Times*. I should have anticipated the difficulty of getting through to the extremely busy and overtaxed Don Yamamoto, much less in the last two days before the New Year. I should have carefully set up his access to back me up and confirm my actual role. I should have waited to call the *Times* to inform them of my resignation and to have plenty of time to describe the full story about my true role for the Ivory Coast.

I should have . . . could have . . . would have . . . oh, what's the difference. I screwed up. I violated all my own rules. What I would have done for another client, insisted on doing for another client, I didn't do for myself.

DEFENDING MYSELF

As noted above, in the last quarter of the story, on the inside page, of course, the *Times* did give me a chance to defend myself—far more than most such stories would have done. I was grateful for that. But still, it was what it was—me defending myself, with less credibility than if there were third parties validating the positive side of my client work.

Instead of State's Yamamoto describing my constructive efforts, I was left saying, only in generalities, "I felt great pressure that I could accomplish the avoidance of bloodshed. . . . I thought I could do some good."

On Equatorial Guinea and Obiang, I was a lot more emotional.

"I'm a liberal Democrat. I've been a liberal Democrat all my life. I haven't changed my values. But what am I supposed to do if the leader of a country comes to me and says he wants to get right with the world, and get right with the United States? Am I supposed to say no, and let him go on doing what he's doing? Or should I try to help him get right?"

At least I ended on a strong note.

"Do I often find myself in a position of disputing facts that are not consistent with easy labels?" I said. "That's what I do for a living. Controversy is what I do for a living."

Controversy, yes.

But putting myself in the center of a media crisis, no, not good.

REMEMBERING *ABSENCE OF MALICE*

Near 11:00 p.m., on December 30, somewhat desperately after reading and analyzing the story, I tried to reach Ginger Thompson, sending her an email expressing my displeasure. She emailed me back to say she was "sorry you are unhappy with the story." She said she would be "happy to chat tomorrow morning."

Out of sheer desperation, I called the D.C. *New York Times* bureau and asked that the bureau chief, Dean Baquet, someone I had known for many years, since he was an editor at the *Los Angeles Times*, please call me. (Baquet has since been promoted and was named in 2011 as the managing editor, the number-two position, of the *Times* in its New York headquarters.) The phone rang a few minutes later and it was Dean. I told him I appreciated his taking the time to call that late at night. I told him I was unhappy with the story I had just read posted online, trying to control my anger.

I asked him where the story was being played in the morning paper. Normally, if I were calling on behalf of a client on a story I worked on and had optimism about, I would be thrilled if I heard it was a page-one story—knowing the immense impact on other journalists, broadcast and cable TV, and international media and the Internet that anything on page one of the *New York Times* has.

This time, however, my heart sank even lower, if that were possible, when Dean said, "I am pretty sure: page one, Lanny."

"Dean," I said, and I am sure I sounded plaintive, "at the very least can you change the headline on the online edition if it's too late in tomorrow morning's paper? As Ginger Thompson knew, I was not, in fact, a 'lobbyist for' Gbagbo's position on the election—I didn't advocate his position on the election at all. In fact, I publicly stated at a press conference and in a press release that I was not defending his position. I avoided doing that while working behind the scenes with the State Department to try to help President Obama get through on the phone to Gbagbo. Ginger knows all that. I sent her my resignation letter, which the *Times* posted last night."

"Oh, come on, Lanny," Dean said. "You registered as a foreign lobbyist for Gbagbo!"

I didn't bother to argue that my engagement letter was with the Ivory Coast Embassy in Washington, not with Gbagbo, and that I never talked to Gbagbo. I realized this was hopeless—and Baquet was too nice a guy this late at night on December 30 to hang up on me.

"Lanny," Dean said quietly, "you have plenty of space in the story where you get a chance to tell your side."

He was right—they did give me plenty of room to explain myself. I just wished I had had the time to get third parties to do it for me, rather than myself.

I had only myself to blame—not the *New York Times*. I had violated my own rules, for what I thought were good reasons, and hadn't given all the reporters all the facts up front—about what I was really doing behind the scenes in sufficient time to get them into the *Times* story.

"Go to bed, Lanny," Dean said, with obvious empathy that I appreciate to this day. "It's not as bad as you think. You do a good job of explaining what you do for a living and why you do it. This too shall pass."

His tone and kindness shook me out of my self-pity and anger.

"I sure hope so. Thanks, Dean."

I hung up the phone, too mentally and physically weary to feel anything.

Page one?

Newspapers delivered all over the country—page one, *New York Times*, my all-time favorite newspaper, the newspaper my late dad would insist I read cover to cover and that he called "the greatest newspaper in the history of the world" (typical understatement from my dad).

I thought about all my friends in Washington, in other places, picking up the *Times* and reading this story—me on "the dark side"!

Suddenly I was thinking of the most painful scene in one of my favorite movies about journalism gone wrong—*Absence of Malice*. It portrayed a young woman who is fearful that her secret abortion might be publicized in the next day's *Miami Herald*. She waits up till dawn and then she runs to the curb when the paperboy throws the paper down. In horror she reads the story. And what does she do? She runs down the street, picking up as many papers as she can from other curbs in the hope that no one will read the story.

For a moment, I thought of doing the same thing in the early morning in the mountains of western Maryland—running down lonely rural roads as the sun was rising, picking up every *New York Times* I could find on the doorstep of every home.

Until I realized that very few people read the *New York Times* in very conservative and very Republican Garrett County, Maryland.

What a mess, I thought.

I asked myself: What lessons can I learn here? What lessons does this experience teach to others?

I didn't see it coming.

I should have seen it coming.

I would have seen it coming had I been a crisis manager advising a client.

What would I have advised a client in my situation?

Ask for additional time to reach out to "third-party validators"— clients, experts, documents, State Department officials—who could tell the "rest of the story" about the five examples, particularly the Ivory Coast. Go to the editor, if necessary, to ask for additional time— as I had done on behalf of Macy's and Representative Rangel, and won the extra time in return for giving the reporter all the information and access she wanted.

But I didn't have someone advising me.

I was representing myself—and had a fool for a client.

I got lost and forgot my own rules.

And I paid the price.

Then I had a thought, like a bright light going off and on before falling asleep:

Stop blaming the New York Times. *Start applying the crisis management rules that you advised your clients to follow—take responsibility, get the facts out, and clean the mess up, starting the next morning.*

"YOU'RE A LAWYER—"F%#K THEM"

As the sun rose on the morning of December 31, 2010, I groggily served myself my two addictions—got a cup of coffee and opened up my BlackBerry.

There is actually a third morning fix I need that comes with the BlackBerry: reading Mike Allen's Politico.com Playbook column, which mixes news, grapevine rumors, happy birthdays, and latest happenings with "people in the news." I was not the only political junkie who needed his or her morning Mike Allen fix. Millions of others, I knew, did the same thing—and certainly the entire political/punditry/media class inside the Washington Beltway.

But on this morning, as if I needed any further bad news, there I was in Mike Allen's *Politico* Playbook with the *Times* headline and story.

WASHINGTON, INC.—N.Y. TIMES A1 "CLIENT LIST PUTS
POWERFUL LOBBYIST ON DEFENSIVE,"
BY GINGER THOMPSON AND ERIC LIPTON.

The rest of the Allen story about me consisted of quotations directly from the *Times* story—no commentary by Allen other than a sassy headline among the many at the top of his column: LANNY DAVIS: VOICE FOR THE VOICELESS (100K/MONTH).

I knew, of course, the *New York Times* front-page story had already traveled around the world in seconds. But Allen's story, I knew, would be read by all the media and political junkies in Washington, and get repeated and reposted on the Internet countless times before I even had a chance to get the counterpoint facts out.

So I realized it was time to get to work—to correct the record.

I was receiving a blitz of email messages, many of them hate mail from people who read the *Times* story and therefore believed I had been defending Gbagbo's position and, worse, the brutal violence launched or facilitated under his leadership group in the Ivory Coast. I was appalled by that violence—and by being associated with it and with him.

I received hundreds of mindless messages with the same words, verbatim, all generated from a website, many from names that seemed made-up, none with identifiable addresses or return email addresses, asking me to stop representing Gbagbo, whom I did not represent.

But many email messages were positive, from friends and distant acquaintances and perfect strangers from all over the country, who saw the *Times* story as one-sided and lacking balance.

From Alan Dershowitz, the famous Harvard professor and friend, came the brief message: "I think you handled the lobbying brouhaha well. Best, Alan."

Another acquaintance wrote that I should be proud of the work I do as an attorney and advocate. "I'm sure Atticus Finch would agree."

Another from a complete stranger, who identified himself as a "public defender in Manhattan." He wrote that he was "personally offended when I read the article about you in the *Times* this morning.

"ABA [the American Bar Association] Model Rule [of Professional Ethics] 1.2(b) clearly states, 'A lawyer's representation of a client . . . does not constitute an endorsement of the client's political, economic, social or moral views or activities.'

"In light of that rule, I think the article in the *Times* is ridiculous and irresponsible, as are the people who criticize you for representing unpopular clients."

But my favorite email of all was from the conservative, nationally syndicated radio talk show host from Philadelphia, Michael Smerconish, whose show I had been on many times during the Democratic primary campaign when I was supporting Hillary Clinton for the nomination. Smerconish is now a regular guest and sometime substitute host on MSNBC shows.

Smerconish is a man of few words. He wrote: "Am reading your detractors. Fuck them. You are a lawyer. Happy New Year."

It made me smile—at a time when I couldn't imagine anything could make me smile.

TIME TO GET TO WORK—GET THE FACTS OUT

But back to what I knew needed to be done in crisis management on my own account—and done immediately, and that was to get a corrective quotation out from the State Department, consistent with the truth, as Don Yamamoto would most certainly confirm. I figured the State Department spokesman, P. J. Crowley, hadn't been briefed and had gotten it wrong.

I did not want to wait a day longer, given the viral nature of the Internet and the fact that front-page *Times* stories travel around the world and into the minds of the media elite, often as accepted truth. I was determined to get a correction published immediately.

But whom could I get to publish this correction? Who would even answer the phone on New Year's Eve? Who had the ability to get my facts out to potentially millions of readers on New Year's Eve, especially to the media and opinion-influencing elite?

Only one man I knew . . . in America.

Mike Allen.

The same Mike Allen who had just written the sassy summary of the *Times* story in *Politico*'s Playbook—the same who was legendary for working 24/7, waking at 2:00 or 3:00 a.m. to write his column to be posted and read by millions before breakfast.

I called Allen. I was not surprised—he picked up after the first ring.

I told him briefly about what I actually did with the State Department behind the scenes, and that it was all included in my resignation letter that the *Times* had received.

I told him, however, that I was told that the *Times* never called Deputy Assistant Secretary Yamamoto, as it promised to do; then used a misleading lead-in to the P. J. Crowley quotation. Moreover, I was pretty sure Crowley had made the comment with the "but" conjunctive word without having talked to Yamamoto or even having read my resignation letter.

Allen expressed surprise that the *Times* had gone with the Crowley quotation while never calling Yamamoto.

"Can you get P. J. Crowley to issue a clarification and talk to me?" he asked.

"I hope so—I will try to reach him."

It was a gamble. I was assuming that Crowley would be reachable on New Year's Eve and would be willing to correct his quotation after being better briefed.

I tried reaching Crowley by email and cell phone, but I only got the answering machine on his cell, and left him a long message on his voicemail.

I could only hope he'd be picking up messages, would get better briefed, and would return Allen's call.

I also tried to reach Don Yamamoto, but could only leave him a message on his cell phone, asking him to please take a call from Mr. Crowley or call him to brief him about my actual role in the Ivory Coast matter.

You have to be an optimist to do all this on New Year's Eve and expect anyone will respond, much less even pick up voicemail messages or read emails—anyone, that is, other than me and Mike Allen!

A few hours later, Mike Allen called me back.

"Done," he said. "P. J. Crowley gave me a more complete quote than the one used by the *New York Times*, and with no 'but' in the middle of the quote."

"Tell me, Mike," I pleaded, relieved. "What did he say?"

All he said in response: "You will feel the love."

That New Year's Eve, as the clock ticked to midnight and 2010 approached 2011, I sat with my family at our lake house, recovering from the previous week's ordeal, and the usual watching of Times Square and the throngs waiting for the great ball to slowly drop as the countdown is shouted.

I tried to cheer up.

But each time I heard the word "Times" before the word "Square," I had a hard time cheering.

Happy New Year!

A NEW YEAR . . . AND VINDICATION

I woke up at dawn on New Year's Day, January 1, 2011, got my cup of coffee, and turned on my BlackBerry, and there it was—Mike Allen's *Politico* column Playbook—with the header LANNY DAVIS BACKSTORY ON NEW YORK TIMES STORY.

There it was—P. J. Crowley's more fulsome quotation, not taken out of context by a biased lead-in. Reported Mike Allen:

The State Department's P. J. Crowley tells us by phone:

"Certainly, Lanny was helpful. He did open another alternative channel of communications for us, and was providing the right advice to his client."

Yes! I thought. Thank goodness. Now why hadn't the *Times* gotten that quotation—completely validating my explanation of my actual role and contradicting the *Times'* lead-in that I was on the "wrong side" in the Ivory Coast matter?

Continuing, Crowley told Allen:

> President Gbagbo has declined to engage our ambassador, Phillip Carter. Absent that avenue, Lanny became another route to encourage President Gbagbo to leave. Unfortunately, every indication is that his client wasn't heeding his advice.

Yesss!!! I thought. Again—these statements from Crowley contradicted the *Times'* reporting in its December 30 online story that I had defended Gbagbo, and would now be available to intercept any search engine that picked up the *New York Times* story.

Oh, thank you, P.J., I thought.

That should do it, I thought. Or so I thought.

Just one more thing to do—a letter to the editor of the *New York Times* to restate P. J. Crowley's quotation supporting my role in the Ivory Coast matter (for those few Americans who don't read Mike Allen in *Politico* every day) and correct my advocacy of democratic and human rights reforms in Equatorial Guinea. (I knew that with a 125-word limit, I couldn't address more than two issues.)

So I wrote the following letter, which was published on January 5, 2011:

> *Your article about me [on December 30, 2010] did not include important facts:*
>
> *My mission for Ivory Coast was limited to finding a peaceful solution—as I said publicly at the outset, not to state who had won and who had lost the election, or who was right or who was wrong. The State Department representative with whom I worked thanked me for that effort.*

My representation of Equatorial Guinea resulted in a public speech by President Teodoro Obiang ... at a June 2010 global forum in Cape Town, South Africa. The speech committed to a broad program of political, legal and economic reforms. A month later, Archbishop Desmond Tutu wrote a letter and offered to assist President Obiang in carrying out his reform program.

Lanny J. Davis
Washington, Dec. 31, 2010

When that letter was published, I thought: That should be enough damage control. The key facts were now in the newspaper of record, the *New York Times* itself. I was thankful that my exercise in self-crisis management on the Ivory Coast story was over.

Or so I thought.

13.

FIGHTING THE BIG LIE
ON THE INTERNET:
THE SWARM OF BEES

Another Round of My Own Making

I had thought I was through with the Ivory Coast matter, and with the fallout from the resulting negative stories in the *New York Times*. I thought wrong.

My learning moment came from a rather unexpected source: the famous and brilliant Garry Trudeau, the Pulitzer Prize–winning creator of the political-satiric *Doonesbury* comic strip.

Early in the morning of Friday, May 6, 2011, my BlackBerry buzzed several times with messages from various friends, all telling me I had been the object of what one referred to as a "cheap shot" about my Ivory Coast–related work in *Doonesbury*.

My first reaction was to feel complimented—I made it into *Doonesbury*! So I went to the *Washington Post* to read it.

The strip depicted two cartoon characters—the driver, Duke, was talking to his son, Earl. (As Trudeau put it in a subsequent email to me, Duke and Earl were emblematic of "lobbyists who accept money to represent the interests of authoritarian regimes.")

In the cartoon that day, Earl is speaking to Duke in the first three panels:

"A lot has happened since you went offline, pop. The Arab Spring has really thinned our competition on K Street.

"Remember that big Ivory Coast account we lost to Lanny Davis Associates? Davis bailed! Dictators are just too toxic now. If this keeps up we'll have the dirtbag space all to ourselves. Of course, the downside is there are fewer dirtbags to rep."

Then in the fourth and last panel:

Duke: "Why does this not worry me?"

Earl: "Well, you're right—we're already seeing emerging dirtbags."

I had just been referred to in *Doonesbury* as representing the "dirtbags" in the Ivory Coast. And, of course, I was being likened to the sleazy lobbyists Duke and Earl.

I realized that I hadn't done such a good crisis management job after all. Trudeau must not have seen Mike Allen's P. J. Crowley quotation or my *New York Times* letter to the editor, or Googled to find them popping up.

I assumed Trudeau would not have written the strip had he known the facts. Perhaps I was influenced because we had one important part of our lives in common: We worked for the *Yale Daily News* as undergraduates at Yale. Trudeau, four years after I had served as "chairman" of the *News*, had begun a comic strip in the *YDN* called *Bulldog Tales*, with some of the characters taken from the Yale Bulldogs football team. ("B.D." was Brian Dowling, Yale's great quarterback at the time.) After Trudeau graduated Yale, *Bulldog Tales* was converted into *Doonesbury*, and the rest is history.

A close friend of mine who knew about the pain I had experienced after the *Times* story called and, anticipating my anguish, advised me to ignore the *Doonesbury* shot and not react. In retrospect, I should have taken his advice.

But my crisis management instincts, again with myself as my client, took over. Since *Doonesbury* was syndicated in fourteen hundred newspapers across the country, I decided it was worth my contacting Trudeau and, perhaps, based on our common *Yale Daily News* ties, he would find a way—even tongue in cheek—to correct the record once I brought the facts to his attention.

So I decided to send him a personal email. I didn't have his address, but I found the email of his syndicator agent, and I sent him the following email on Friday afternoon, May 6:

> Friday afternoon, May 6, 1:40 p.m.
>
> *Gary—it's been a long time since we have met and since* Bulldog Tales *and the Yale days. . . .*
>
> *Your* Doonesbury *today (May 6 in* Wash Post*) made a reference to my work for Ivory Coast [that] was misleading and included a cheap shot about my representing "dictators."*
>
> *As has now been made public in a statement issued by P. J. Crowley, the then State Department spokesman, I was actually working closely, behind the scenes, to help the State Department reach the then leader of Ivory Coast, Laurent Gbagbo, to ease him out and to avoid bloodshed. I was asked to facilitate a phone call from President Obama to Mr. Gbagbo. When the latter refused twice, I immediately resigned the account within 10 days (started on December 19 and ended on December 29, with a letter that was published in the* NY Times *on Dec. 30). I will send you the actual statement issued by P. J. Crowley in the next email and will try to find a copy of my resignation letter.*
>
> *Can you please try to correct this—the fact that I did not defend a dictator, that I was working behind the scenes to help the State Department ease him out and help President Obama call him to accomplish this and avoid bloodshed, and that this is now a matter of public record? I would certainly appreciate a note to this effect at the end of the next* Doonesbury *you publish.*

I know you are a brilliant satirist, and I don't mind—even complimented—being the object of it, as long as you are accurate and not misleading.

So to repeat: I will send you the P. J. Crowley January 2 statement and hope you will find a way to correct the record—in fairness.

Thanks and would love to talk to you some day soon. My contact information is below.

> *Regards,*
> *Lanny*

I wasn't optimistic that the email would ever get passed on to Trudeau, but I hoped, if it did, he would at least verify the P. J. Crowley statement and find a way to correct the record.

Boy, was I wrong.

The following Monday morning, May 9, I received a phone call from a *Politico* writer named Chris Frates, who wrote a Political Intelligence column. He told me he was writing a brief piece about Trudeau attacking me in *Doonesbury* and asked me whether I wished to comment.

Instead of declining to give more traction to the largely unnoticed *Doonesbury* reference to me—advice I would have given to a client—I wanted to be sure that *Politico*, the place where Mike Allen had published the quote from P. J. Crowley, the official State Department spokesman, acknowledging that my behind-the-scenes work for the State Department regarding the Ivory Coast was helpful, would get it right.

Worse, I wrote out my response while I was feeling angry and put upon—a mistake that every crisis manager warns a client to avoid. Here are the words quoted by Frates in his story, a clear result of writing in heat:

> "Garry Trudeau may think his cartoon is an excuse for not checking the facts and a cheap shot. He should be beyond that.
> "All he needed to do is check the Internet and he would have

seen P. J. Crowley, State Department spokesman, in *POLITICO* on January 1 that my role on Ivory Coast was to help the State Department behind the scenes to convince the Ivory Coast leader to agree to a peaceful solution. Ten days later, when he refused to accept a phone call from President Gbagbo at my behest, I resigned.

"Garry Trudeau can't use carelessness as an excuse when he engages in satire at my expense," Davis said.

That, I hoped, was the end of that.

If it had been a client who did what I did, I would have called him or her and predicted: "You just managed to give the misinformation more life. Trudeau is bound to respond—and not positively."

If it had been a client, I would have also thought but not said: You idiot!

Instead, I hoped, naively, that Trudeau would react and tell *Politico*: "Oops, I did Lanny wrong. I apologize."

It didn't happen.

"NOT REALLY IN THE FAIRNESS BUSINESS"

Three days after my email to Trudeau and the Frates article, on Thursday, May 12, at about 5:00 p.m., I received an email from Trudeau, which began with the memorable words:

> *Dear Lanny:*
> *Normally I resist engaging with the folks I write about—I'm not really in the fairness business—but in deference to our shared* YDN [Yale Daily News] *ties, here's an explanation. I suspect you'll find it unsatisfying.*

He continued with harsh criticism of my work on Ivory Coast, despite my having proven to him through the quote I had sent him from

P. J. Crowley, spokesman for the State Department, that I had played a constructive role behind the scenes to try to ease Gbagbo out of power peacefully.

But the phrase that struck me as memorable—and emblematic about those who seemed indifferent to false published statements or innuendo about others—was his phrase "I'm not really in the fairness business."

I realized that as a political satirist and cartoonist he had license to make fun and not always be fair. But were there no boundaries of fairness even for a satirist? I wondered. Shouldn't there be—at least after the subject of the satiric attack asks for the record to be corrected because it is a particularly damaging and false accusation, with the truth available in the public record?

Frates called me almost as soon as I received the Trudeau email. Trudeau had sent him a copy of his email to me. Frates asked me if I wanted to reply—he was going to write a brief story, including these awful quotations.

In retrospect, I should have let it go, as I would have advised a client to do. But believing I had to challenge Trudeau's inaccurate characterizations within the *Politico* article, I wrote an email responding to Trudeau and sent a copy to Frates.

It didn't occur to me, at least then, that if I replied to Trudeau and we went another round in *Politico*, we would both look foolish, like two little boys throwing sand into each other's eyes in the sandbox.

But I just couldn't resist. His statement that he wasn't in the "fairness business" was just too emblematic of the troubling pattern of indifference to the absolute values of truth and fairness—even by a cartoonist engaged in satire:

> May 12, about 6 p.m.
> *Dear Garry,*
> *I appreciate your taking the time to reply. I too will copy Chris.*

*I understand you are not in the "fairness business." You are a
satirist and cartoonist, not a journalist.*

*But not being in the fairness business doesn't mean you
should feel good about attacking someone personally when you
get your facts wrong that form the basis of your personal attacks.
Then to make matters worse, you repeat the falsehoods, and add
to them, in your email, copied to a reporter, even when published
facts are available that contradict your assertions.*

I then listed the various facts that were in the public record about
the true role I played in trying to help the State Department, including quoting again the P. J. Crowley statement published in *Politico* on
January 1, acknowledging my "constructive" role behind the scenes
helping the State Department.

To my relief, Frates called me back and told me Trudeau would not
continue another round with a response.

If he had, I can't say that I could have resisted making still another
response.

Thank goodness I wasn't tested.

Well, I kind of was. Twice more in 2012 I was told that Trudeau made
similar disparaging references to me. But now I knew better. Trudeau
wouldn't change his views. Facts didn't seem to matter. And certainly
not because of fairness, since I knew, in his own words, he wasn't "in the
fairness business." So (fortunately for me) I didn't respond.

THE "SWARM OF BEES": FIGHTING THE BIG LIE
ON THE INTERNET

One good thing about this experience with Garry Trudeau and my
mismanagement of the *New York Times* story is that it taught me to
focus on the fundamental question about the new profession of "legal
crisis management" I had chosen: What was it really all about?

Ironically, it was Garry Trudeau's reference to not being in the "fairness business" that reminded me of the simple answer: What this crisis management business was all about—what I was fighting for in all the "crisis tales" described in this book—was, simply, truth and fairness in print newspapers, on Internet news websites, in the blogosphere, on social media, everywhere.

Fighting for truth and fairness—not sometimes, not in relative terms, but always, as absolute values, without compromise.

"Absolute" is a word I usually avoid.

But the values—the goals—of truth and fairness, when it comes to publication of false or misleading accusations that damage a person's reputation, should be absolutes, whether in a satiric cartoon that falsely smears someone's reputation or on the Internet in anonymous comments posted in the middle of the night.

I feel that there can be no justification, ever, for half-truths and almost-fairness.

Once confronted with facts that cannot be disputed, even assuming reasonable differences on conclusions or inferences from those facts, the obligation to publish corrections and clarifications—all the facts needed to avoid a misleading negative impression—is, in my judgment, absolute. It is not sufficient for the editors, whether print, broadcast, or website, to invite the victim of the misleading report to write his or her own "comment" or correction. That has much less credibility than the publication itself acknowledging the error and, in the process, standing up for the absolute values of truth and fairness in all published information.

It was during the immediate aftermath of the Ivory Coast story that I first thought of the metaphor of what it felt like to be in the middle of a story that misstated the truth and that went viral on the Internet—the sensation of being in the middle of a swarm of bees, swirling around your head, stinging away endlessly. No matter how much you swat at the swarm—with facts, telephone calls, corrections, follow-up stories to try to correct the record—while you may kill a few bees here and there with the facts, they will continue to swarm.

So it goes, being in the middle of the misinformation echo chamber of false or misleading accusations on the Internet. You can try putting facts out, try correcting the record with facts on an Internet site, or in another publication telling the truth, or try getting them onto Twitter or Facebook or other social media.

But the Google-like search engines will continue to register "hits" of the prior stories, repeating the inaccuracies, leading people to perceive them as truth by virtue of their repetition on the Internet, and thus the factual misstatement bees will continue to swarm.

The result, for the victim of the swarm—I can speak from personal experience, such as continuing false assertions of my defending "dictators" or supporting the Honduran "coup," as well as from listening to crisis clients over the years—is often a sense of hopelessness, futility, resignation. It seems, at times, that no matter how hard you try, some people just don't consider correcting the record and being fair all that important.

The disease of ignoring facts, unfortunately, was no longer all that unusual. Too often, repeated hits on the Internet even of a false assertion become proof of the truth, simply by virtue of repetition. Too often, many otherwise respectable journalists do not take the extra time to go to the "source of the Nile," to trace the repeated "facts" to be sure the original information is, in fact, verifiably true.

Post first and check the facts second—that seems to be the growing rule, rather than the exception, of the jungle of today's Internet culture.

Here is just one personal example of how good people and good organizations can go wrong under the pressure of that culture. In mid-September 2010 I was accused, in an article posted on an Internet news site called *Campus Progress*, sponsored by a major liberal Democratic organization, of publishing an op-ed piece without revealing that I was a paid lobbyist for a client whose interests would be advanced by the position I was taking in the op-ed piece.

The accusation was false. I had written the column in June 2010—four months before I had been retained by the client in question, a coalition of for-profit or "career" colleges, and before I had any inkling that I even might be retained by these colleges.

Several hours after this false accusation was posted on *Campus Progress*, I received a call from the reporter asking me to comment on my failure to disclose the client relationship. When I told her the truth—that the op-ed piece had been published four months before, and that she could have confirmed that fact by checking my lobbying registration report or calling me directly, this is what she said. I am not making this up:

"Well, I posted first, *but I then called you to verify the facts, didn't I?*"

There it was. There it is.

Post first, check the facts second.

To their credit, the editors and the reporter for *Campus Progress* posted the correction shortly after my conversation. But in today's Internet culture, that was, unfortunately, too late. That didn't stop the misinformation bees from continuing to swarm for months and months. I kept getting calls based on the original post from people who hadn't seen the correction or had seen the false accusation posted and repeated on other Internet sites. The "correction" was simply lost in the continuing misinformation Internet swarm.

What to do to beat it? Is anything possible?

My advice is as simple as it is difficult to follow:

Don't give up.

Believe in the fundamental values underlying crisis management—truth and fairness.

Even though you know all the bees cannot be killed and they will continue to swarm somewhere, somehow, on the Internet, to be unearthed by a search engine—keep fighting.

Even though Google will continue to show the stories with the false or misleading assertions and people will believe them just because of repeated hits—keep fighting.

Even though political cartoonists "not in the fairness business" or website editors or anonymous bloggers and commentators will ignore corrections—keep fighting.

Those who repeat the misinformation, even when they know it is counter to the facts, will at least also know that you are not going to stop swatting, that you will be there to continue to confront and challenge them.

And crisis managers, by following the basic rules outlined in this book, will at least stand a chance of inserting into the echo chamber true facts that will show up, or stand a chance of showing up, on a Google search or on some other search engine.

Another possible tool with which to oppose the Internet swarm is to fight the search engines using their own techniques against them.

There is now a cottage industry of reputation-protecting companies that have reverse-engineered the algorithm of the search engines to push distorted negative stories off page one, where data show more than 90 percent of searchers stop their research, and even onto page three or higher, where data shows fewer than 1 percent of the searchers will go. To oversimplify the technique, these companies create hundreds, thousands maybe, of "mentions" of the accurate facts and stories on various Internet sites, whether news organizations, websites, Twitter, Facebook, or other social media. The result is to produce sufficient hits of the accurate, positive mentions to push down the misinformation hits to pages two, three, or higher of the Google or other Internet search engine.

Such "brand" or "reputation" management techniques may seem manipulative. But what this is all about is getting truth to rise to the surface and dominate inaccuracies. And that's a good thing.

FOLLOW THE RULES—FIGHT BACK

The rules of crisis management described in the tales told in this book, and the lessons learned, some the hard way by making mistakes, can be boiled down to the first foundational rule about the truth: "Tell it all, tell it early, tell it yourself." All the rest are overlapping and mutually reinforcing—a menu of options that should be selected, in various combinations, depending on the facts and circumstances. These crisis tales teach the reasons the fundamental rules of crisis management must be followed, always and without exception.

The HealthSouth and Martha Stewart tales prove not only the value of a crisis manager's getting access to all the facts to develop an effective strategy, but also the value of an attorney's leading the crisis management effort—one who is actually providing legal advice and thus can claim attorney-client privilege and get access to all the facts, good and bad, known by the legal team. But these two tales also show how careful an attorney–crisis manager has to be—as was the case in the HealthSouth and Martha Stewart cases—for one mistake could cost the client company its very existence or, in the case of someone under criminal investigation, his or her personal freedom.

But in both the Martha Stewart and HealthSouth tales, the lesson learned was also that media and crisis management requires cooperation, communication, and trust between all attorneys, otherwise the risk of going public may outweigh the crisis management advantages of being proactive. These tales also show that in today's world of the Internet, with the damage that can be done to reputations and even the risk of losing one's freedom, successful crisis management depends on defense lawyers' being open to a media strategy—or at least open enough to listen.

But it's not enough to do a good job, to gather all the facts, with the advantage of attorney-client privilege, and find ways to get them out ahead of the story. The second rule is: You have to find a simple way of expressing those facts—a headline that is easy to understand

and that accurately summarizes the truth, putting the story into perspective.

In the Royal Caribbean case, the expression "We are a cruise ship—not *CSI*" summarized that message perfectly. Royal Caribbean had done its best to cooperate with investigators and to take care of Mrs. Smith while trying to be sensitive to the travails of the grieving widow. But it wasn't reasonable for the cruise ship to be held to the standard of the FBI or *CSI*'s TV investigative team. When it came to Pakistan's Prime Minister Bhutto's conveying to President Clinton the succinct reason for returning the $600 million for the undelivered F-16s, the expression "the money or the planes, what's fair is fair" was easy to remember and, as it turned out, easy for President Clinton to grasp, repeat, and make into U.S. policy.

Once the simple message is developed, the third rule teaches us that you have to find a way to get your facts out to get in front of the story—if possible, as was the case with the Macy's racial discrimination lawsuit story, in a comprehensive predicate story, taking the risk of allowing a reporter to have total access to all the facts, good and bad. But then there is the human element that must be taken into account—the outrage that victims of negative, distorted media attacks feel, which fuels their desire to strike back. So it was with Representative Charles Rangel, and NFL Players Association leader Gene Upshaw, and Redskins owner Dan Snyder, whose anger initially resulted in statements and actions that made a bad story worse.

But Mr. Rangel ended up taking his punishment with grace and dignity and winning reelection twice and continuing to serve in the U.S. Congress. Gene Upshaw sadly passed away too soon and too young, but not before he knew he had basically beaten the campaign of personal invective, distortion, and misinformation against him by certain retired players, who mysteriously went silent once he was gone. And Dan Snyder stubbornly fought for the truth and took the heat for doing so. Then he told his story of why he sued to clear his name—and then when the newspaper that had smeared him admitted in court that it really didn't mean the plain words it had published falsely accusing him, he was willing to walk away from the suit and move on.

Then came the moving experience of Mississippi senator Trent Lott, whose remarkable interaction with the Reverend Jesse Jackson during his personal and political crisis resulted not in a "solution" to that crisis but in a personal catharsis, allowing him and his wife and family to move on with closure, grace, and peace.

The inspiring example of William Morgenstern of Rent-Way shows what can happen if you have the facts on your side and you can use all techniques—legal, media, and political—to get the truth out. In the case of Morgenstern, that choice was even more difficult since he and most of those around him believed that no one would believe the truth, since the optics were so bad and he was putting himself at legal risk if he went proactive and transparent. But he did it anyway, because he believed in the power of truth and his basic core values and character would not let him do otherwise.

Finally, my experiences in dealing with foreign clients or governments proved, most of all, the limitations on effective crisis management when the true facts are trumped by media coverage concerning facts involving a faraway land and government. This is especially the case when the crisis manager is prevented from telling the full story, early and completely, due to international and governmental secrecy requirements, as was the case with my representation of both the Honduran Business Council and Ivory Coast's Washington, D.C., embassy. Effective crisis management is made even more difficult when you find yourself as part of the crisis story and then foolishly attempt to represent yourself, ending up with a fool for a client, with your judgment clouded by your own emotions, ego, and blindness.

Perhaps one unfortunate lesson to be learned from attempting to apply crisis management techniques to helping a bad government get better is that such an effort carries too high a personal cost and too little chance to be given a fair hearing in the media. The "human rights" international media/NGO complex is just too ideological, absolutist, and powerful to be resisted when it turns on anyone trying to do good by working for someone with a bad reputation, even if the improvement is real and in the U.S. national interest.

So as I learned from my work on trying to get Equatorial Guinea right on human rights and democracy, even after my work was endorsed by the saintly Archbishop Desmond Tutu, my efforts, which actually achieved progress in bringing Equatorial Guinea from the dark side to the bright side, ended up being described as my going from the bright side to the dark side.

To repeat the quotation I gave to Ginger Thompson of the *New York Times*: "I'm a liberal Democrat. I've been a liberal Democrat all my life. I haven't changed my values. But what am I supposed to do if the leader of a country comes to me and says he wants to get right with the world, and get right with the United States? Am I supposed to say no, and let him go on doing what he's doing? Or should I try to help him get right?"

Sadly, I learned the lesson that good intentions, even good results, can be painted darkly. I would certainly advise anyone who is asked to try to help a "bad" government on democracy and human rights to think twice before doing it—even if you are working with the U.S. State Department—unless you are willing to risk being repeatedly falsely labeled as taking money to defend the "bad guys" by a "swarm of misinformation bees" on the blogosphere and social media—and in *Doonesbury*!

Of course this is not good for the world or humankind—for the cause of those who are victims of human-rights-abusing governments. But it is one of the unfortunate realities of the business that there are those who don't think it is their duty to be in the "fairness business" and stick to the facts.

Whatever the difficulties in achieving success in crisis management, one thing is clear: If you don't follow one or more of the rules described in this book, there will be no chance to correct the public record and to clear the honor and name of people falsely and unfairly maligned. Even if swatting the "swarm of bees" with facts seems hopeless, and even if sometimes it *is* hopeless, the ultimate lesson of my crisis tales—and of this book—is that in the final analysis, even if there are those on the Internet who aren't in the truth and fairness business, the rest of us must be . . . no matter how difficult.

HOPE SPRINGS ETERNAL

Just as I was ready to give up on that idealistic goal that the facts and the truth still count, I read an inspiring example proving that fighting back against the swarm of disinformation and distortion still matters and can produce results.

On Wednesday afternoon, December 14, 2011, a *Washington Post* political blogger/reporter posted a note about Republican presidential candidate Mitt Romney on the *Post*'s *blogPost* website. The report on *blogPost* made a terrible accusation against Romney—that his campaign had produced an ad that used a favorite expression of the Ku Klux Klan. As it turns out, that assertion was 100 percent false.

The *Post* blogger/reporter made the mistake because she had relied on other Internet postings, assuming them to be true, including one on a highly respected site stating that "the Romney campaign wasn't commenting" about the ad or the KKK expression it used. When her editor noticed the posting, he asked her to contact the Romney campaign to verify the report. Instead of calling, she used email, and the error was compounded. The Romney campaign did respond, denying the charge, but the email got filtered into a spam file.

It wasn't until Thursday that the truth was confirmed—that the statement on *blogPost* about Romney and the KKK expression was false.

So what did the *blogPost*'s editor do? What did the *Washington Post* and its executive editor, Marcus Brauchli, say?

Did the editor say, "Oh, this is just the Internet, fact-checking and truth don't really matter if it's just a blog on the Internet"?

No.

Did he say, as one reporter writing for an Internet site who had gotten it wrong said to me, "Well, even though we posted something inaccurate based on what we read on the Internet, I did call you after and to confirm, so that makes it okay"?

No.

Or did he say, reminiscent of what, say, a political-satiric cartoonist might say: "Since this site is described by us as just a 'sounding board for news and conversation that's reverberating online,' we don't need to admit our mistakes and correct the record, since we are not in the fairness business"?

No.

First, the editor of *blogPost* posted the following statement the next day, on Thursday, December 15:

> This posting contains multiple, serious factual errors that undermine its premise. [Mr. Romney's ad never used the KKK expression.] . . . The *Post* should have contacted the Romney campaign for comment before publication. Finally, we apologize that the posting began by saying, "someone didn't do his research" when, in fact, we had not done ours.

Second, Brauchli said: "We had a reporter failure and we had an editor failure. . . . We believe in being excessively contrite when the *Post* falls short of its own standards."

And third, here, in part, is what the *Post*'s ombudsman, Patrick Pexton, wrote in the *Post* on Friday, December 16, 2011,

> The errors are pretty obvious. You remember the old saw that police and parents used to scare us when we were in high school driver education: "Speed kills." Well, when reporting, too much

speed can kill a publication's reputation for even-handedness and fact-checking. *Reporters love to be first and hate to be last, but accuracy and fairness must always triumph over speed.*

Another problem here is that too many reporters see the computer as their main tool of the trade. I'm old-fashioned, and I think the telephone is still the first tool of the trade if you can't do a personal interview. Fine to use the Internet for some basic research, or in a pinch to email a source for a comment, but it's faster and often better to call. You get more nuance, more spontaneity, and you usually get a real human being to answer a question. E-mail is too easily ignored; a person on the phone is harder to put off. . . . We believe in being excessively contrite when the *Post* falls short of its own standards.

Thank you, *Washington Post*, thank you, Mr. Brauchli, and thank you, Mr. Pexton, for the sentence I highlighted above: *Reporters love to be first and hate to be last, but accuracy and fairness must always triumph over speed.*

You have proven that far from being hopeless, it is worth it to keep swatting at that swarm of misinformation bees on the Internet and to never give up . . . because somewhere, somehow, someday, the *Washington Post*'s example of caring about truth and fairness and taking responsibility for correcting errors will be the rule of the Internet, and not the exception.

AFTERWORD

PENN STATE

Overcoming Fear to Get the Truth Out

_____

It was late morning on Tuesday, January 17, 2012, in a small conference room at a building adjacent to Teterboro Airport in northern New Jersey: an odd venue for the outpouring of emotion by the thirteen men and women who were sitting around the conference table. They were different ages, from different backgrounds, different perspectives, and life experiences.

What this group of people had in common was that they were all Penn State graduates and were all members of the board of trustees of Pennsylvania State University, otherwise known as Penn State.

They all shared a recent traumatic experience. Each had voted to remove their beloved Joe Paterno as football coach after nearly a half century of coaching the Penn State team—the legendary football coach whose merged identity with the university was symbolized by the expression he used and made famous: "We are Penn State."

On this morning at a small suburban airport terminal conference room, each member of the board was there for one purpose: to tell the truth to two reporters for the *New York Times* about why—and how—they had terminated "Coach Pa," as he was known and as many referred to him that day, as football coach late on the evening of November 9, 2011.

The weight of their decision would have been heavy enough without the emotional ties that each felt to Joe Paterno. They also felt they owed a legal duty as trustees of the university under state law to protect the interests of the university, past, present, and future—a university first established by President Abraham Lincoln 156 years ago, in 1864, during the Civil War, and today comprising twenty-four campuses—with almost one hundred thousand students all across the state of Pennsylvania—the main campus located at State College in the north central area of the state.

Sitting at the head of the long conference table were two young men, Pete Thamel and Mark Viera, sportswriters for the *New York Times*. In front of them was a tape recorder, although they were also taking notes on old-fashioned steno pads.

The journalists had come prepared to ask questions on a chronological basis—what happened day-by-day, minute-by-minute if necessary, the classic "tick-tock" journalistic narrative—in order to tell the collectively remembered story of the decision to remove Coach Paterno. But that wasn't the plan I had arranged, with the consent of each of the board members. They were supposed to tell their individual stories one at a time, around the table, a story each one had described to me as the most "difficult," "gut-wrenching," "heartbreaking," and "awful" decision of their lives.

The two reporters had agreed to that format, with the understanding that they were free to ask follow-up questions individually or to the group and to write the story—of course—as they saw fit.

"I THOUGHT ABOUT THE MOTHERS OF THOSE BOYS"

As each person spoke for about fifteen to twenty minutes over the next three-plus hours, voices cracked and individuals had to stop to regain their composure.

Then came Stephanie Nolan Deviney, a brilliant trial attorney from Exton, Pennsylvania. She described her horror when she learned, on Saturday, November 5, 2011, from the published grand jury report or "presentment," about the sexual assaults that had occurred on the Penn State campus on small boys, one described graphically to the grand jury that occurred in 2001 involving a small ten- to twelve-year-old boy. She had read in the presentment that Coach Paterno had testified before the grand jury that he knew about his former assistant football coach's engaging in sexual conduct with this young child alone in the shower in the Penn State athletic facility where the coach had his offices. She said that bothered her—that the coach had apparently not done more to protect this victim and future victims over all these years. Yet she also knew she admired Coach Paterno for all that he had done for Penn State and for all that he meant to Penn State's national reputation for producing "student athletes" and for research and academic excellence.

On Tuesday night, November 8—the night before she was due to go to Penn State for a full board meeting that she knew would have to decide whether to remove Paterno as football coach—Stephanie Nolan Deviney said she still hadn't made up her mind about how she would vote. Then late in the evening, before going to bed, she said she had gone into the bedroom of her then sleeping seven-year-old son to kiss him on the forehead.

She paused, collecting herself, before continuing. The two *New York Times* reporters looked at her, waiting. Then she said: "I thought of the mothers of those boys in the presentment. And I thought about what they must feel when they kiss their sons good night."

She kissed her son on the forehead and made up her mind. There was only one decision as a trustee—and as a mother—she realized, painfully, that she could make.

THE SANDUSKY PRESENTMENT NEWS EXPLODES
IN THE MEDIA

On Saturday morning, November 5, 2011, a Pennsylvania grand jury, meeting in the state capital, Harrisburg, issued a criminal indictment of three individuals in the form of a twenty-three-page narrative report, called a presentment. The presentment report appeared early that morning on the Internet site of the Harrisburg clerk of the court—allegedly posted in error late Friday night. It explained in narrative fashion the background and factual basis for the three indictments.

The first was an indictment of Jerry Sandusky, the nationally renowned former Penn State defensive coordinator under Joe Paterno for twenty-three years, who had retired twelve years before, in 1999. Sandusky was accused by the grand jury of having sexually assaulted at least eight young boys between the ages of ten and thirteen, beginning as early as 1995 or 1996 and as recently as 2005 or 2006, many on the Penn State campus and specifically in the Lasch Building, the main athletic facility presided over by Joe Paterno. Sandusky had been given an office in that building next to Paterno's after his retirement, and full privileges and access to all its facilities, including the wrestling room, swimming pool, and showers, as well as to the field and bench of the football team during practices and games.

The presentment stated in graphic, horrific detail the testimony from these eight individuals, now in their late teens or twenties, about how Jerry Sandusky had allegedly sexually molested and, in some cases, brutally raped them, some in the Lasch Building showers. Sandusky was indicted on forty-five counts of criminal sexual assault involving these eight victims.

The other two men indicted in the presentment were two senior Penn State officials—Senior Vice President for Finance Gary Schultz, to whom (on the organization chart) the Penn State University campus police reported; and the athletic director, Timothy Curley, to whom Coach Joe Paterno reported. Both were indicted for two alleged crimes: (1) perjury before the grand jury on the issue of what they had been told by Coach Paterno regarding an alleged sexual assault by Sandusky on a young ten- to twelve-year-old boy on Friday evening, February 9, 2001; and (2) unlawfully failing to report what they had been told to the State Department of Public Welfare or to law enforcement authorities, as state law seemed to have required them to do.

At a nonpublic board "seminar" meeting in May 2011, the board had been told only vaguely by the president of Penn State, Dr. Graham Spanier, or they had read in a local Harrisburg newspaper months before, that there was a grand jury investigation involving Sandusky and young boys. But President Spanier was said to have played down the significance of the investigation and its impact on the university. He reportedly told them nothing about the Sandusky shower incident with a young boy—which he recalled being told at the time involved only "horseplay" between Sandusky and the boy—that he knew had occurred in February 2001. Thus when the presentment was published that Saturday morning and became a raging national and international story all over the media, the Internet, and social media, the board was caught totally unprepared and was shocked, like everyone else—despite the fact that they had a legal obligation under state law as "trustees" to be informed and prepared at all times to protect the interests, brand, and reputation of Penn State University.

From the morning of the presentment's publication, in the media and from a flurry of telephone calls and emails between themselves and from their families and friends, members of the board of trustees, like the rest of America, were horrified to read the awful details of what a "graduate assistant"—the anonymous expression used in the presentment—had seen Sandusky do to a young ten- to twelve-year-old boy while, he thought, he was alone in the Lasch Building shower room on a Friday night. The "graduate assistant" was quickly identified in the media as a twenty-seven-year-old Paterno assistant named Mike McQueary. McQueary told the grand jury that he had visited his locker in the Lasch Building about nine or nine-thirty in the evening on Friday, February 9, 2001.* He said he went to retrieve a few things from his locker, just off the shower room. The presentment said that McQueary was "surprised to find the lights and showers on." It continued:

> He then heard rhythmic, slapping sounds. He believed the sounds to be those of sexual activity. . . . He looked into the shower. He saw a naked boy, Victim 2, whose age he estimated to be ten years old, with his hands up against the wall, being subjected to anal intercourse by a naked Sandusky. The graduate assistant was shocked but noticed both Victim 2 and Sandusky saw him. The graduate assistant left immediately, distraught.

Emotionally shaken, McQueary first went to visit his father and reported what he had seen. They agreed that his first call should be to Coach Paterno. The next morning, Saturday, February 10, McQueary visited Coach Paterno at his home. He told the grand jury that he told the coach that Sandusky was engaged in sexual activity with the young boy, but he did not go into any graphic detail.

The presentment stated that Coach Paterno had waited until Sunday to call his immediate supervisor—what the law required him to do—the athletic director, Tim Curley, to report what he had heard from McQueary. Paterno told the grand jury that he told Curley "that the graduate assistant had seen Jerry Sandusky in the Lasch

---

* The original presentment had mistakenly dated McQueary's sighting of Sandusky's sexual assault as Friday night, March 1, 2002. That error was subsequently corrected by the time Sandusky went to trial in June 2012.

Building showers *fondling or doing something of a sexual nature to a young boy.*"*

The grand jury indicted Curley and Schultz because, as the presentment explained, they did not believe either man's testimony was entirely truthful when they denied knowing that Sandusky had engaged in sexual conduct with the young boy on that Friday evening, February 9. Curley said that Paterno had not referred to sexual conduct and he had not told Schultz about sexual conduct between Sandusky and the young boy—and Schultz told the grand jury the same thing—despite Coach Paterno's contrary testimony. The grand jury believed Paterno and accused Curley and Schultz of perjury. They also indicted both men for failing to report what Paterno (and, subsequently, McQueary) had allegedly told them about this sexual assault to the appropriate state agency or to law enforcement authorities.

For the next one hundred hours or so—from Saturday morning, November 5, to Wednesday evening, November 9—virtually all of the thirty-two members of the board put aside their jobs and their families and personal lives and wrestled with what most would describe as one of the most difficult and painful decisions they ever had to make in their lives.

Through these four days, they described holding multiple conference calls, individual calls to fellow trustees and with friends and Penn

---

* These words in the presentment were virtually identical to the actual sworn testimony by Coach Paterno that he gave to the grand jury, unknown by the board or anyone, until December 17, 2011, when Paterno's testimony was read verbatim by an assistant Pennsylvania attorney general at the public preliminary hearing before the presiding judge, held to determine whether the three men who were indicted should stand for trial. As will be seen, the fact that Coach Paterno had admitted to knowing about sexual conduct by Sandusky and a small boy in his own athletic facility building, and that it involved some form of "fondling" of the young boy, was little known even months after the testimony was read publicly on December 17 at the preliminary hearing. Most alumni and, it appears, the media don't know about this Paterno grand jury testimony that he knew about Sandusky's sexually assaulting a young boy that night in the Lasch Building showers in February 2001, yet for more than ten years, aside from one phone call or meeting, he did nothing else.

State alumni, sleepless nights of torment and anguish. On Monday morning, November 7, they insisted that Curley and Schultz be told they were being placed on "administrative leave" (removed from their positions, but with pay).

Finally, board members agreed that they had to meet in person to make the most difficult decisions of all. On Wednesday evening, November 9, they met at the university's historic administration office building, called "Old Main," gathering in a big conference room to continue their discussions. Late that afternoon, they met with Penn State president Graham Spanier, who had served for more than sixteen years, gaining national stature during that time for his outstanding leadership in making Penn State one of the nation's great universities academically, in faculty, and in research. His friend for years, the board chair Steve Garban, reported to him that the board could not give him the vote of confidence that he had asked for—mainly because he had failed to keep them informed on a timely basis, going all the way back to his decision not to inform them about the 2001 Sandusky incident and because of his issuance of a statement of "unconditional support" of Messrs. Curley and Schultz shortly after the presentment was published on Saturday, November 5, without consulting the board. Mr. Spanier offered to step aside and the board agreed.* He saw his decision as necessary because the "buck" stopped with him as president, even though he always contended that he would have immediately reported Sandusky had he known that he had sexually assaulted the young boy in that shower in 2001. (Long after Spanier's resignation, he still had many friends who believed his assertion that had he truly known that Sandusky had been sexually assaulting the young boy in the shower, he would have immediately called the authorities.)

By about 10:00 p.m. on November 9, the trustees had made what they described as the most "painful" decision of all: to require that

---

* The board technically terminated him "without cause" so that he maintained his rights to compensation and other benefits under the existing contract.

their beloved football coach, Joe Paterno, step down after almost a half century.

They communicated that decision to Coach Paterno at 10:30 p.m. by telephone. They did so because they believed at the time that there was no better alternative way to deliver the news. That unfortunate timing and method of communicating the decision would come back to haunt them, the subject of criticism by Paterno and non-Paterno supporters alike.

Vice Chair John Surma announced the board's decision to remove Coach Paterno and terminate President Spanier at a nationally televised press conference at about 10:45 p.m.

The immediate reaction on campus was a firestorm—literally and figuratively. Students and Paterno supporters from the town—it was hard to distinguish the two—started some fires and there were some minor instances of vandalism.

By the next morning, the actual firestorm became virtual on the Internet, in social media, and throughout the national network of dedicated and loyal Penn State alumni, numbering more than half a million. The alumni blogosphere and social networks lit up with outraged reaction on the removal of Coach Paterno, especially when the Paterno family made it known to the media that the coach had fulfilled his legal obligation by reporting the incident the following day to Mr. Curley, the athletic director, who was his immediate supervisor. Sources quoted from the family stated that it was the university administration that had failed to follow up and conduct a thorough investigation to stop Sandusky from his additional alleged sexual assaults of young boys on the Penn State campus and elsewhere.

Famous Penn State alumni—such as All-Pro player for the Pittsburgh Steelers Franco Harris, who played for and loved Joe Paterno—condemned the board for its decision, demanded an apology to Joe Paterno, and demanded his immediate reinstatement.

Less than two weeks after Coach Paterno's removal, on November 21, 2011, an "independent task force" of the board, headed by trustee Kenneth Frazier and including board trustees, faculty, and students, announced it had retained as "special investigative counsel" the law firm headed by Louis Freeh, former director of the FBI under President Bill Clinton and former U.S. District Court judge. His written mandate, as guaranteed by Ken Frazier, was total independence. Judge Freeh would have access to all records at the university, all university employees would be urged to cooperate with his team thoroughly, and he would publish the report of his investigation without prior review by the board. Thus, the board would not be in a position even to read the report in advance in order to have time to prepare an appropriate response—something that some later came to regret. It was generally understood by board members and the media that Mr. Freeh's mandate from the independent task force was to conduct an investigation and make factual findings in his report based on evidence.

During the next several weeks and through early January, the anger grew, and there were personal calls and emails to individual members of the board that were so hateful and threatening that some feared for their and their families' safety, and asked for (and received) special law enforcement surveillance of their homes just in case.

The outrage expressed publicly and individually by Penn State alumni who loved Coach Paterno about the board's decision to remove him as football coach might have seemed excessive at times. But it also accurately reflected the admiration for all that Coach Paterno had done for Penn State through the years—not just the successful football teams, but his commitment to academic excellence by his football players, his generous financial donations to the university, and his willingness to help raise considerable funds for Penn State.

Making matters worse, there was also a vacuum of facts and understanding about why the board made the decision it did. For example, very few alumni knew that the board's decision meant that Coach Paterno had been removed as coach for only the last three games of the season, since he had already announced that Wednesday, November 9, he was resigning at the end of the year, and that he hadn't been "fired," as the media widely reported. Rather, Coach Paterno remained a professor with full compensation rights under his continuing contract (worth, as would later be reported, millions of dollars to him and his family). And few knew that the coach had told the grand jury under oath the previous January that back in 2001, he knew that Sandusky had been seen engaging in conduct of a "sexual nature" involving "fondling" with a young boy alone in the Lasch Building showers.

What alumni and the media got from the board was silence and "no comments" after press inquiries, and unanswered accusations that the board had been guilty of a "rush to judgment," without giving the coach an opportunity to be heard and to defend himself, which was often said to be a violation of the coach's due process rights. The reason for the silence was understandable concern by legal advisors about any public statements during a criminal proceeding, with individuals set to be tried, and also about the inevitable filing of civil lawsuits against the university by the victims of Sandusky's alleged sexual assault.

However, by early December, the media—especially in the four media markets of Philadelphia, Harrisburg, Pittsburgh, and State College—had become increasingly frustrated, as were Penn State alumni, by the board's silence and by the university's failure to respond to basic questions about what happened, when, how, and why. Reporters couldn't even find out how much the university was paying outside attorneys and consultants as well as Coach Paterno and Messrs. Spanier, Curley, and Schultz.

THE ASSIGNMENT—BUT CAN THE "RULES" APPLY?

It was about that time—in early December 2011—that I was called by the university's general counsel, Cynthia Baldwin, a former Pennsylvania Supreme Court justice and former board member, and asked to consider offering crisis management advice to the new president, Rodney Erickson, about how to deal with the immediate crisis among alumni and the media regarding the board's decision to remove Coach Paterno and how it was done.

Justice Baldwin, a person of high integrity with love for her alma mater as strong as anyone I met during my experience working for Penn State, recognized the need for greater transparency to address the crisis and "turn the corner" to remind all that the story of Penn State should not forever be defined by this tragic event. She knew that President Erickson would welcome that approach of openness and honesty—she wisely understood that was his basic nature as a natural leader. And, as she said, she thought my reputation for recommending transparency as almost always the first rule of crisis management would be compatible with all of Erickson's basic instincts.

Rodney Erickson had been the provost of Penn State University since 1999, a position, in effect, with responsibility for overseeing the deans, faculty, and all academic disciplines and departments at the university. Before that, he had been a professor of geography and business administration for more than twenty-five years and had served as dean of the graduate school since 1985. On Wednesday afternoon, November 9, when the decision to require then president Spanier to step down had been made by the board, Vice Chair John Surma had approached Rod Erickson and asked him whether he would be willing to serve as the "interim" successor as president. Erickson had agreed, understanding the difficult situation he would face but also appreciating the importance of the university's having immediate continuity of leadership in the face of this crisis. Several weeks later, by the time I met with him in early December, Rod Erickson had been named the official next president of Penn State.

Several days after my phone conversation with the university general counsel, I met with President Erickson on the State College campus in his spacious office in Old Main. As I walked into the office, it occurred to me that just a few weeks before, the office had been occupied for more than sixteen years by former president Spanier.

In about five minutes, maybe just two minutes, I made up my

mind about Rod Erickson. He was, simply put, the real deal—sincere, authentic, straightforward, and both soft-spoken and gentle in tone but with what I immediately sensed was a toughness grounded in principles that guided him, which he would not compromise. One such principle, I confirmed to my relief, was his commitment to openness and transparency—the latter word the key one he communicated when he held his first press conference after it was announced he was taking over for President Spanier.

President Erickson answered all my questions without hesitation, in the fewest possible words, with clear-eyed truth. I realized that he was typecast for this particular situation and this particular crisis—fostering the opposite of the opaque, somewhat secretive culture that critics perceived existed during the administration of President Spanier and under Coach Paterno's football program.

His answers to my questions convinced me that Rod Erickson had no advance knowledge of Sandusky's specific conduct or anyone's knowledge about that until the presentment was published on November 5, although he recalled vaguely reading about reports of a grand jury investigation around March 2011 (in a local Harrisburg newspaper, the *Patriot Gazette*), but his impression was that the investigation had been long-running and didn't seem to be going anywhere. He also said he knew nothing at the time about the extent of Coach Paterno's knowledge about the Sandusky incident.

I accepted the assignment, hoping that I could help President Erickson establish a new culture of transparency, as a first step toward the ultimate goal of "turning the corner" after the Sandusky trial and after the Louis Freeh report was completed and being able to tell the positive narrative about Penn State as a great university that should not be defined by this tragic situation.

As a first step, with Justice Baldwin's assistance and advice in drafting, President Erickson agreed to a new written, public policy of "full disclosure unless . . ."—with the "unless" specifically defined as information barred by law, contractual provisions, or personal privacy rights. His administration team, led by the able and straight-talking Thomas G. Poole, the vice president for administration, worked with our crisis management team to develop a new website to post all questions and answers that the press and alumni were asking that could be answered consistent with this "full disclosure unless . . ." policy. Ultimately, we called the new website *Openness*—an unsubtle message that directly communicated the theme of the new Erickson administration. But the main questions—the two "elephants in the room"— remained unanswered: Why did the board reach its decision on Coach Paterno, and why did it deliver the news the way it did? The ultimate crisis management goal—to put the bad story behind them and to hit the "reset" button, allowing Penn State to resume a positive narrative about the university—would be stymied until those two questions were answered in detail by the board.

The conclusion that the board had to break its legally enforced silence was further reinforced when President Erickson held three town meetings sponsored by the Penn State alumni association: in Pittsburgh on January 11, Valley Forge on January 12, and New York City on January 13. During these meetings, he was unable to answer these two major questions—which were often shouted at him by angry alumni—since Erickson had not been in the room during the board's deliberations between November 5 and 9. The most he could do was stand in the front of the room, refer generally to the board's fiduciary responsibilities to serve the best interests of the university, and then, in effect, serve as a sponge for the anger in the room.

The media coverage of Erickson's town meetings was, not surprisingly, somewhat negative; the stories depicted Penn State alumni fury with the board of trustees and frustration with President Erickson's inability to answer basic questions on Paterno's removal. The clips from TV interviews and angry outbursts from the audience were reminiscent of the Tea Party meetings over health care in the summer of 2010. But ironically, the one positive outcome was that President Erickson was depicted sympathetically by the media as doing his best under the circumstances, and even the angry alumni seemed to give him a pass and express sympathy that the board was maintaining its silence and he couldn't do anything about that.

"TELL IT ALL . . . YOURSELF . . . PERSONALLY"

On early Friday morning, January 13, 2012, I was on the Acela express train from Washington, D.C., to New York City to meet President Erickson to join him for a private lunch with leading Penn State alumni from the business and professional community. Shortly after the train left Union Station in Washington, I received a call from Steven Garban, the chairman of the board of trustees, asking whether I would offer advice to him and the vice chair, John Surma, on what the board could or should do to halt the downward spiral of negative media coverage that was harming the university's reputation, short- and long-term. I said I could offer some options. I agreed to be available to talk again to him and Vice Chairman Surma later in the day, after 4:00 p.m., when I would be on the Acela returning to Washington from New York City. We set the call for about 6:00 p.m.

When I arrived in New York, I met President Erickson at a Midtown dining club where he was scheduled to meet with several dozen leading Penn State alumni, many of whom were New York City professional and business leaders. We talked beforehand about the tough experiences he had had during the town meetings. We agreed that unless the board explained itself better, there was little he could do about his sensation of being a punching bag.

After the private alumni luncheon, I was struck by two things that helped me understand the crisis management challenge we faced: the profound sadness in the room at what had happened to the reputation and brand of their beloved university, and the "awesome"—that was the word that kept occurring to me as I talked to people at my table and then listened to the Q-and-A discussion after the lunch—dedication, loyalty, and just plain love these men and women, young and old, had toward Penn State University. I was astonished and impressed by the intensity of this devotion. It was almost as if Penn State was a best friend who had been hurt or attacked, with a reflexive, near-automatic response of defensiveness and protectiveness based on unconditional love. Yes, there were some who were disappointed about the decision to replace Coach Paterno, and some expressed anger, too, especially about the way the board had chosen to communicate the decision late at night over the telephone. Others supported the decision.

I learned once again the crisis management necessity of getting the facts out and getting in front of the story. Even among these so-phisticated business leaders there was real frustration at the board's unwillingness to explain itself.

President Erickson lived up to, indeed exceeded, my expectations when he spoke briefly and I could observe him in person answering questions. His honesty and dignity impressed everyone. He defused whatever anger was in the room quickly. I could hear comments after the lunch about this great and soft-spoken man who was doing his best to shepherd Penn State through the intense media crisis it was going through.

I had also arranged a sit-down after the luncheon for President Er-ickson with a young *New York Times* reporter, Mark Viera, who had written a few stories in the aftermath of the Sandusky news and pre-sentment. I had also learned from a reporter friend on the *Times* that Viera was a Penn State grad. I hoped the result would be a sympathetic personal portrait of President Erickson in the *Times*. I knew if that oc-curred, since the *Times* was so influential with other reporters, it might provide a much-needed positive counterpoint to the overwhelming negative media coverage of the Penn State crisis and the town meetings.

The Erickson interview with Viera went well. Viera's questions were mostly about Rod's background and personal history and his feelings about the tough position he was in, having to face alumni anger without having the answers about the board's decision-making process and rationale. (As I had hoped, the portrait of Erickson appeared in the much-read Sunday, January 15, *Times*, placed in the sports section due to the media focus on the Paterno decision, and was as positive and sympathetic as could be expected within the overall media-portrayed negative context of the Penn State story.)

I boarded the return train at 4:00 p.m., but it was crowded and noisy, with happy-hour festivities going on. As 6:00 p.m. approached, I realized I needed some privacy. The only place where I could find that was the bathroom at the end of the car. I took the call at 6:00 p.m., and it was Garban and Surma, who immediately got to the point (a style that I became accustomed to in all my dealings with Garban). Garban said he understood the board was being hammered because it wasn't responding to questions and that this was hurting President Erickson's effectiveness. He reminded me that the board's outside attorneys were concerned about any board member speaking to the press due to continuing criminal proceedings against individuals who deserved a fair trial and threats of civil litigation by the victims against the university. So what did I recommend—both as a lawyer, who understood these legal concerns, and as a media strategist?

Tell the truth, I said to him and Surma.

Follow the basic rules of crisis management—assemble the facts, get out in front at long last, and develop simple messages to explain what happened and why. Sooner or later, the facts about what happened on the evening of November 9 would come out. I would work with the attorneys to assure them that the board would be expressing its feelings and perspective on its decisions and that these would inevitably become public, sooner or later.

This was always my main argument to attorneys concerned about speaking to the media during a legal crisis: If the facts were coming out anyway, why not get them out yourself sooner rather than later so you had a chance to shape the story and put the negative facts, if there were any, in an appropriate context first?

I said I would arrange an immediate sit-down among members

of the board and one or more reporters from leading media organizations. I promised I would work closely with university attorneys, remembering the mistake I had made and vowed never to make again during the Martha Stewart experience. I said I would be present during the interview to ensure that nothing prejudicial to the criminal or civil court proceedings was stated.

"Okay," Surma said, typically using as few words as possible to convey his message. "Let's go ahead."

Steve Garban agreed. He asked what the next step would be, sounding relieved. I told them that we needed to move quickly. I told them they were in a deep hole that was getting deeper with every "no comment" response. I told them we should get started if possible the next morning. I said I needed to talk to as many board members as possible on a conference call so I could hear their answers directly: how they voted the way they did on November 9 and why they delivered the news to Coach Paterno the way they did.

That meant a Saturday-morning conference call. I expected some resistance—knowing how difficult it would be on a Friday night to assemble a significant number of board members on the next day, Saturday morning.

But Garban and Surma said they would make that happen.

CATHARSIS ON THE TELEPHONE

On Saturday, January 14, at 9:00 a.m., I sat alone at the kitchen table, as my wife and two sons were getting ready to go skiing. I sat with a notebook in front of me and made the conference call. For five minutes, the board secretary announced the names of the persons calling in. I knew there were thirty-two members of the board, including the governor, but I didn't know how many would be calling in on such short notice. I tried to keep track, but I lost count after twenty or so names were announced.

Finally, I heard the voice of John Surma, telling me that he had told everyone what my advice was and they were ready to answer my questions. I told them I was there to urge them to tell the truth to the media—to defend themselves from the attacks and get their story out, for better or worse, once and for all. I heard someone say, quietly, "Thank God." Another said, "Thank you," and a third voice said, "Finally." There were murmurs of approval from other voices on the conference call.

My original plan for the call, naturally, was to begin with the first rule of crisis management: Understand all the facts and compile a complete factual narrative. My plan was to then walk them through the kind of day-by-day "tick-tock" from November 5 to 9 that I expected a reporter would want to do, with various people jumping in to help me construct a collective narrative and explanation in preparation for a reporter's asking the same questions.

The work product I was aiming for after I completed the interviews was a written statement of what happened, which I would prepare and get circulated, ultimately to be approved by all the attorneys. Once approved, the statement could be issued publicly to the media and widely disseminated to Penn State alumni through its website, its five-hundred-thousand-plus email list, and social media. I believed, however, that there was little time to get this done, given the growing anger and frustration of the media and Penn State alumni.

But then something else started to happen—something I hadn't planned, something that happened naturally and, as it turned out, something much better. Emotion took over. One person began to speak, telling a personal story from the first news of the presentment on Saturday to the sleepless nights to the final evening when the painful decision was made to remove Coach Paterno. The words were about feelings and anguish and conflict and torment—not just about facts.

It was like listening to a group of people giving something akin to religious testimony, each experiencing a catharsis. So I allowed it to happen, naturally, as one person ended and another person picked up and started talking, one at a time, sometimes for twenty or thirty minutes.

The perspectives were different, based on different personal backgrounds, different life experiences, and different relationships with Coach Paterno and the football program. Some had little or no relationship with either. But one thing they all had in common: the pain and emotional conflict each experienced as they approached the moment when the decision to vote on removing or not removing widely revered Coach Paterno was made.

I sat at my kitchen table on that Saturday morning, listening, mesmerized, as some voices broke, some expressing such deep emotion that they had to stop talking for a minute or two before continuing. As time passed, it occurred to me that each person was sharing some of these thoughts and emotions for the first time, and it was a good thing for each of them to do so and listen to others do so.

By about 1:00 p.m., we were only halfway through, and everyone sounded exhausted, as was I. When I asked whether we should suspend the discussion, since I said I had heard enough of the story to understand what we needed to do with the media, there was no hesitation. Those who hadn't spoken wished to continue and have their say. And those who had spoken still wanted to listen to the rest speak. So we scheduled another call for the next morning.

I was moved, even honored, by this experience. Here I was, a stranger to almost all of them on the phone, and they were sharing their raw emotions with me, trusting me to make the right judgment about what they could or should say to the media.

WASHINGTON POST INTERVIEW: "I WISH I HAD DONE MORE"

Later that day, I received a message from Sally Jenkins, a *Washington Post* sports columnist, asking me to call her about an exclusive interview she had just completed with Coach Joe Paterno.

She asked me if the board had a response to Coach Paterno's contention that he had done the right thing legally by reporting what he heard from McQueary about Sandusky's conduct to his immediate supervisor, Tim Curley, the athletic director. Did I disagree? I told her I couldn't answer such a question on behalf of the full board—that I was not authorized to do so. I wanted to tell her to hold off on writing her story till after the board had a chance to tell its story in the media, but I decided that would be inappropriate.

I knew that medical reports would be widely read in newspapers and on the Internet the next day, saying that Coach Paterno was very ill with lung cancer, and that Jenkins's interview would be seen as a real journalistic coup. I also felt bad for the coach and his family, knowing he was very sick with lung cancer.

The Jenkins interview appeared on the *Post* website that night and was published the next day. The article was understandably sympathetic to Coach Paterno. One comment Coach Paterno made that was quoted by Jenkins in her exclusive interview turned out to be more significant than I realized later on when I first read it in the *Post*. . . .

He said: "In hindsight, I wish I had done more."

Early the next morning, Sunday, the board conference call resumed, with virtually everyone calling in, including those who had already told their stories to me, while the rest recounted their own personal narratives. Again I was struck that the individual board members seemed to need the cathartic experience not only of describing their own difficult journey to the decision to remove Coach Paterno, but also of listening to the others' perspectives and emotional experiences.

At about 1:00 p.m., all had spoken. I had already made up my mind the night before that the first rule of crisis management—get the facts out—needed a modification. Instead of "facts," I realized what we needed to "get out" were the individual emotions and feelings underlying the decision to remove Coach Paterno. It was no longer about trying to prove that the board had made the "right" decision. No matter how the board explained it, there would be passionate alumni and students who loved Coach Paterno and who would not ever agree with the board's decision. At least, I hoped, even these critics would come to appreciate the sincerity and deep anguish each board member had experienced in making a decision they considered to be the right one.

So the key crisis management strategy hit me—and, more accurately, it happened as a result of my listening to the true, deeply felt emotions of all the board members who had made the difficult decision to remove Coach Paterno, even just for the last three games of the season while still continuing his contract, worth millions of dollars of payments to him and his family. The revelation was that this was *not* a strategy designed to *defend* the decision—or to criticize or condemn Coach Paterno, whose great work for the university and his legacy of the "Grand Experiment" of demanding that athletes also achieve the goal of academic excellence were facts that would not change, even though, in his own words, he should have "done more" once he had heard about Sandusky's evil conduct in the shower that Friday night in February 2001. Rather, it was a strategy to explain *feelings and emotions* that provided the context for that difficult decision. I knew this would not satisfy the most severe alumni critics of the decision. But I hoped it would at least, over time, allow all to understand better what board members had felt and had gone through in making a decision that in their hearts they thought was the right thing to do for the best interests of the university in the long term—their "fiduciary duty" as trustees of the university, past, present, and future.

I believed that would be the necessary first step in the healing for alumni and students and the board of trustees—*healing that, I recognized, had become the chief immediate priority of this crisis management challenge.* I told the board members on the phone that in the sit-down with a reporter that I wanted each person to initiate as soon as possible, I wanted each person to repeat the same process they had just been through—one story at a time, one person and emotional sharing at a time, but this time in front of a reporter, on the record. There was no dissent.

328 | LANNY J. DAVIS

I realized that since the board was meeting in State College that coming Thursday and Friday, January 19–20, it would be important to get the board's story out—the emotional authenticity of what they experienced when they made their difficult decisions on November 9—if possible before the board meetings. There would be a substantial media contingent there, as well as some of the most vocal alumni critics. All would be pressuring the board to explain itself. A comprehensive story in a national newspaper would serve as an ideal predicate story from which all other stories could be derived. Ideally, then, a major article about the board's reasons for the decisions it made on November 9—individually expressed, as I had heard them—should be published before the board's Thursday meeting. But how to get this done within a day or two? It seemed impossible.

I asked board members on the Sunday call if a few could volunteer to meet with a reporter or reporters as soon as Tuesday, meaning the article would possibly be published on the day before the board met in State College.

I already had the *New York Times* in mind as the ideal newspaper to write the story because of its national circulation, its first-in-the-class reputation for excellence as the "newspaper of record," and especially, its top-rated sports department. The article, I believed, would probably appear as a lead article in the *Times*' well-read sports section and not on the front page as a hard news or political story.

I asked for volunteers, expecting only a handful to be willing. To my surprise (and relief), many of them offered to be there and participate. Early Monday morning, John Surma gave me the astonishing news: Thirteen board members had volunteered to attend and do the interviews. Surma suggested we locate the interview at Teterboro Airport so that those trustees who would be in State College could board the university's private jet and fly to New Jersey.

I immediately called a friend at the *Times* for advice on who could do the story. After consulting with an editor, my friend called me back with the name of a leading sports reporter, Pete Thamel, who was assigned to do the story. Also assigned to coauthor would be Mark Viera, the same young *Times* reporter and Penn State alumnus who had interviewed President Erickson on Friday afternoon and whose sympathetic portrait had appeared on Sunday.

Within hours, our plans were set: The two reporters would meet the thirteen board members at Teterboro Airport on Tuesday morning—just three days after the first conference call on Saturday morning.

"A RESPONSIBILITY TO EVERY CHILD"

Tuesday morning, January 17, 2011, the thirteen board members sat around a conference table in a business office at Teterboro Airport. Thamel and Viera were at the head of the table with their tape recorder.

I reminded both reporters of the ground rules that we had agreed to: Everything was on the record, but they agreed (as did their editor, with whom I had talked the day before) that the tape recording could be used only for accuracy and had to be destroyed after publication. I certainly did not want the recording to be posted on the Internet and perhaps misused or taken out of context.

I had also agreed that a *New York Times* photographer could accompany the two reporters. But when he asked for one group shot of all the trustees sitting at the conference table, instinctively I said no. I saw the best course was to stick with individuality as the way this story would be told. That meant the photographs had to be individual and personal as well, not a set-up group shot. I wanted the photographs to be taken as each person was telling his or her story. That way, their true emotions would be depicted individually—the visual version of the personal stories and emotions that would be appearing in print. Around the table, one at a time, the trustees told their stories to the reporters as they had told them to me.

Board chairman Steven Garban began and within minutes choked up when he admitted that his friendship and love for Paterno might have compromised his independence and judgment. Garban was a former captain of the Penn State football team, and he had maintained a close friendship with Joe Paterno over the thirty-three-year career he spent working with and for the university. He showed that he was truly an honorable man and honest about his mistakes of judgment.

Paul Suhey, a former football captain, close friend of the entire Paterno family, and an orthopedic surgeon in the State College area, described the love he had for Coach Paterno. He said he always thought of the coach as a second father who took care of him, and he felt Paterno was centrally responsible for his successful career. Suhey described how sick he felt as he read the presentment, sick for the child victims of Sandusky. But he also described his personal torment in supporting any decision to remove his beloved football coach, Joe Paterno. "I knew we had a problem," he said, with keeping Coach Paterno as coach, but he stopped, tearing up, and couldn't continue.

Karen Peetz, a senior executive at Bank of New York Mellon, was mentored by Graham Spanier when she was a student and all-star athlete at Penn State. For her, the decision to support Spanier's stepping down as president was personally very difficult, but she knew there was no choice. She felt that as highly as she regarded President Spanier, even up to the moment of decision, she felt he had not shown the level of leadership that had been required. "Part of being a leader at that level is to be a risk manager and to think through what might happen," she said. "We were up against the challenge of our lives."

As each trustee told his or her story, one word was repeated more than any other: "children." Two other words were repeated by many board members: "done more." The main reason they supported Coach Paterno's removal as coach was that he had not "done more" for the children—the same words the coach himself had used in his interview with Sally Jenkins.

One of the most powerful statements made that morning came from Kenneth C. Frazier, an African-American attorney from the inner city of Philadelphia, who described his love and appreciation for

Joe Paterno in very personal terms. He went on to attend Harvard Law School and became first general counsel and then CEO of a famous medical device and supply company, Merck Corporation.

When asked about whether Coach Paterno's supporters were right that he had done his legal duty and could not be blamed for not doing more, Ken Frazier continued: "To me, it wasn't about guilt or innocence in a legal sense," regarding Paterno's decision not to go to the police for more than ten years while other children were being brutally sexually assaulted by Sandusky. "It was about these norms of society that I'm talking about: that every adult has a responsibility for every other child in our community. And we have a responsibility not to do the minimum, the legal requirement. We have a responsibility for ensuring that we can take every effort that's within our power not only to prevent further harm to that child, but to every other child."

Both reporters looked up, stunned by the eloquence and passion of that statement. I saw them look down and write some notes in their notebooks. I knew that Frazier's statement would be highlighted in the story.

After all the board members' individual stories were over, the two reporters began asking questions. As I expected, they wanted to nail down the "tick-tock" chronology of what had happened each day between the publication of the presentment on Saturday morning, November 5, and the November 9, 10:00 p.m., decision of the board to remove Coach Paterno. The reporters heard three reasons that various board members had articulated for removing the coach for the last three games of the season.

First, some board members thought the coach's announcement that he would stay as coach until the end of the year, and that the board should essentially mind its own business, was an unacceptable challenge to the board's legal responsibility as university trustees under state law. Since Curley had been placed on administrative leave, meaning there was no longer an athletic director in place who would have the authority to make the decision on Paterno's employment status, the ultimate responsibility for determining Coach Paterno's fate, in fact, rested with the board.

A second reason was concern that Coach Paterno's presence on the sidelines of the forthcoming Saturday's football game would be a distraction for the players, and would inevitably focus attention on Sandusky.

But the third reason—the one that seemed to move them most—was the phrase that Coach Paterno himself had used in his *Washington Post* interview by Sally Jenkins. Coach Paterno "should have done more" over more than ten years than his minimal legal duty of reporting the horrific Sandusky sexual assault on a young boy in the Lasch Building shower. As they saw it, he should be held accountable for that failure of leadership.

Then the reporters turned to Vice Chair John Surma to recount the last moments of the decision and the aftermath, in which he played the central role.

He said that he had asked everyone in the room, and Pennsylvania governor Tom Corbett on the telephone, whether there were any dissenting votes about asking Coach Paterno to step aside and no longer serve as Penn State's football coach.

He said that there was only silence. He could hear, he said, a few whispers of "yes," or "I agree." Okay, he told the reporters, that was that. The time was about 10:00 p.m., Wednesday, November 9. No one had dissented: thirty-two people from diverse backgrounds—from the Penn State University student representative, to leaders of the Agriculture and Engineering departments, to alumni elected representatives, to leaders of major companies, to the governor of Pennsylvania.

"I was lying in my bed that night shaking," said Ira M. Lubert, a board member and businessman, reflecting on what he went through when the decision they had made sunk in. "And I couldn't sleep—thinking, 'We just terminated Joe Paterno.'"

Then John Surma was asked by one of the two reporters to describe the controversial manner in which the news was communicated to Coach Paterno, over the telephone, at 10:30 that night.

"We had a bunch of bad choices," he said.

One that seemed unthinkable was for a delegation of board members to go to Paterno's home after 10:00 p.m., walk through the gauntlet of cameras, reporters, students, bright lights, and shouting Paterno supporters gathered on the front lawn, knock on the door, and deliver the news. There were also security concerns with doing so—as it turned out, well founded, given the fires and student anger exhibited shortly after the news of the coach's removal became public.

It was also a problem, said a few other board members to the reporters, to wait to tell the coach in person until the next morning. That would risk the coach's learning about the decision from someone else or, worse, from the media.

So, Surma explained, the phone call that night seemed to be the only available alternative, the best among what were all bad choices. There was some difficulty getting through to the coach on his home phone. Finally, an envelope with Steve Garban's cell phone number was given to Fran Ganter, the associate athletic director for football, who knew the Paternos well. He was asked to go to the Paterno home, just a few minutes from Old Main, where the board was meeting, and ask Coach Paterno to call Garban on his cell phone.

Within about a half hour, sometime around 10:30 p.m., Garban's phone rang. Garban sadly handed the phone to John Surma.

Surma had written down three points on a three-by-five card that he planned to say to Coach Paterno.

Point one was that the board had decided unanimously to remove Coach Paterno as football coach of Penn State, effective immediately.

Point two was that the board regretted having to deliver the message over the telephone.

Point three was that the coach's employment contract would continue, including all financial benefits and his continued status as a tenured faculty member.

As Surma explained, in his mind and that of other trustees, points two and three were important to convey to the coach—emphasizing that, while they had asked him to step down as coach immediately and not coach the last three games of the season, they were still intent on treating him and his family with dignity, in recognition of his years of service to the Penn State community and his contributions to the university for more than a half century.

When Surma picked up the phone and heard Paterno's voice, he immediately stated that he had three things to tell him and, without pausing, stated point one. But as soon as he got to the last words, "effective immediately," Paterno hung up the phone. Surma never got to points two and three.

Moments later, the phone rang again. It was Sue Paterno, Joe Paterno's wife. She had been friends with most of the board members for many years.

Surma answered the phone and heard her say, "After sixty-one years, he deserved better," she said. Then she hung up on Surma.

Even then, two months later, the reporters could see the trauma felt by Surma and others in the room with this abrupt and awkward method of communicating such a devastating message to the revered football coach for almost half a century. They still felt bad about how the message had been delivered—and even worse when Surma repeated the words from Sue Paterno, which seemed to ring true to everyone in the room.

The fact that they still felt they had no better alternatives didn't seem to help much. "It was regrettable," said the attorney Stephanie Deviney, as everyone nodded.

Pete Thamel, the lead *Times* reporter, broke the silence and said quietly, "Thank you, all. We have work to do—we are writing for publication in tomorrow's *Times*."

The board members stood and quietly left the conference room. It was a sensation similar to that of leaving a funeral service.

"CHOOSE SOMETHING LIKE A STAR"

One board member, Anne Riley, stayed behind as everyone else filed out, to say a few words to me.

When Anne introduced herself on the phone on Saturday morning just three days before, to tell her story, she said, simply, "I am an English teacher." She said she had attended Penn State and then had taught English at State College High School for thirty-one years and had retired from teaching in 1997. She remained active and involved in her community. She was first elected by the alumni to the seat designated "alumni trustee" in 1997, and had served five three-year terms. She was running for reelection in 2012.

Anne had described her great and continuing anguish in not dissenting from the decision to remove Coach Paterno, since her family, especially her dad, had been close to Coach Paterno and his family for more than forty years. Her dad, she said, had died in Coach Paterno's kitchen of a sudden heart attack as he and the coach were reviewing the last chapter of a book he had written on the history of Penn State football. She had been told that the coach had tried to revive him as he waited for the ambulance to arrive.

"I loved Coach Paterno, and this was awful for me," she told me on the phone on Saturday and repeated to the *Times* reporters. She came to her decision with great difficulty, moved by her conviction, as the coach himself told the *Post*'s Jenkins, that he should have "done more" for the children than just fulfilling his minimal legal duty to call the athletic director. She was also conscious of her legal, fiduciary duty as a trustee for the best interests of the university. She also felt bad about the removal of former president Graham Spanier, whom she admired greatly and still considered a close friend. She suffered greatly when she made the decision—and she continued to suffer long after the decision by alumni who were angry with her for making the decision. Out of all the board members, I felt a special affection and admiration for Anne Riley. Maybe because she had such a difficult emotional experience, perhaps worse than most of the board—not only making the decision but in the aftermath, where she lived firsthand, as a member of the State College community, dealing with the anger and (at times) hate expressed toward her often in person for the decision she made with the rest of the board on Coach Paterno.

I must say I also felt a special affection for her because she was so proud of being an English teacher, and I was reminded of the most memorable teacher I ever had, who had the most influence on me and my love of writing for the rest of my life—my English teacher Mr. T. C. Abbey, from my high school, Newark Academy.

The day before, Monday, I had received a call from Anne Riley. She wanted me to advise her about what to do about the huge volume of hate emails she was receiving each day, mostly from Penn State alumni upset about the Paterno decision. She said she was frightened by some of them. I told her I would make provisions for her safety and that the university's attorneys would look into the more threatening ones (which we did). During the conversation, she reminded me, again, "I am an English teacher—it helps me put things in perspective." I told her that my favorite poet was Robert Frost and about my favorite high school English teacher, Mr. Abbey, and how he had taught me to love Frost's poetry. She said she too loved Frost, especially his insights into human choices and contradictions and the difficulty of ensuring perfect outcomes to life's crises.

I had a feeling she was trying to teach me about crisis management's limitations.

So after everyone left the room, Anne hung back and handed me a piece of paper with some printed words on it. It was a Robert Frost poem titled "Choose Something Like a Star," which I had not read before.

She waited while I read it.

It began with the line "O Star (the fairest one in sight)," and ended, referring to that fairest of all stars:

It asks a little of us here.
It asks of us a certain height,
So when at times the mob is swayed
To carry praise or blame too far,
We may choose something like a star
To stay our minds on and be staid.

"It's a beautiful Frost poem, Anne," I said. "And just right for the occasion, especially, for you, the last two lines."

She nodded—satisfied, as every good English teacher would be, that I had gotten the lesson she wanted me to learn from the poem.

THE BOARD STORY IS FINALLY OUT—OR IS IT?

Later that day, I took several calls from Thamel and Viera, answering factual questions, including a few about the personal backgrounds of the trustees who had appeared for the interview.

I arrived at State College late that evening and checked into the Nittany Lion Inn. At about midnight, I found the thirty-two-hundred-word article posted on the *New York Times* website. I was very happy with it. It conveyed the personal, individual anguish of each board member, while still comprehensively reporting the flow of calls, deliberations, and decisions made between November 5 and the evening of November 9.

But it wasn't until the next morning, in the Wednesday, January 18, 2012, *New York Times*, that I saw the actual newspaper version of the story. There it was, filling the entire front page of the sports section. Then I flipped the page and saw a second full page on the back page. The banner headline on the first page read:

PENN STATE'S TRUSTEES RECOUNT PAINFUL DECISION
TO FIRE PATERNO

And there, in the middle of the page, in a large font, was Ken Frazier's quotation, just as I had suspected as soon as I saw the reporters' reaction after Ken spoke:

> We have a responsibility for ensuring that we can take every effort
> that's within our power not only to prevent further harm to that
> child, but to every other child.

And then I noticed that sprinkled on both pages, front and back, were individual photographs of various board members as they were speaking, not posed, their faces reflecting real pain, pain that was individual and authentic—just as the stories were individual and authentic. In other words, these personalized photos made the point even better than the text—the core message that I wished to communicate on behalf of the board: Whether you agree or disagree with the board's decision on Joe Paterno, they did it with anguish for highly personal and authentic reasons. I was also pleased to see that the reporters had chosen to include the key phrase that Paterno "should have done more"— his own words to the *Post*'s Sally Jenkins in his interview a few days before.

So it seemed we had accomplished the *beginning* of what we knew would be a long process of helping the university "turn the corner" and get the Sandusky story behind it. Before there could be any chance of finality, we knew, we had to wait for the Sandusky trial and verdicts and the Louis Freeh report, however either turned out.

But as to this first step, getting the board's true feelings and reasons for doing what it had done published, we had achieved the classic "predicate" story in the *New York Times*—more so than we could have ever imagined when we thought about getting a foundational story written. And all within three to four days.

But now, we knew, we had to follow up on the *Times* story to get the story out into the public domain and into the minds of average Penn State alumni, who might not have read, or might not have read closely and remembered, the *Times* story just a few days later. We knew the board's story needed to be repeated again and again in every possible venue—print media, broadcast TV news and cable, leading national media and Internet sites in sports, editorial pages, social media, and delivered directly and repeatedly for weeks and months to the more than five hundred thousand alumni who received the university's publications and whose email addresses were available.

We also planned to put President Erickson and several trustees (such as Anne Riley!) on national TV programs with mass audiences, such as ABC's *20/20* or CBS's *60 Minutes*. We knew that the national audience constituted the pool of potential student applicants, football players, and faculty—and they needed to have their questions answered, too. Rod Erickson was ideally suited for TV—his open and honest manner of speaking was exactly right for these kinds of focused interviews.

On the day of the publication of the *Times* story, we gave Pennsylvania reporters from the major newspapers and wire services, as well as the State College paper and the Penn State student newspaper, the *Daily Collegian*, each a chance to do their own personal interviews with various board members. We knew Pennsylvania reporters would be unhappy with the *Times*'s getting access to board members first when all of them had repeatedly asked for, and been refused, the same opportunity. But we explained to them that the university needed to get the full story out nationally, all at once, with the imprimatur of the power and respectability of a national newspaper.

On the second and final day of the public board meeting, Friday, January 20, 2012, a new chairman of the board was elected—Karen Peetz, the Bank of New York Mellon executive who had participated in the *Times* interview at Teterboro. She laid out a program of reform and transparency for the board going forward, including the new *Openness* website, more avenues of communication with alumni and students and faculty, and more oversight and participation by board members with various new committees, including a board "Outreach

Committee"—meaning outreach to the broader Penn State community as well as the media.

Karen Peetz's approach, style, and demeanor—and the substance of her opening remarks as the new chair of the board—evoked the impression (intended) of reform, responsiveness, sensitivity, and participation by the board, by students and faculty, by alumni. The reaction from many in the media and among most alumni was very positive toward Karen Peetz as well as toward the new vice chair, Keith Masser, a farmer who, in plain language, made a brief speech to the board after his election, promising a new era of reform and transparency and doing the right thing for the interests of the university—past, present, and future.

After the board meeting on Friday, January 20, there was a meeting of the newly created committee under Chairperson Peetz, the Outreach Committee. I set out a plan going forward in a variety of arenas to begin the process of new leadership and a new culture of leadership at Penn State.

First we needed to get out more pervasively the narrative described in the *Times* story. The plan included repeats in other national newspapers and cable programs, and the need for one written comprehensive statement summarizing the board's reasons for doing what it did—knowing that relatively few people had actually read the *New York Times* story and there needed to be multiple, repeated efforts to communicate with the Penn State alumni and the greater community of students and faculty.

I presented an extensive program for explaining the board's decision through the media, on broadcast and cable TV, on the social networks, and in the blogosphere, along with outreach to students, faculty, and alumni and openness to the media to respond to all questions except those barred by law or contract. The board would also meet with reporters and editorial writers as the university waited for the Sandusky trial and the Freeh report publication. But most important, they would have to be ready to hit the "reset" button after the

Freeh report was completed—with a rollout of all the positive achievements among students and faculty, and, particularly, in research that had made Penn State one of the great universities in the world—one that was not known just for football.

We also had plans for Penn State's Sandusky experience to become a national teaching moment on the issue of child sexual abuse—especially how to see warning signs of early conduct by pedophiles and predators and to learn about taking personal responsibility, as Ken Frazier had so eloquently put it, to go to the authorities in time to save the children, current and future.

President Erickson had also approved Penn State's holding a national conference on child sexual abuse. We had already obtained the participation in such a conference of the famous and influential National Center for Missing and Exploited Children (NCMEC). The purpose of the conference was to bring together experts to address the issue of protective measures and recognition of early warning signs of child sexual abuse. The president and cofounder of NCMEC, Ernie Allen, had already communicated with President Erickson and expressed the center's willingness to lend its prestige and reputation. That conference was ultimately held on October 29 and 30, 2012.

Those were our plans—to get the story out repeatedly in all media venues—as soon as the board meeting ended on January 20, 2012.

Until Coach Paterno died two days later.

THE PASSING OF COACH PATERNO

Early in the morning on January 22, 2012, Coach Joe Paterno passed away from lung cancer.

There was widespread grief and sympathy among hundreds of thousands of Penn Staters who loved Coach Pa not just for the national football program he created that made Penn State a household name across the country, but for the record of financial generosity

342 | LANNY J. DAVIS

he had shown the university through substantial gifts and especially for his stand in insisting on academic excellence in combination with athletics—one of the first coaches in America to take such a stand.

Understandably and predictably, Paterno's passing added to the anger of many alumni about his removal. Some even blamed the board for accelerating the coach's decline and passing due to the added stress triggered by his removal. At the nationally televised memorial service held on the Penn State campus several days later, attended by fifteen thousand people, Nike founder and chairman Phil Knight was given a standing ovation when he criticized the administration of the university for failure to conduct a thorough investigation.

The board felt they could and should do nothing more to defend themselves in the aftermath of the Knight denunciation and other similar ones that occurred during and after the memorial service for Coach Paterno. The threatening email traffic to the board members had dramatically increased, and the antiboard slate of candidates for the three alumni seats, called the "Penn Staters for Responsible Stewardship," gained even more supporters and traffic on their website.

Moreover, alumni critics were now insisting that the board posthumously apologize to Coach Paterno for his removal and, the newest demand, rename Beaver Stadium, the football stadium, as "Joe Paterno Stadium." Eight years before, a life-size bronze statute of Joe Paterno had been placed in front of the entrance of Beaver Stadium, turned slightly in the crouched position so familiar to those who had watched him on the sidelines during Penn State football games. Penn State fans were accustomed to walking by the statue and waving to, patting, and photographing their beloved Coach Pa. Now there was a substantial clamor, triggered by the coach's passing, that there also be a huge "Joe Paterno Stadium" sign on the outside of the front entrance behind the statue.

The board's response was not to yield to the pressures of the moment and to postpone any decision until after the Freeh investigatory report was published, which was expected in early summer. But the board also decided that it was time to lower its profile to reduce tensions with alumni, hoping the *Times* story would quiet things down. Of course, I knew that there was no way the *Times* story alone could do that. Our plan, postponed by Coach Paterno's passing, was still to repeat the story in many other venues in order to get the facts out and understood by a wider audience.

Two months after Coach Paterno's passing, after a significant amount of time spent editing and reediting to arrive at words and phrases that all thirty-two board members could endorse, the board did agree in March to publish a single, comprehensive explanation of all its decisions between November 5 and 9, explaining in one written document the specific reasons it had dismissed President Graham Spanier and removed Coach Paterno as coach. This had been conveyed in the *Times* story, but in this document it was explained comprehensively, reflecting the collective reasons of the full board.

The written document, however, was never widely circulated. The board decided against being too aggressive, for example, by issuing a press release or an op-ed piece to enhance its impact. Again they understandably wanted to reduce tensions among alumni and not exacerbate the situation. They did email the statement to more than five hundred thousand alumni and members of the Penn State community and posted it on the board website.

Meanwhile, the antiboard, pro-Paterno alumni organization called Penn Staters for Responsible Stewardship continued to criticize the board's decision on Coach Paterno and to promote its three-person slate of candidates for alumni trustees. Its website continued to be highly critical of board trustees who had voted to remove Coach Paterno.

Results of the election were announced on May 4, 2012. A record turnout—more than three times the usual number—of thirty-seven thousand alumni ballots were cast. Only one member of the antiboard slate from the Penn Staters for Responsible Stewardship was elected among the top-three vote-getters. But the only incumbent board member in an alumni seat who chose to run again was defeated: my friend the English teacher, Anne Riley.

TWO VERDICTS: THE SANDUSKY JURY, LOUIS FREEH

Six weeks after Anne Riley's defeat, on Friday evening, June 22, a Centre County jury in Bellafonte, Pennsylvania (near State College), unanimously convicted Jerry Sandusky, former Penn State defensive coach, of forty-five counts of child sexual assault of ten young boys, several of them after Coach Paterno had been told of Sandusky's sexual assault on a young boy in February 2001.

About three weeks later, on July 12, 2012—almost exactly eight months after the board made its decision to require President Graham Spanier to step down and to remove Coach Joe Paterno as Penn State football coach—the special investigative counsel to the board, former federal judge and FBI director Louis Freeh, published a 267-page report detailing his factual findings and conclusions based on those facts. These findings, Freeh wrote, were based on an investigation that had lasted almost eight months, involving, by his team's count, more than 420 interviews and analyzing more than 3.5 million pieces of pertinent electronic data and documents, including emails between former president Spanier, Athletic Director Curley, and Finance Vice President Schultz, and many others within the administration and athletic department going back to the 1990s and especially focused on the time before and after McQueary's report of what he had seen Sandusky doing to the young child in the shower on the evening of February 9, 2001.

The Freeh report made a number of findings that senior leaders of the university, including Messrs. Spanier, Curley, Schultz, and Coach Paterno, should have done more to report and hold Sandusky accountable and to protect the child victims. But many people, including some who supported the board decision to remove Coach Paterno, were uneasy about Freeh's decision to go beyond making specific findings of fact based on specific evidence and to offer his conclusions, especially at a time when Curley and Schultz were still awaiting a criminal trial.*

The Freeh report's conclusions made the crisis management mission of "putting the bad news behind you" even more difficult, since it reopened the feelings of anger and frustration and divisions among Penn State alumni that we hoped had begun to die down. But the Freeh report had the significant benefit of refocusing the public's and Penn State alumni's concern for the child victims.

THE PATERNO STATUE COMES DOWN— AND THE NCAA SANCTIONS

Ten days after the Freeh report was published, on early Sunday morning, July 22, as the State College community still slept, without warning or leaks to anyone, the iconic and lifelike statue of Coach Joe Paterno that had stood for nine years before the front entrance of Beaver Stadium was taken down by bulldozers, as was the plaque behind it.

President Erickson made the decision himself. The board meeting that had just ended included a debate about what to do about the statue as well as the issue of renaming the stadium, with no decision

---

* On November 1, 2012, former Penn State president Graham Spanier was indicted by a Harrisburg, Pennsylvania, grand jury on eight counts of perjury, obstruction, and endangering the welfare of children—all the allegations relating to his failure to take further action, ask more questions, and ultimately to report the McQueary report of Sandusky's engaging in what the grand jury stated was his knowledge of sexual assault on a young boy in a shower in February 2011. (Note that Spanier denied he was ever told about any sexual assault—he said he only knew about "horseplay.") Additional charges were made by the outgoing attorney general Linda Kelly against Schultz and Curly, including similar counts as made against Spanier. At the end of 2012, it appeared that the trials of Schultz and Curly might be postponed until later in 2013 so that all three men could be tried together.

made. But President Erickson decided that was his decision to make—and be held accountable for—as president of the university and only with the best interests of the university in mind.

With a Harry Truman attitude—"the buck stops here"—and an inner strength based on core principles, he made the decision and took the heat. As anticipated, many students and alumni were upset. But the public statement by President Erickson, issued immediately, helped calm the vast majority of Penn State alumni and assure the greater community that he had acted in a balanced fashion, considering both the interests of the child victims and the long-term interests of the university, but also the sensitivities of the Paterno family and Joe Paterno's great contributions to Penn State, which would not be erased by whatever he did or did not do regarding the Sandusky matter. President Erickson said in his written statement, in part:

> I now believe that, contrary to its original intention, Coach Paterno's statue has become a source of division and an obstacle to healing in our university and beyond. For that reason, I have decided that it is in the best interest of our university and public safety to remove the statue and store it in a secure location. I believe that, were it to remain, the statue will be a recurring wound to the multitude of individuals across the nation and beyond who have been the victims of child abuse.
>
> On the other hand, the Paterno Library symbolizes the substantial and lasting contributions to the academic life and educational excellence that the Paterno family has made to Penn State University. The library remains a tribute to Joe and Sue Paterno's commitment to Penn State's student body and academic success, and it highlights the positive impacts Coach Paterno had on the University. Thus I feel strongly that the library's name should remain unchanged.
>
> I fully realize that my decision will not be popular in some

Penn State circles, but I am certain it is the right and principled decision. I believe we have chosen a course that both recognizes the many contributions that Joe Paterno made to the academic life of our university, while taking seriously the conclusions of the Freeh Report and the national issue of child sexual abuse. Today, as every day, our hearts go out to the victims.

I read that statement on the Sunday morning it was issued—reflecting the reality that the statue would be a continued reminder of the past and Erickson's focus needed to be on the future and a new positive narrative about the great Penn State University, but also balanced by recognition that the library should continue to bear Coach Paterno's name and honor his indisputable contribution to the academic excellence and the "grand experiment" of the student athlete that was an undisputed great element of his legacy.

When I saw that balance in his statement as I read it online that Sunday morning, I thought, Perfect.

I also thought, once again, as I had from the first five minutes of my meeting with President Erickson some seven months before, that this was the right man for the right time for Penn State.

THE NCAA NEAR-DEATH-PENALTY SANCTIONS

The next day, Monday, Mark Emmert, president of the National Collegiate Athletic Association, announced the NCAA's sanctions against Penn State for the absence of control and supervision, at the highest levels of the university, by those who were allegedly responsible for permitting, facilitating, and concealing Jerry Sandusky's child sexual assaults for a period of almost fifteen years. The NCAA's only basis for its factual findings was the Freeh report—it undertook no hearings and offered no opportunity for rebuttal by the university, and NCAA president Emmert was reportedly given the power by the NCAA board to determine the sanctions himself without seeking approval from the NCAA board or offering any right of appeal of his decisions. The key finding, based on evidence cited exclusively in the Freeh report:

> The NCAA concludes that this evidence presents an unprecedented failure of institutional integrity leading to a culture in which a football program was held in higher esteem than the values of the institution, the values of the NCAA, the values of higher education, and most disturbingly the values of human decency. . . . [I]t was the fear of or deference to the omnipotent football program that enabled a sexual predator to attract and abuse his victims.

Even those who believed the university deserved some sanctions told me they felt uneasy about the process used by Emmert and the NCAA to make these factual findings and to impose these sanctions. He based his action entirely on the Freeh report, which itself drew conclusions and inferences, as we have seen, without providing for due process for those who were accused. So, too, Emmert reached his conclusions on his own, having been delegated the power to do so by the NCAA board of directors, without giving the university a hearing or an opportunity to rebut or present mitigating reasons regarding the level of sanctions.

The sanctions, which were described as short of the "death penalty"—banning all football at Penn State for a period of time—certainly did serious damage to the program. The sanctions included a $60 million fine (to be paid over a five-year period beginning in 2012 into an endowment for programs preventing child sexual abuse or assisting the victims of child sexual abuse); a ban on participation in postseason bowl games for four years; the vacating of all football victories since 1998 (not coincidentally, the year of the Sandusky child-shower investigation that resulted in no charges being filed); a four-year reduction in the number of available football scholarships; waiver of transfer rules (which would allow current Penn State football players to transfer if they wished and be eligible to immediately play football); and the establishment of an independent overseer or monitor, appointed by the NCAA, to ensure Penn State's reformation of its internal procedures and culture to be certain this never happened again.

Many believed the sanctions were excessive and unfair, or at the very least disproportionate, given the small number of people from Penn State who were even alleged to have been knowledgeable about Sandusky's predatory conduct toward children. There was no doubt that those who most suffered from the NCAA sanctions were, in fact, innocent of anything to do with Sandusky and his evil conduct: the players, and the new coach, Bill O'Brien, a charismatic leader who uprooted his family and his career in Boston, where he was offensive coordinator for the New England Patriots, to make the courageous decision to bring back the greatness of Penn State football, with the hope that he would have a fighting chance to rebuild the program.

In addition to the fury the Emmert sanctions triggered in the Penn State community and among alumni, the initial reaction was anger aimed at President Erickson for "voluntarily" signing what was termed a "binding consent decree" imposing the sanctions. But within a day, President Erickson's decision was mostly forgiven after he explained that he had no real choice but to consent. Erickson stated that NCAA president Emmert had told him that if he didn't sign the decree and consent immediately, the NCAA would impose the "death penalty" for Penn State football for several years. This would have deprived the university of the much-needed revenue generated by the football program (about $60 million per year—not coincidentally, the amount of the fine). Emmert subsequently confirmed that was the choice President Erickson faced.

Not only would such a death penalty have deprived the university of the $60 million from the football program, which is used to subsidize all the other athletic programs at Penn State and additional resources for academic programs as well, but the loss of Penn State football would also have substantially damaged the hundreds of small businesses and people in the local State College community who benefited by the revenues and jobs created by the football program.

Erickson and the board were also inaccurately accused by critics of having "accepted" the conclusions of the Freeh report. But surely in this context, the word "accepted" should have meant "received" as opposed to "approved." It should be recalled that the original mandate, to ensure Judge Freeh's independence both optically and in fact, allowed his report to be published without preview by the board or attorneys, thus not permitting the president, the board chair, or its attorneys reading the Freeh report the day before its public release to be able to prepare a measured response. They never stated they agreed with all its findings and conclusions.

From the first morning I met him in early December 2011 all the way through his decision to take down the statue and consent to the sanctions, Rod Erickson had shown himself to be a simple man willing to act on his own principles and sense of right and wrong, regardless of criticism or consequences—the right man for the right time in the worst crisis in Penn State's 168-year history.

On August 2, 2012, George Mitchell, the former Democratic majority leader of the U.S. Senate from Maine, who had been appointed to head the baseball-steroids investigation and had served as a special envoy to the Middle East for Secretary of State Hillary Rodham Clinton, was appointed by the NCAA to monitor Penn State.

By the end of 2012, there were still hopes in the Penn State community that Senator Mitchell would be in a position to assess compliance at the university—and as many hope, earlier than the full five years, there might be forgiveness of some of the sanctions.

As the season began, Penn State had lost a number of star players who, as a result of the NCAA sanctions, were allowed to transfer out of

Penn State and play football elsewhere without having to miss a season and still be eligible for scholarship help. But Coach Bill O'Brien and those players who stuck with him and Penn State provided their own "profiles in courage." By the end of the season they managed a winning record in 2012 and they had proven that character can be demonstrated best in adversity. The inspiring examples of the coach; the acting athletic director who had chosen him, David Joyner, who was a former football captain and All-American under Coach Paterno; the players who stuck with the program throughout the season; and the nearly 100,000 fans and alumni who still flocked to Beaver Stadium every Saturday to cheer on the Nittany Lions all proved once again— and some said decisively—that Penn Staters should not and would not be defined by the evil Sandusky, but rather by the greatness of Penn State's history and the richness of its student body, faculty, and reputation as a research university.

In the final analysis, by the end of 2012, there was real hope that healing had begun and was proceeding. Fund-raising was up, student applications poured in, and the future seemed brighter. There clearly seemed to be light at the end of the long tunnel. In short, the ultimate goal of the crisis management team (bolstered in the middle of the year by the addition of the outstanding national public relations firm the Edelman Group, and media- and politically savvy David LaTorre from Harrisburg, Pennsylvania) was closer than ever before—namely, healing and restoration of the positive Penn State narrative. More and more Penn State alumni embittered by the decision to replace Joe Paterno even for just three games were more focused on the future than the past, and more and more the famous slogan of proud self-identity by Penn State alumni could be heard throughout the stadium and among alumni across the nation: "We are Penn State."

ANNE RILEY—ON STARS AND FIREFLIES

Some time after the NCAA sanctions were announced, I called to check in on my friend and favorite English teacher, Anne Riley, the former Penn State board trustee who voted to remove Coach Paterno and was defeated for reelection. We talked for a while about how she felt after not being reelected to the board ("not surprised," she said) and what she now felt about the NCAA sanctions.

She still spoke with obvious pain in her voice about the continued hostility by a few remaining diehards toward her—in emails and occasionally on the streets of State College—about her decision on Coach Paterno. But, she said, her conscience was still clear. She still believed she had no choice but to follow her fiduciary duty as a trustee and to support decisions that were intended to be in the best long-term interests of the university. She did emphasize to me that, in retrospect, she believed that her longtime friend, former president Spanier, had not been treated fairly in the Freeh report, even after his indictment for perjury and obstruction in November 2012.

We talked awhile about the job of crisis manager, and she noted that the NCAA sanctions evoked a new level of anger and reopened the wounds. She noted that there was something contradictory and unfair about the NCAA's sanctions, which, she said, penalized the innocent for actions of others that they had nothing to do with. But then we agreed that poetry is a place that is supposed to explain life's contradictions and imperfect outcomes, and that Robert Frost's poems remained a source of that insight.

"Your crisis management rules about getting all the facts out might not always work perfectly," she noted. I couldn't argue, telling her it was true that the Penn State nightmare was not yet over and might not be for a long time.

Anne then asked me if I knew the Frost poem "Fireflies in the Garden." I told her no. She said she would send it to me.

Within a few days, I received a copy of it in the mail, with a hand-written note—"this one is *loaded* w/metaphor re PSU year."

Fireflies in the Garden

Here come real stars to fill the upper skies,
And here on earth come emulating flies,
That though they never equal stars in size,
(And they were never really stars at heart)
Achieve at times a very star-like start.
Only, of course, they can't sustain the part.

Perfect, I thought. Facts and truth, like stars, should be constants and should matter. But like fireflies, in the new Internet world of the swirling "swarm of bees" of misinformation fueled by emotions, they can't always "sustain the part."

ACKNOWLEDGMENTS

This book would not have been possible without two people: Ron Goldfarb, my agent and friend, and Mitchell Ivers, my editor at Threshold Editions, Simon & Schuster, both of whom thought my crisis tales would be interesting to read while also teaching the fundamental rules for managing crises in business, politics, and life. I also want to express my gratitude to all the great people at Simon & Schuster and Threshold Editions and Gallery Books who saw worth in my manuscript and who worked so hard—and with such patience—in making this book a reality, especially Louise Burke, president and publisher of Threshold Editions and Gallery Books; Natasha Simons, editorial assistant, Gallery Books; Al Madocs, production editor; and Sally Franklin, managing editor.

Also thanks to my attorney colleagues over the years who worked with me on many of the crises described in this book and helped me develop a brand-new form of crisis management—combining law practice, allowing me to advise clients under the protection of the attorney-client privilege, and thus to get direct access to all the facts, plus using media and political experience to resolve the crisis: Adam Goldberg, my former deputy at the Clinton White House; Josh Galper and Caroline Nolan, who learned their journalistic skills at my alma maters—the *Yale Daily News* and Yale Law School; and Eileen O'Connor, a veteran CNN reporter and Georgetown Law graduate. Thanks also to my partners in Purple Nation Solutions, a public affairs/

strategic communications firm affiliated with my law firm; Eleanor Spector McManus, an award-winning producer for the *Larry King Live* show, also from CNN; and Michael S. Steele, former Republican National Committee chair and former lieutenant governor of Maryland.

Thanks to four people who helped me learn crisis management skills, combining law, media, and politics while serving as special counsel to President Clinton in 1996 to 1998: Lanny Breuer, also special counsel to the president; Charles Burson, then counsel to Vice President Al Gore; Cheryl Mills, deputy White House counsel; and Mike McCurry, President Clinton's press secretary and the wisest counselor and best friend anyone could have during a crisis—business, political, or personal.

Thanks to Michael Smerconish—attorney, outstanding radio-talk-show host, and TV cable analyst—whose message during my own personal experience in the center of a media crisis described in this book gave me heart during a particularly difficult time.

Thanks especially to my assistant, Maddie Melendez, the person whose daily crisis was and remains managing me (akin to managing a hurricane, as she always points out)—keeping me on course and on schedule.

Thanks also to those business executives, attorneys, and friends from politics and media with whom I have worked in dealing with the various crises described in this book, especially Anne Riley, the English teacher from State College, Pennsylvania, whose wisdom and courage inspire me still and who reminded me of my favorite English teacher in high school, Mr. Abbey, and of the continuing wisdom of our favorite poet, Robert Frost.

Thanks to my family for making it all possible—keeping me grounded and always feeling lucky because of them: my children—daughter, Marlo, forty-four; and son-in-law, David; son Seth, forty-two; and daughter-in-law Melissa; sons Joshua, fifteen, and Jeremy Joseph ("JJ"), eight; and my six grandchildren—Jake, Sydney, and Devon (Marlo and David); and Zachary, Noah, and Gabriel (Seth and Melissa).

And finally, special thanks to my best friend, advisor, and wife, Carolyn Atwell-Davis, who has proven to be the ultimate crisis manager in being married to me for more than twenty-eight years.

I give credit to all of the above for whatever is good about this book; and take full responsibility for whatever is not.

INDEX